Essential Angular for ASP.NET Core MVC

Adam Freeman

Apress®

Essential Angular for ASP.NET Core MVC

Adam Freeman
London, UK

ISBN-13 (pbk): 978-1-4842-2915-6   ISBN-13 (electronic): 978-1-4842-2916-3
DOI 10.1007/978-1-4842-2916-3

Library of Congress Control Number: 2017949481

Cover image by Freepik (`www.freepik.com`)

Managing Director: Welmoed Spahr
Editorial Director: Todd Green
Acquisitions Editor: Gwenan Spearing
Development Editor: Laura Berendson
Technical Reviewer: Fabio Claudio Ferracchiati
Coordinating Editor: Mark Powers
Copy Editor: Kim Wimpsett

Distributed to the book trade worldwide by Springer Science+Business Media New York, 233 Spring Street, 6th Floor, New York, NY 10013. Phone 1-800-SPRINGER, fax (201) 348-4505, e-mail `orders-ny@springer-sbm.com`, or visit `www.springeronline.com`. Apress Media, LLC is a California LLC and the sole member (owner) is Springer Science + Business Media Finance Inc (SSBM Finance Inc). SSBM Finance Inc is a **Delaware** corporation.

For information on translations, please e-mail `rights@apress.com`, or visit `www.apress.com/rights-permissions`.

Apress titles may be purchased in bulk for academic, corporate, or promotional use. eBook versions and licenses are also available for most titles. For more information, reference our Print and eBook Bulk Sales web page at `www.apress.com/bulk-sales`.

Any source code or other supplementary material referenced by the author in this book is available to readers on GitHub via the book's product page, located at `www.apress.com/9781484229156`. For more detailed information, please visit `www.apress.com/source-code`.

Printed on acid-free paper

Dedicated to my lovely wife, Jacqui Griffyth.
(And also to Peanut.)

Contents at a Glance

Contents

About the Author

Adam Freeman is an experienced IT professional who has held senior positions in a range of companies, most recently serving as chief technology officer and chief operating officer of a global bank. Now retired, he spends his time writing and long-distance running.

About the Technical Reviewer

Fabio Claudio Ferracchiati is a senior consultant and a senior analyst/developer using Microsoft technologies. He works for BluArancio (`www.bluarancio.com`). He is a Microsoft Certified Solution Developer for .NET, a Microsoft Certified Application Developer for .NET, a Microsoft Certified Professional, and a prolific author and technical reviewer. Over the past ten years, he's written articles for Italian and international magazines and coauthored more than ten books on a variety of computer topics.

CHAPTER 1

Understanding Angular and ASP.NET Core MVC

This book is about using Angular and ASP.NET Core MVC together to build rich applications. Individually, each of these frameworks is powerful and feature-rich, but using them together combines the dynamic flexibility of Angular with the solid infrastructure of ASP.NET Core MVC.

Who Is This Book For?

This book is for ASP.NET Core MVC developers who want to add Angular to their projects but don't know where to start. Angular is a complex framework that can be overwhelming to learn, and this book provides a solid foundation by using ASP.NET Core MVC to support an Angular application. By the end of this book, you will understand how ASP.NET Core MVC and Angular can work together and will have gained a basic understanding of how Angular development works.

What Does This Book Cover?

This book explains how to use Angular in an ASP.NET Core MVC project. I demonstrate how to create a Visual Studio or Visual Studio Code project that contains Angular and ASP.NET Core MVC and show you how to get them working together. I show you how to use Entity Framework Core to store the application data and ASP.NET Core Identity to authenticate and authorize users. Each ASP.NET Core package adds its complexities, and I show you how these can be managed to deliver functionality to Angular.

This book also introduces Angular development, focusing on just those features that are required by most applications. I explain how Angular applications work, how to structure an Angular application, and how individual building blocks can collaborate to create complex features.

The examples are based around SportsStore, which will be familiar if you have read any of my other books. SportsStore is a fictional online store that contains the features that most projects need. The SportsStore examples in this book have been adapted so that I can highlight problems between Angular and ASP.NET Core MVC and explain how to solve them.

What Doesn't This Book Cover?

This book is not a deep-dive into Angular or ASP.NET Core MVC. I assume you are already familiar with C# and ASP.NET Core MVC development, and I describe only the essential Angular features.

© Adam Freeman 2017
A. Freeman, *Essential Angular for ASP.NET Core MVC*, DOI 10.1007/978-1-4842-2916-3_1

I have written other books that provide the deep-dive for each framework. If you are unfamiliar with ASP.NET Core MVC development, then you should read *Pro ASP.NET Core MVC* before this book. Once you have mastered the basics of Angular development, then *Pro Angular* provides a comprehensive tour of Angular features.

What Do You Need to Know?

Before reading this book, you should have a working knowledge of ASP.NET Core MVC development and have a good understanding of JavaScript, HTML, and CSS.

Are There Lots of Examples?

There are *loads* of examples. The best way to learn is by example, and I have packed as many of them as I can into this book. To maximize the number of examples in this book, I have adopted a simple convention to avoid listing the same code over and over again.

To help you navigate the project, the caption for each listing includes the name of the file and the folder in which it can be found, like in Listing 1-1.

Listing 1-1. The Contents of the CheckoutState.cs File in the Models/BindingTargets Folder

```
namespace SportsStore.Models.BindingTargets {

    public class CheckoutState  {

        public string name { get; set; }
        public string address { get; set; }
        public string cardNumber { get; set; }
        public string cardExpiry { get; set; }
        public string cardSecurityCode { get; set; }
    }
}
```

This is a listing from Chapter 9, and the caption tells you that it refers to a file called CheckoutState.cs, which can be found in the Models/BindingTargets folder. A project that combines Angular and ASP.NET Core MVC can have a lot of files, and it is important to change the right one. (Don't worry about the code in this listing or the folder structure for the moment.)

When I make changes to a file, I show the altered statements in bold, like in Listing 1-2.

Listing 1-2. Adding Methods in the SessionValuesController.cs File in the Controllers Folder

```
using Microsoft.AspNetCore.Http;
using Microsoft.AspNetCore.Mvc;
using Newtonsoft.Json;
using SportsStore.Models;
using SportsStore.Models.BindingTargets;

namespace SportsStore.Controllers {

    [Route("/api/session")]
    public class SessionValuesController : Controller {
```

```
        [HttpGet("cart")]
        public IActionResult GetCart() {
            return Ok(HttpContext.Session.GetString("cart"));
        }

        [HttpPost("cart")]
        public void StoreCart([FromBody] ProductSelection[] products) {
            var jsonData = JsonConvert.SerializeObject(products);
            HttpContext.Session.SetString("cart", jsonData);
        }

        [HttpGet("checkout")]
        public IActionResult GetCheckout() {
            return Ok(HttpContext.Session.GetString("checkout"));
        }

        [HttpPost("checkout")]
        public void StoreCheckout([FromBody] CheckoutState data) {
            HttpContext.Session.SetString("checkout",
                JsonConvert.SerializeObject(data));
        }
    }
}
```

This is another listing from Chapter 9, and the bold statements indicate the changes that you should make if you are following the example.

I use two different conventions to avoid repeating code in long files. For long class files, I omit methods and properties, like in Listing 1-3.

Listing 1-3. Restricting Access in the SupplierValuesController.cs File in the Controllers Folder

```
using Microsoft.AspNetCore.Mvc;
using SportsStore.Models;
using SportsStore.Models.BindingTargets;
using System.Collections.Generic;
using Microsoft.AspNetCore.Authorization;

namespace SportsStore.Controllers {

    [Route("api/suppliers")]
    [Authorize(Roles = "Administrator")]
    public class SupplierValuesController : Controller {
        private DataContext context;

        // ...methods omitted for brevity...
    }
}
```

This listing from Chapter 11 shows you that a new attribute must be applied to the SupplierValuesController class but doesn't list the constructor or other methods, which remain unchanged.

This is the convention that I follow to highlight changes to a region within a file, such as when new statements are required in a single method in a long file, like in Listing 1-4.

Listing 1-4. Configuring the JSON Serializer in the Startup.cs File in the SportsStore Folder

```
...
public void ConfigureServices(IServiceCollection services) {
    services.AddDbContext<DataContext>(options =>
        options.UseSqlServer(Configuration
            ["Data:Products:ConnectionString"]));

    services.AddMvc().AddJsonOptions(opts => {
        opts.SerializerSettings.ReferenceLoopHandling
            = ReferenceLoopHandling.Serialize;
        opts.SerializerSettings.NullValueHandling = NullValueHandling.Ignore;
    });
}
...
```

This is a listing from Chapter 5 that requires a new statement in the ConfigureServices method of the Startup class, which is defined in the Startup.cs file in the SportsStore folder, while the rest of the file remains unchanged.

Where Can You Get the Example Code?

You can download the example projects for all the chapters in this book from https://github.com/apress/esntl-angular-for-asp.net-core-mvc. The download is available without charge and includes all the supporting resources that are required to re-create the examples without having to type them in. You don't have to download the code, but it is the easiest way of experimenting with the examples and makes it easy to copy and paste code into your own projects.

Where Can You Get Corrections for This Book?

You can find corrections for this book in the Errata file in the GitHub repository for this book (https://github.com/apress/esntl-angular-for-asp.net-core-mvc).

Contacting the Author

If you have problems making the examples in this chapter work or if you find a problem in the book, then you can e-mail me at adam@adam-freeman.com, and I will try my best to help. Please check the errata for this book at https://github.com/apress/esntl-angular-for-asp.net-core-mvc to see if it contains a solution to your problem before contacting me.

Summary

In this chapter, I described the purpose and content of this book, explained how you can download the project used for each chapter of the book, and described the conventions I use in the code listings. In the next chapter, I show you how to set up your development environment in preparation for creating a combined Angular and ASP.NET Core MVC project in Chapter 3.

CHAPTER 2

■ ■ ■

Getting Ready

In this chapter, I explain how to set up the tools and packages required for Angular and ASP.NET Core MVC development. There are instructions for Windows, Linux, and macOS, which are the three operating systems that can be used for .NET Core projects. For quick reference, Table 2-1 lists the packages and explains their purpose. Follow the instructions for your preferred operating system to install the tools that are required for the rest of this book.

Table 2-1. *The Software Packages Used in This Book*

Name	Description
Visual Studio	Visual Studio is the Windows-only IDE that provides the full-featured development experience for .NET.
Visual Studio Code	Visual Studio Code is a lightweight IDE that can be used on Windows, macOS, and Linux. It doesn't provide the full range of features of the Windows-only Visual Studio product but is well-suited to Angular and ASP.NET Core MVC development.
.NET SDK	The .NET Core Software Development Kit includes the .NET runtime for executing .NET applications and the development tools required to build and test applications.
Node.js	Node.js is used for many client-side development tools, delivered through its package manager, NPM. It is used to prepare the Angular code for the browser.
Git	Git is a revision control system. It is used by some of the NPM packages commonly used for client-side development.
Docker	The Docker package includes the tools required to run applications in containers. The databases in this book are run inside Docker containers, which makes them easy to install and manage.

Getting Ready on Windows

The following sections describe the setup required for Windows. All the tools used are available for free, although some are offered in commercial versions with additional features (but these are not needed for the examples in this book). If you are using Windows, you can use Visual Studio, which is the traditional IDE for .NET projects, or Visual Studio Code, which offers a lighter-weight alternative.

© Adam Freeman 2017
A. Freeman, *Essential Angular for ASP.NET Core MVC*, DOI 10.1007/978-1-4842-2916-3_2

Installing .NET Core

The .NET Core Software Development Kit (SDK) includes the runtime and development tools needed to start the development project and perform database operations. To install the .NET Core SDK on Windows, download the installer from https://download.microsoft.com/download/B/9/F/B9F1AF57-C14A-4670-9973-CDF47209B5BF/dotnet-dev-win-x64.1.0.4.exe. This URL is for the 64-bit .NET Core SDK, which is the version that I use throughout this book and which you should install to ensure that you get the expected results from the examples. Rather than type in a complex URL, you can to go to https://www.microsoft.com/net/download/core and select the 64-bit installer for the .NET Core SDK. (Microsoft also publishes a runtime-only installer, but this does not contain the tools that are required for this book.)

Run the installer. Once the install process is complete, open a new PowerShell command prompt and run the command shown in Listing 2-1 to check that .NET Core is working.

Listing 2-1. Testing .NET Core

```
dotnet --version
```

The output from this command will display the latest version of the .NET Core runtime that is installed. If you have installed only the version specified, this will be 1.0.4.

Installing Node.js

Node.js is a runtime for server-side JavaScript applications and has become a popular platform for development tools. In this book, Node.js is used by the Angular build tools to compile and prepare the code that ASP.NET Core MVC will send to the browser.

It is important that you download the same version of Node.js that I use throughout this book. Although Node.js is relatively stable, there are still breaking API changes from time to time, and they may stop the examples from working. To install Node.js, download and run the installer from https://nodejs.org/dist/v6.10.3/node-v6.10.3-x64.msi. This is the installer for version 6.10.3. You may prefer more recent releases for your projects, but you should stick with the 6.10.3 release for the rest of this book. Run the installer and ensure that the npm package manager and Add to PATH options are selected, as shown in Figure 2-1.

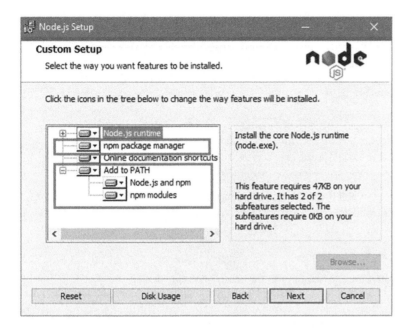

Figure 2-1. *Installing Node.js on Windows*

The NPM package manager is used to download and install Node packages. Adding Node.js to the PATH ensures that you can use the Node.js runtime at the command prompt just by typing node. Once you have completed the installation, open a new command prompt and run the command shown in Listing 2-2.

Listing 2-2. Checking That Node.js Is Installed Correctly

```
node -v
```

You should see the following version number displayed: v6.9.2. If the installation has been successful, then proceed to the "Installing NPM Packages" section.

Installing Bower

Once you have installed Node, run the command shown in Listing 2-3 to install the Bower package, which is used to manage client-side packages.

Listing 2-3. Installing the Bower Package

```
npm install -g bower@1.8.0
```

Installing Git

The Git revision control tool is required to download the client-side packages used by the Bower package installed in the previous section. Download and run the installer from `https://git-scm.com/downloads`. When the installation is complete, open a new command prompt and run the command in Listing 2-4 to check that Git is installed and working properly.

Listing 2-4. Checking the Git Install

```
git --version
```

This command prints out the version of the Git package that has been installed. At the time of writing, the latest version of Git for Windows is 2.13.0.

Installing Docker

Docker is available in Community and Enterprise editions, the difference being the support and certifications offered for the Enterprise edition. Both editions provide the same set of core features, and I use the free Docker Community edition throughout this book.

Go to `https://store.docker.com/editions/community/docker-ce-desktop-windows`, click the Get Docker CE for Windows (stable) link, and run the installer that is downloaded. Docker will start automatically when the installation is complete. You may be prompted to enable Hyper-V, as shown in Figure 2-2. Click the Ok button.

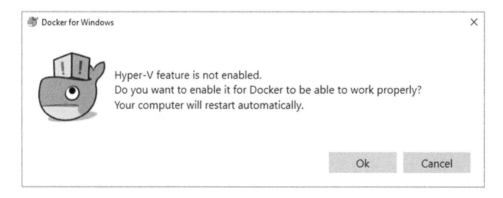

Figure 2-2. *Enabling Hyper-V*

Once the installation has completed, right-click the Docker icon in the taskbar and select Settings from the pop-up menu. Navigate to the Advanced section and increase the memory allocated to Docker so that it is at least 3500MB, which is the minimum required to run SQL Server, as shown in Figure 2-3. Click the Apply button to save the configuration change and restart Docker with the new configuration.

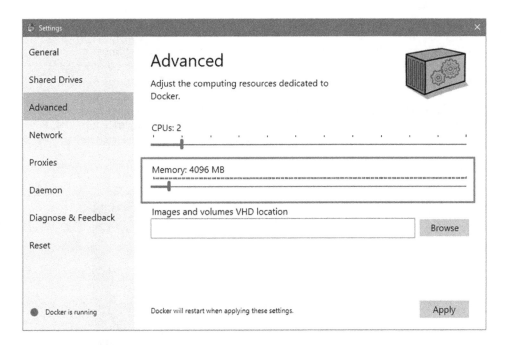

Figure 2-3. *Assigning memory to Docker*

Once Docker has restarted, open a new PowerShell command prompt and run the command shown in Listing 2-5 to check that the installation was successful.

Listing 2-5. Checking That Docker Is Working

```
docker run --rm hello-world
```

Docker will download the files it needs to run a simple Hello World application. Docker will write out messages like these, indicating that everything is working as expected (the command produces more output than is shown here, but this is the important part):

```
...
Unable to find image 'hello-world:latest' locally
latest: Pulling from library/hello-world

c04b14da8d14: Pull complete
Digest: sha256:0256e8a36e2070f7bf2d0b0763dbabdd67798512411de4cdcf9431a1feb60fd9
Status: Downloaded newer image for hello-world:latest

Hello from Docker!
This message shows that your installation appears to be working correctly.
...
```

Installing Visual Studio 2017

Visual Studio is the traditional development environment for ASP.NET Core and Entity Framework Core projects. It offers a full-featured development experience, but it can be resource hungry. Consider using Visual Studio Code if you want a lighter-weight development experience, which I describe in the next section.

Download the installer from `https://www.visualstudio.com/vs`. There are different editions of Visual Studio 2017 available, but the free Community edition is sufficient for the examples in this book. Run the installer and ensure that the .NET Core Cross-Platform Development workload is selected, as shown in Figure 2-4.

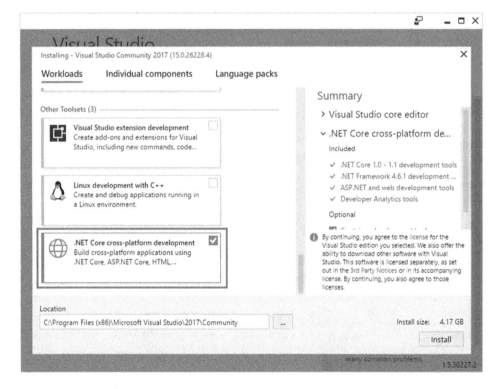

Figure 2-4. *Selecting the Visual Studio packages*

Click the Install button to begin the process of downloading and installing the Visual Studio features.

Adding the Visual Studio Extensions

Two Visual Studio extensions are essential for working on ASP.NET Core MVC projects. The first is called Razor Language Service, and it provides IntelliSense support for tag helpers when editing Razor views. The second is called Project File Tools, and it provides automatic completion for editing `.csproj` files, which simplifies the process of adding NuGet packages to projects.

Select Extensions and Updates from the Visual Studio Tools menu, select the Online section, and use the search box to locate the extensions. Click the Download button, as shown in Figure 2-5, to download the extension files.

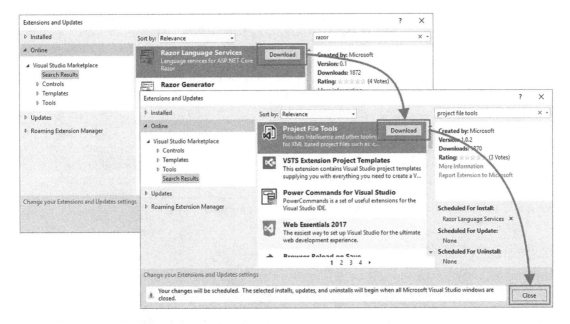

Figure 2-5. *Downloading Visual Studio extensions*

Click the Close button to dismiss the list of extensions and then close Visual Studio, which will trigger the installation process for the extensions you downloaded. You will be prompted to accept the changes that will be made and the license terms, as shown in Figure 2-6. Click the Modify button to install the extensions. Once the process has completed, you can start Visual Studio and begin development.

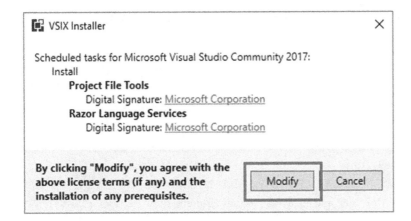

Figure 2-6. *Installing Visual Studio extensions*

Installing Visual Studio Code

Visual Studio Code is a lightweight editor that doesn't have all the features of the full Visual Studio product but works across platforms and is perfectly capable of handling ASP.NET Core MVC and Entity Framework Core projects.

I find myself increasingly using Visual Studio Code, in part because it means I can use the same IDE on different platforms and in part because it is more responsive and less resource hungry than Visual Studio 2017.

To install Visual Studio code, visit `http://code.visualstudio.com` and click the download link for Windows. Run the installer and then start Visual Studio Code.

Once the installation is complete, start Visual Studio Code, click the Extensions button in the sidebar, and locate and install the C# package, which provides support for working with C# code files.

Getting Ready on Linux

The following sections describe the setup required for Linux. Microsoft has taken Linux support for .NET Core seriously because of its popularity as a deployment platform, which makes it a good platform for development, too. .NET Core supports a range of Linux distributions, and I have used Ubuntu 16.04 for this book, which is the current Long-Term Support (LTS) release at the time of writing.

Installing .NET Core

The .NET Core Software Development Kit (SDK) includes the runtime and development tools needed to start the development project and perform database operations. The easiest way to install .NET Core on Linux is to visit `https://www.microsoft.com/net/core`, select your distribution from the list, and copy and paste the commands into a command prompt to ensure you don't mistype any configuration arguments.

To install .NET Core SDK on Ubuntu 16.04, open a command prompt and enter the commands in Listing 2-6 to configure package management so that Microsoft packages can be installed.

Listing 2-6. Preparing Package Management for .NET Core

```
sudo sh -c 'echo "deb [arch=amd64] https://apt-mo.trafficmanager.net/repos/dotnet-release/
xenial main" > /etc/apt/sources.list.d/dotnetdev.list'
sudo apt-key adv --keyserver hkp://keyserver.ubuntu.com:80 --recv-keys 417A0893
sudo apt-get update
```

Run the command shown in Listing 2-7 to download and install the .NET Core SDK package. It is important that you use the version number shown in the listing so that you get the expected results from the examples in this book.

Listing 2-7. Installing the .NET Core Package

```
sudo apt-get install dotnet-dev-1.0.4
```

Once the package has been downloaded and installed, run the command shown in Listing 2-8 to check that .NET Core is installed and working.

Listing 2-8. Testing the .NET Core Package

```
dotnet --version
```

The output from this command will display the latest version of the .NET Core runtime that is installed. If you have installed only the version specified, this will be 1.0.4.

Installing Node.js

N The easiest way to install Node.js is through a package manager, using the procedures described at `https://nodejs.org/en/download/package-manager`. For Ubuntu, I ran the commands shown in Listing 2-9 to download and install Node.js.

Listing 2-9. Installing Node.js on Ubuntu

```
curl -sL https://deb.nodesource.com/setup_6.x | sudo -E bash -
sudo apt-get install nodejs
```

Once you have installed Node.js, run the command shown in Listing 2-10 to check that the installation was successful and that you have the right version.

Listing 2-10. Checking That Node.js Is Installed Correctly

```
node -v
```

You should see that version 6.*x.x* is installed. Version 6.10.3 is the latest at the time of writing, but there may be updates pushed into the package manager feed for version 6.*x* by the time you read this.

Installing Bower

Once you have installed Node, run the command shown in Listing 2-11 to install the Bower package, which is used to manage client-side packages.

Listing 2-11. Installing the Bower Package

```
sudo npm install -g bower@1.8.0
```

Installing Git

Git is already installed on most Linux distributions. If you want to install the latest version, then consult the installation instructions for your distribution at `https://git-scm.com/download/linux`. For Ubuntu, I used the command in Listing 2-12.

Listing 2-12. Installing Git

```
sudo apt-get install git
```

Once you have completed the installation, open a new command prompt and run the command in Listing 2-13 to check that Git is installed and available.

Listing 2-13. Checking the Git Install

```
git --version
```

This command prints out the version of the Git package that was installed. At the time of writing, the latest version of Git for Linux is 2.7.4.

Installing Docker

To install Docker on Linux, visit https://www.docker.com/community-edition, select the distribution that you are using from the list, and follow the installation instructions, copying and pasting the commands to avoid typos.

For Ubuntu 16.04, open a new command prompt and enter the commands in Listing 2-14 to configure the package manager and install the prerequisite packages that Docker relies on.

Listing 2-14. Preparing the Package Manger and Installing Prerequisite Packages

```
sudo apt-get -y install apt-transport-https ca-certificates curl
curl -fsSL https://download.docker.com/linux/ubuntu/gpg | sudo apt-key add -
sudo add-apt-repository \
     "deb [arch=amd64] https://download.docker.com/linux/ubuntu \
     $(lsb_release -cs) stable"
sudo apt-get update
```

To install Docker, run the command shown in Listing 2-15.

Listing 2-15. Installing Docker

```
sudo apt-get -y install docker-ce
```

Once Docker is installed, run the commands shown in Listing 2-16 so that you can use Docker without sudo.

Listing 2-16. Configuring Docker So That Root Access Is Not Required

```
sudo groupadd docker
sudo usermod -aG docker $USER
```

Log out of your current session and log back in again for the commands in Listing 2-16 to take effect. Once you have logged back in, run the command shown in Listing 2-17 to check that the installation has been successful.

Listing 2-17. Checking That Docker Is Working

```
docker run --rm hello-world
```

Docker will download the files it needs to run a simple Hello World application. Docker will write out messages like these, indicating that everything is working as expected (the command produces more output than is shown here, but this is the important part):

```
...
Unable to find image 'hello-world:latest' locally
latest: Pulling from library/hello-world

c04b14da8d14: Pull complete
Digest: sha256:0256e8a36e2070f7bf2d0b0763dbabdd67798512411de4cdcf9431a1feb60fd9
Status: Downloaded newer image for hello-world:latest

Hello from Docker!
This message shows that your installation appears to be working correctly.
...
```

Once you have confirmed that Docker is installed and working properly, then run the command shown in Listing 2-18 to install Docker Compose, which is required for the examples in this book.

Listing 2-18. Installing Docker Compose

```
sudo curl -L https://github.com/docker/compose/releases/download/1.13.0/docker-compose-
`uname -s`-`uname -m` -o /usr/local/bin/docker-compose
sudo chmod +x /usr/local/bin/docker-compose
```

Once the installation is complete, run the command shown in Listing 2-19 to check that Docker Compose works as expected.

Listing 2-19. Checking Docker Compose

```
docker-compose --version
```

If the installation has been successful, you will see this response: `docker-compose version 1.13.0, build 1719ceb`.

Installing Visual Studio Code

To install Visual Studio code, visit `http://code.visualstudio.com` and click the download link for your platform. Run the installer and then start Visual Studio Code, which will present a standard integrated development environment.

Once the installation is complete, start Visual Studio Code, click the Extensions button in the sidebar, and locate and install the C# package, which provides support for working with C# code files.

Getting Ready on macOS

The following sections describe the setup required for macOS, which provides a good platform .NET development through Visual Studio Code. Although my main development machine runs Windows, my laptop runs macOS, and I use it for development when traveling.

Installing .NET Core

Before installing .NET Core, open a new command prompt and run the command in Listing 2-20 to install the HomeBrew package manager.

Listing 2-20. Installing the Package Manager

```
/usr/bin/ruby -e \
  "$(curl -fsSL https://raw.githubusercontent.com/Homebrew/install/master/install)"
```

Once installation is complete, run the commands shown in Listing 2-21 to install the OpenSSL library, which is a prerequisite for some .NET Core features.

Listing 2-21. Installing the OpenSSL Package

```
brew install openssl
mkdir -p /usr/local/lib
ln -s /usr/local/opt/openssl/lib/libcrypto.1.0.0.dylib /usr/local/lib/
ln -s /usr/local/opt/openssl/lib/libssl.1.0.0.dylib /usr/local/lib/
```

To install .NET Core on macOS, download the SDK installer from https://go.microsoft.com/fwlink/?linkid=848823. This URL is for the .NET Core SDK version I use throughout this book and that you should install to ensure you get the expected results from the examples.

Run the installer. Once the process is complete, open a Terminal window and run the command shown in Listing 2-22 at the prompt to check that .NET Core is working.

Listing 2-22. Testing .NET Core

```
dotnet --version
```

The output from this command will display the latest version of the .NET Core runtime that is installed. If you have installed only the version specified, this will be 1.0.4.

Installing Node.js

To install Node.js on macOS, download and run the installer available from https://nodejs.org/dist/v6.10.3/node-v6.10.3.pkg. Once the installation is complete, open a new Terminal window and run the command shown in Listing 2-23 at the command prompt once the installer has completed.

Listing 2-23. Checking That Node.js Is Installed Correctly

```
node -v
```

You should will see the following version number displayed: v6.10.3.

Installing Bower

Once you have installed Node, run the command shown in Listing 2-24 to install the Bower package, which is used to manage client-side packages.

Listing 2-24. Installing the Bower Package

```
sudo npm install -g bower@1.8.0
```

Installing Git

The Git revision control tool is required to download the client-side packages used by the Bower package installed in the previous section. Download and run the installer from https://git-scm.com/downloads. When the installation is complete, open a new command prompt and run the command in Listing 2-25 to check that Git is installed and working properly.

Listing 2-25. Checking the Git Install

```
git --version
```

This command prints out the version of the Git package that has been installed. At the time of writing, the latest version of Git for macOS is 2.13.0.

Installing Docker

Go to https://store.docker.com/editions/community/docker-ce-desktop-mac, click the Get Docker for CE Mac (stable) link, and run the installer that is downloaded. Drag the whale to the Applications folder, as shown in Figure 2-7.

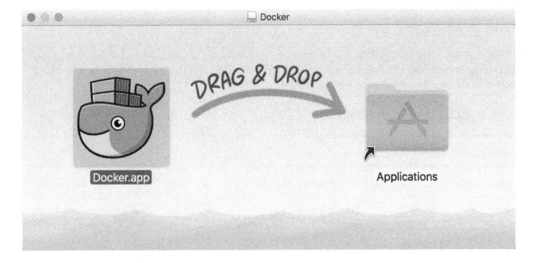

Figure 2-7. Installing Docker

Open Launchpad and click the Docker icon to perform the setup process. Once Docker has started, click the Docker menu bar icon and select Preferences from the pop-up menu.

Navigate to the Advanced section and increase the memory allocated to Docker so that it is at least 3500MB, which is the minimum required to run SQL Server, as shown in Figure 2-8. Click the Apply button to save the configuration change and restart Docker with the new configuration.

Figure 2-8. *Assigning memory to Docker*

Click Apply & Restart to change the memory and restart the Docker process. When Docker is running again, dismiss the Preferences window, open a new Terminal window, and run the command shown in Listing 2-26 to check that the installation was successful.

Listing 2-26. Checking That Docker Is Working

```
docker run --rm hello-world
```

Docker will download the files it needs to run a simple Hello World application. Docker will write out messages like these, indicating that everything is working as expected (the command produces more output than is shown here, but this is the important part):

```
...
Unable to find image 'hello-world:latest' locally
latest: Pulling from library/hello-world

c04b14da8d14: Pull complete
Digest: sha256:0256e8a36e2070f7bf2d0b0763dbabdd67798512411de4cdcf9431a1feb60fd9
Status: Downloaded newer image for hello-world:latest

Hello from Docker!
This message shows that your installation appears to be working correctly.
...
```

Installing Visual Studio Code

Developing for .NET on macOS is done using Visual Studio Code. To install Visual Studio Code, visit http://code.visualstudio.com, click the download link, run the installer, and then start Visual Studio Code.

Once the installation is complete, start Visual Studio Code, click the Extensions button in the sidebar, and locate and install the C# package, which provides support for working with C# code files.

Summary

In this chapter, I explained how to install the tools and packages that are required to use Angular and ASP. NET Core MVC, and in the next chapter, I show you how to create a project that combines them.

CHAPTER 3

■ ■ ■

Creating the Project

In this chapter, I show you how to create a project that contains ASP.NET Core MVC and Angular applications, which means both parts of the project can be developed using Visual Studio or Visual Studio Code. This project forms the foundation for the rest of this book, as I explain how to use Angular and ASP.NET Core MVC to create a rich web application. Table 3-1 puts the combined project in context.

Table 3-1. *Putting a Combined Project in Context*

Question	Answer
What is it?	A combined project includes Angular and ASP.NET Core MVC in a single folder structure.
Why is it useful?	A combined project makes it easy to develop both parts of an application using a single IDE, such as Visual Studio, as well as simplifying the process of using an ASP.NET Core MVC web service to provide data to Angular.
How is it used?	The Angular application is created first, followed by ASP.NET Core MVC. Additional NuGet packages are used to allow both parts of the project to work together at runtime.
Are there any pitfalls or limitations?	A combined project makes managing the development process easier, but you still need a good working knowledge of both Angular and ASP.NET Core MVC to create an effective application.
Are there any alternatives?	You can develop the Angular and ASP.NET Core MVC parts of the application separately, although this tends to complicate the development process.

■ **Tip**   You can download the complete project for this chapter from `https://github.com/apress/esntl-angular-for-asp.net-core-mvc`. This is also where you will find updates and corrections for this book.

Preparing to Create a Project

There are several different ways to create a project that combines Angular and ASP.NET Core MVC. The approach that I use in this book relies on the @angular/cli package, used in conjunction with the .NET tools for creating a new MVC project.

© Adam Freeman 2017

A. Freeman, *Essential Angular for ASP.NET Core MVC*, DOI 10.1007/978-1-4842-2916-3_3

```
┌─────────────────────────────────────────────────────────────────────────┐
│               USING THE DOTNET NEW ANGULAR COMMAND                         │
└─────────────────────────────────────────────────────────────────────────┘
```

Microsoft provides a template that can be used to create a similar project structure (which you can use by running `dotnet new angular` at the command line). The process I use in this chapter is more manual, but it means you will understand how the different building blocks fit together and have a better idea of where to look when you don't get the results you expect. Once you are familiar with how Angular and ASP.NET Core MVC can work together, using this template is perfectly reasonable, with the caveat that you are unable to specify the versions of ASP.NET Core MVC and Angular that are used in the project.

The @angular/cli package provides a command-line interface that simplifies the process of creating and working with a new Angular project. During development, the Angular code is compiled, packaged, and delivered to the browser using webpack, a popular tool for creating JavaScript bundles that contain only the code required to run a project.

To create a project that combines Angular and ASP.NET Core MVC, I start with @angular/cli and access he underlying webpack configuration, which can then be used to integrate the Angular tools and libraries into the ASP.NET Core project.

To start this process, open a new command prompt and run the command in Listing 3-1 to install the @angular/cli package. If you are using Linux or macOS, you may need to use `sudo` to run this command.

Listing 3-1. Installing the @angular/cli Package

```
npm install --global @angular/cli@1.0.2
```

This command takes a while to run because the package has a lot of dependencies, all of which have to be downloaded and installed.

Creating the Project

The process for creating a combined Angular and ASP.NET Core MVC project requires careful attention: both development platforms have their tools and conventions, and getting them to work together requires a specific set of steps to be performed in order. In the sections that follow, I walk through the process and explain each step.

■ **Tip**   You must follow each step exactly as shown, without missing a step or changing the order. If you get stuck, then you can download a ready-made project from the source code repository, which is linked from the Apress.com page for this book.

Creating the Angular Part of the Project

The first step is to create a new Angular project, which is done using the @angular/cli package installed in Listing 3-1. Open a new command prompt, navigate to the folder where you keep your development projects, and run the command shown in Listing 3-2.

Listing 3-2. Creating an Angular Project

```
ng new SportsStore --skip-git --skip-commit --skip-tests --source-dir ClientApp
```

The ng command is provided by the @angular/cli package, and ng new creates a new Angular project. The arguments that start with --skip tell @angular/cli not to perform some of the standard setup steps that are usually included in projects, and the --source-dir argument specifies the name of the folder that will contain the source code for the Angular application. The Angular code lives in a folder called ClientApp in projects that combine Angular and ASP.NET Core MVC.

The command in Listing 3-2 creates a folder called SportsStore that contains the tools and configuration files for an Angular project, along with some placeholder code so that the tools and project structure can be tested. The ng new command downloads a large number of packages, which can take a long time to complete.

The rest of the setup is performed inside the project folder, so run the command shown in Listing 3-3 to change the working directory.

Listing 3-3. Changing the Working Directory

```
cd SportsStore
```

Getting the Angular tools to work with the .NET tools requires additional NPM packages. Run the command shown in Listing 3-4 to install these packages.

Listing 3-4. Adding NPM Packages to the Project

```
npm install --save-dev webpack@2.3.2 aspnet-prerendering@2.0.3 aspnet-webpack@1.0.28
webpack-hot-middleware@2.17.1
```

Microsoft provides some of these NPM packages, and they are used to set up and run the Angular development tools inside the ASP.NET Core runtime. These packages work directly with webpack, which is usually hidden when working with projects created using @angular/cli. Run the command shown in Listing 3-5 in the SportsStore folder to create a webpack configuration file that can be used to build and run the project, a process known as *ejecting* the project from @angular/cli.

Listing 3-5. Ejecting the Project

```
ng eject
```

The ejection process updates the package.json file, which NPM uses to keep track of the packages used by the project. In some cases, the ejection process will add additional NPM packages to the project.json file, so run the command shown in Listing 3-6 to ensure that any new packages are downloaded and installed.

Listing 3-6. Updating the NPM Packages

```
npm install
```

Creating the ASP.NET Core MVC Part of the Project

Once the Angular project has been set up, the next step is to create an MVC project in the same SportsStore folder. Run the command shown in Listing 3-7 in the SportsStore folder to create a basic MVC project.

Listing 3-7. Creating the ASP.NET Core MVC Project

```
dotnet new mvc --language C# --auth None --framework netcoreapp1.1
```

Run the command shown in Listing 3-8 in the SportsStore folder to add a Microsoft package to the project. This NuGet package is the .NET counterpart to the NPM packages installed earlier and is used to integrate the Angular tools into Visual Studio.

Listing 3-8. Adding a NuGet Package to the Project

```
dotnet add package Microsoft.AspNetCore.SpaServices --version 1.1.0
```

The application will be stored using Microsoft SQL Server and accessed using Entity Framework Core. Run the commands shown in Listing 3-9 in the SportsStore folder to add the NuGet packages required to add these features to the application.

Listing 3-9. Adding the Data NuGet Packages to the Project

```
dotnet add package Microsoft.EntityFrameworkCore --version 1.1.1
dotnet add package Microsoft.EntityFrameworkCore.Design --version 1.1.1
dotnet add package Microsoft.EntityFrameworkCore.SqlServer --version 1.1.1
```

Not all the required packages can be added using the command-line tools. Open the project using Visual Studio or Visual Studio Code. If you are using Visual Studio, then select File ➤ Open ➤ Project/Solution, navigate to the SportsStore folder, and select the SportsStore.csproj file. To edit the NuGet packages, right-click the SportsStore project item in the Solution Explorer, select Edit SportsStore.csproj from the pop-up menu, and make the changes shown in Listing 3-10.

If you are using Visual Studio Code, open the SportsStore project, click SportsStore.csproj in the file list to open the file for editing, and make the changes shown in Listing 3-10.

Listing 3-10. Adding NuGet Packages in the SportsStore.csproj File in the SportsStore Folder

```
<Project Sdk="Microsoft.NET.Sdk.Web">
  <PropertyGroup>
    <TargetFramework>netcoreapp1.1</TargetFramework>
  </PropertyGroup>
  <ItemGroup>
    <PackageReference Include="Microsoft.AspNetCore" Version="1.1.1" />
    <PackageReference Include="Microsoft.AspNetCore.Mvc" Version="1.1.2" />
    <PackageReference Include="Microsoft.AspNetCore.SpaServices" Version="1.1.0" />
    <PackageReference Include="Microsoft.AspNetCore.StaticFiles" Version="1.1.1" />
    <PackageReference Include="Microsoft.EntityFrameworkCore" Version="1.1.1" />
    <PackageReference Include="Microsoft.EntityFrameworkCore.Design"
        Version="1.1.1" />
```

```
    <PackageReference Include="Microsoft.EntityFrameworkCore.SqlServer"
        Version="1.1.1" />
    <PackageReference Include="Microsoft.Extensions.Logging.Debug" Version="1.1.1" />
    <PackageReference Include="Microsoft.VisualStudio.Web.BrowserLink"
        Version="1.1.0" />

    <DotNetCliToolReference Include="Microsoft.EntityFrameworkCore.Tools"
        Version="1.0.0" />
    <DotNetCliToolReference Include="Microsoft.EntityFrameworkCore.Tools.DotNet"
        Version="1.0.0" />
  </ItemGroup>
</Project>
```

If you are using Visual Studio, the new packages will be downloaded when you save the SportsStore.csproj file. If you are using Visual Studio Code, use a command prompt to run the command shown in Listing 3-11 in the SportsStore folder.

Listing 3-11. Restoring Packages

```
dotnet restore
```

Configuring the Project

Now that the project foundation is in place, it is time to configure the different parts of the application to work together.

Preparing the Project (Visual Studio)

If you are using Visual Studio, select File ➤ Open Project/Solution, navigate to the SportsStore folder, and select the SportsStore.csproj file. Select File ➤ Save All and save the SportsStore.sln file, which you can use to open the project in the future.

Select Project ➤ SportsStore Properties, navigate to the Debug section of the options window, and ensure that IIS Express is selected for the Launch field, as shown in Figure 3-1.

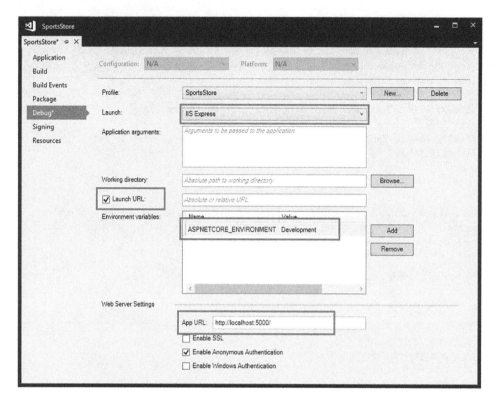

Figure 3-1. *Configuring the application*

Ensure that the Launch URL button is selected and enter `http://localhost:5000` in the App URL field, as shown in Figure 3-1. Finally, click the Add button to create an environment variable called `ASPNETCORE_ENVIRONMENT`, if it doesn't already exist, with a value of `Development`. Save the changes and close the properties window.

Creating and Editing the Configuration Files

Regardless of the IDE you are using, add a TypeScript file called `boot.ts` to the `SportsStore/ClientApp` folder, with the code shown in Listing 3-12.

Listing 3-12. The Contents of the boot.ts File in the ClientApp Folder

```
import { enableProdMode } from "@angular/core";
import { platformBrowserDynamic } from "@angular/platform-browser-dynamic";
import { AppModule } from "./app/app.module";

const bootApplication = () => {
    platformBrowserDynamic().bootstrapModule(AppModule);
};
```

```
if (module["hot"]) {
    module["hot"].accept();
    module["hot"].dispose(() => {
        const oldRootElem = document.querySelector("app-root");
        const newRootElem = document.createElement("app-root");
        oldRootElem.parentNode.insertBefore(newRootElem, oldRootElem);
        platformBrowserDynamic().destroy();
    });
}

if (document.readyState === "complete") {
    bootApplication();
} else {
    document.addEventListener("DOMContentLoaded", bootApplication);
}
```

This file is responsible for loading the Angular application and responding to changes to the client-side code. Next, edit the Startup.cs file to change the code in the Configure method, as shown in Listing 3-13. The additions enable the integration between the ASP.NET Core and Angular development tools.

Listing 3-13. Enabling Middleware in the Startup.cs File in the SportsStore Folder

```
using Microsoft.AspNetCore.Builder;
using Microsoft.AspNetCore.Hosting;
using Microsoft.Extensions.Configuration;
using Microsoft.Extensions.DependencyInjection;
using Microsoft.Extensions.Logging;
using Microsoft.AspNetCore.SpaServices.Webpack;

namespace SportsStore {
    public class Startup {
        public Startup(IHostingEnvironment env) {
            var builder = new ConfigurationBuilder()
              .SetBasePath(env.ContentRootPath)
              .AddJsonFile("appsettings.json", optional: false, reloadOnChange: true)
              .AddJsonFile($"appsettings.{env.EnvironmentName}.json", optional: true)
              .AddEnvironmentVariables();
            Configuration = builder.Build();
        }

        public IConfigurationRoot Configuration { get; }

        public void ConfigureServices(IServiceCollection services) {
            services.AddMvc();
        }

        public void Configure(IApplicationBuilder app,
                IHostingEnvironment env, ILoggerFactory loggerFactory) {
            loggerFactory.AddConsole(Configuration.GetSection("Logging"));
            loggerFactory.AddDebug();
```

```
        app.UseDeveloperExceptionPage();
        app.UseWebpackDevMiddleware(new WebpackDevMiddlewareOptions {
            HotModuleReplacement = true
        });

        //if (env.IsDevelopment()) {
        //    app.UseDeveloperExceptionPage();
        //    app.UseBrowserLink();
        //} else {
        //    app.UseExceptionHandler("/Home/Error");
        //}

        app.UseStaticFiles();

        app.UseMvc(routes => {
            routes.MapRoute(
                name: "default",
                template: "{controller=Home}/{action=Index}/{id?}");
        });
    }
  }
}
```

Open the webpack.config.js file in the SportsStore folder, locate the module.exports statement shown in Listing 3-14, and make the changes in bold. This file contains a lot of configuration statements, but the ones you are looking for are close to the top of the file.

Listing 3-14. Setting the Public Path in the webpack.config.js File in the SportsStore Folder

```
...
module.exports = {
  "devtool": "source-map",
  "resolve": {
    "extensions": [".ts",".js"],
    "modules": ["./node_modules"]
  },
  "resolveLoader": {"modules": ["./node_modules"]},
  "entry": {
    "main": [
        "./ClientApp\\boot.ts"
    ],
    "polyfills": [
      "./ClientApp\\polyfills.ts"
    ],
    "styles": [
      "./ClientApp\\styles.css"
    ]
  },
  "output": {
    "path": path.join(process.cwd(), "wwwroot/dist"),
```

```
    "filename": "[name].bundle.js",
    "chunkFilename": "[id].chunk.js",
    "publicPath": "/app/"
  },
"module": {
    "rules": [{
        "enforce": "pre", "test": /\.js$/, "loader": "source-map-loader",
...
```

Enabling Logging Messages

During development, it can be useful to see details of the build process for the Angular application and details of the queries sent to the database by Entity Framework Core. To enable logging messages, add the configuration statements shown in Listing 3-15 to the appsettings.json file.

Listing 3-15. Enabling Logging in the appsettings.json File in the SportsStore Folder

```
{
  "Logging": {
    "IncludeScopes": false,
    "LogLevel": {
      "Microsoft.EntityFrameworkCore": "Information",
      "Microsoft.AspNetCore.NodeServices": "Information",
      "Default": "Warning"
    }
  }
}
```

Updating the Bootstrap Package

Throughout this book, I use the Bootstrap CSS package to style the HTML elements displayed by the browser. To update the version used in the project, edit the bower.json file in the SportsStore folder and make the change shown in Listing 3-16.

USING THE BOOTSTRAP PRERELEASE

Throughout this book, I use a prerelease version of the Bootstrap CSS framework. As I write this, the Bootstrap team is in the process of developing Bootstrap version 4 and has made several early releases. These releases are labeled as "alpha," but the quality is high, and they are stable enough for use in the examples in this book.

Given the choice of writing this book using the soon-to-be-obsolete Bootstrap 3 and a prerelease version of Bootstrap 4, I decided to use the new version even though some of the class names that are used to style HTML elements are likely to change before the final release. You must use the same version of Bootstrap to get the expected results from the examples, just like the rest of the packages used in this book.

Listing 3-16. Updating Bootstrap in the bower.json File in the SportsStore Folder

```
{
  "name": "asp.net",
  "private": true,
  "dependencies": {
    "bootstrap": "4.0.0-alpha.6",
    "jquery": "2.2.0",
    "jquery-validation": "1.14.0",
    "jquery-validation-unobtrusive": "3.2.6"
  }
}
```

Save the change. If you are using Visual Studio Code, use a command prompt to run the command shown in Listing 3-17 to download the Bootstrap package. (This is done automatically by Visual Studio.)

Listing 3-17. Updating the Client-Side Packages

```
bower install
```

Removing Files

Some files in the project can be removed. Table 3-2 describes the files that are not required in this book. You don't have to remove these files, but it will help simplify the project structure and, in the case of the .editorconfig file, avoid confusion when your code editor doesn't respect your normal preferences.

Table 3-2. *Files That Can Be Removed*

Name	Description
.editorconfig	This file contains project-specific editor configuration settings, and it is used by Visual Studio to override the preferences specified by the Tools ➤ Options menu, including setting the tab size to two spaces.
e2e	This folder contains tests for Protractor, which does end-to-end testing for Angular applications. See www.protractortest.org for details.
protractor.conf.js	This file contains configuration settings for Protractor.
README.md	This file contains welcome text containing an overview of the @angular/cli tools.

Updating the Controller, Layout, and View

The final step in setting up the project is to update the controller and the Razor layout and view to replace the placeholder content and incorporate the Angular application. Edit the Home controller and replace the contents with the code shown in Listing 3-18.

Listing 3-18. Replacing Content in the HomeController.cs File in the Controllers Folder

```
using Microsoft.AspNetCore.Mvc;

namespace SportsStore.Controllers {
    public class HomeController : Controller {

        public IActionResult Index() {
            return View();
        }
    }
}
```

Edit the _Layout.cshtml file in the Views/Shared folder and replace the content with the elements shown in Listing 3-19.

Listing 3-19. Replacing Content in the _Layout.cshtml File in the Views/Shared Folder

```
<!DOCTYPE html>
<html>
<head>
    <meta charset="utf-8" />
    <meta name="viewport" content="width=device-width, initial-scale=1.0" />
    <title>SportsStore @ViewData["Title"]</title>
    <link rel="stylesheet" href="~/lib/bootstrap/dist/css/bootstrap.css" />
</head>
<body>
    @RenderBody()
    @RenderSection("Scripts", required: false)
</body>
</html>
```

Edit the Index.cshtml file in the Views/Home folder and replace the contents with those shown in Listing 3-20.

Listing 3-20. Replacing Content in the Index.cshtml File in the Views/Home Folder

```
@section scripts {
  <script src="~/dist/inline.bundle.js" asp-append-version="true"></script>
  <script src="~/dist/polyfills.bundle.js" asp-append-version="true"></script>
  <script src="~/dist/vendor.bundle.js" asp-append-version="true"></script>
  <script src="~/dist/main.bundle.js" asp-append-version="true"></script>
}

<div class="navbar bg-inverse">
  <a class="navbar-brand text-white">@(ViewBag.Message ?? "SPORTS STORE")</a>
</div>
<div class="p-1">
  <app-root></app-root>
</div>
```

The script elements in this view include bundles of JavaScript files that contain the Angular framework and the client-side application code. These bundles will be created automatically by webpack when the files in the Angular part of the project change.

The app-root element will be replaced with dynamic content produced by the Angular application, as you will see in the next section. The other elements are standard HTML that has been styled with Bootstrap.

Running the Project

If you are using Visual Studio, then start the application by selecting Start Without Debugging from the Debug menu. A new browser window will open and request http://localhost:5000, which was the URL you used to configure the project earlier in the chapter, showing the content in Figure 3-2.

If you are using Visual Studio Code, then use a command window to run the command shown in Listing 3-21 in the SportsStore folder, which will build the project and start the ASP.NET Core HTTP server.

Listing 3-21. Starting the Project

```
dotnet run
```

Open a new browser window and navigate to http://localhost:5000. If you have followed all of the configuration steps, you will see the content shown in Figure 3-2.

Figure 3-2. *Testing the application*

■ **Tip**   It can take a moment for the application to deliver the content to the client for the first HTTP request. Reload the browser page if you just see the SportsStore header but not the "app works!" message.

This may not seem like an impressive result, but the Angular development tools and ASP.NET Core are now working together. Edit the app.component.ts file in the SportsStore/ClientApp/app folder and make the change highlighted in Listing 3-22. (You will have to expand the app.component.html file to see the app.component.ts file in the Solution Explorer if you are using Visual Studio, which nests related files together.)

Listing 3-22. Making a Change in the app.component.ts File in the SportsStore/ClientApp/app Folder

```
import { Component } from '@angular/core';

@Component({
    selector: 'app-root',
    templateUrl: './app.component.html',
    styleUrls: ['./app.component.css']
})
export class AppComponent {
    title = 'Angular & ASP.NET Core MVC';
}
```

As soon as you save the file, you will see the following messages produced by the ASP.NET Core MVC application:

```
...
info: Microsoft.AspNetCore.NodeServices[0]
      webpack built 7db0492261faa4be5ca2 in 13727ms
info: Microsoft.AspNetCore.NodeServices[0]
      webpack building...
info: Microsoft.AspNetCore.NodeServices[0]
      webpack built 13d818ceaf0329cf3f6e in 353ms
...
```

There will also be corresponding messages displayed in the browser's JavaScript console, similar to these:

```
..
[HMR] bundle rebuilding
[HMR] bundle rebuilt in 503ms
[HMR] Checking for updates on the server...
[HMR] Updated modules:
[HMR]  - ./ClientApp/app/app.component.ts
[HMR]  - ./ClientApp/app/app.module.ts
[HMR]  - ./ClientApp/boot.ts
[HMR] App is up to date.
...
```

The file change has triggered the Angular development tools to compile the TypeScript files and generate new JavaScript files that will be loaded and executed by the browser. The changed files are sent to the browser, and the running application is updated on the fly, producing the output shown in Figure 3-3.

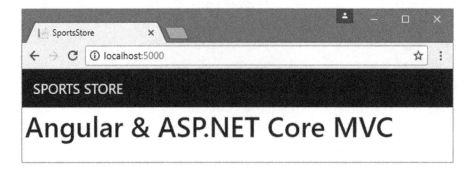

Figure 3-3. *Updating the application*

■ **Caution** The automatic refresh feature is generally reliable, but you may have to reload the browser window to see the effect of some changes or after you restart the ASP.NET Core server.

Understanding the Combined Project and Tools

It is worth taking the time to understand how Angular and ASP.NET Core MVC have been integrated into the project, especially since they rely on different platforms.

Understanding the Structure of the Project

Combining Angular and ASP.NET Core MVC in a single project produces a complex folder structure. When working with a combined project, it is important to remember that you are developing two distinct applications whose files happen to be collocated. Table 3-3 describes the most important parts of a combined project.

Table 3-3. *The Key Files and Folders in a Combined Project*

Name	Description
ClientApp	This folder contains the Angular application and its configuration files.
ClientApp/app	This folder contains the source code for the Angular application, including templates and stylesheets used by Angular components.
Controllers	This folder contains the ASP.NET Core MVC controller classes.
Views	This folder contains the Razor views that are rendered by the MVC controllers.
wwwroot	This folder contains the static content files that the project requires.
wwwroot/dist	This folder contains the JavaScript files produced by compiling the Angular project.
webpack.config.js	This file contains the configuration used to build the Angular application.

You can find the source code for the Angular application in the `ClientApp/app` folder, which is where you will create your TypeScript files, along with any related HTML templates and CSS stylesheets. Only the source code lives this folder; when the code is compiled, the files that are produced are placed into the `wwwroot/dist` folder so they can be included in the responses to HTTP requests.

You can find the source code for the ASP.NET Core MVC application in the `Controllers` and `Views` folders and in the `Models` folder, which you will create in Chapter 4 These folders contain C# and Razor files, which are used to receive HTTP requests from the client and generate responses. The rest of the files in the project are either configuration files that can be ignored for the moment or packages required to support the integration of the Angular and ASP.NET Core tools.

Understanding the Tool Integration

The key to getting Angular and ASP.NET Core to work together is the `Microsoft.AspNetCore.SpaServices` package that was added to the project earlier in the chapter. This NuGet package, which is provided by Microsoft, provides services that are useful when working with single-page application frameworks, such as Angular.

For this chapter, the most important service is the ability to run Node.js packages from inside an ASP.NET Core project, which allows the development tools used by Angular, such as webpack, to be integrated into the ASP.NET Core HTTP request pipeline.

When the first HTTP request is received by the ASP.NET Core part of the application, the middleware added to the request pipeline starts a new Node.js runtime and uses it to run webpack. Webpack compiles the TypeScript files in the `ClientApp/app` folder and creates a set of JavaScript bundles in the `wwwroot/dist` folder.

The HTTP request is handled in the usual way by the MVC framework, which directs the request to the `Index` action on the `Home` controller, which tells Razor to render the `Index.cshtml` file in the `Views/Home` folder and send the output back to the client. The HTML produced by the Razor view contains `script` elements that load the JavaScript bundles created by webpack, which load the Angular application and display the message in the browser, as illustrated in Figure 3-4.

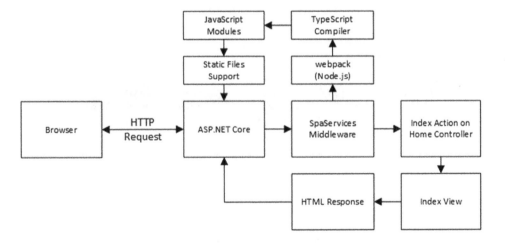

Figure 3-4. *Integrating Angular and ASP.NET Core MVC*

From the perspective of the MVC part of the application, the difference from a regular project is that the `SpaServices` middleware is using webpack to generate some static JavaScript files that are loaded from `script` elements included in a Razor view. From the Angular perspective, the difference from a regular project is that the HTTP requests from the browser are being handled by ASP.NET Core using Razor views, rather than through a static HTML file.

Understanding the Project Change Systems

One source of confusion is that there are three different ways in which changes to files in the projects are displayed in the browser. I describe each of these update mechanisms in the sections that follow.

Updating Angular Files

The SpaServices middleware is configured to support the webpack *hot module replacement* feature (known as the HMR feature), which recompiles TypeScript files and updates the running application automatically when there is a change to the code files in the Angular part of the project.

The JavaScript files created by webpack include code that opens a connection back to the server and waits for a change notification. When a file in the ClientApp/app folder changes, the files are recompiled, and the module files are updated. A signal is sent to the browser, which requests the modified module and uses it to update the code running in the browser without requiring a reload.

The update process was demonstrated in the "Running the Project" section, and it applies not just to TypeScript files but also to HTML and CSS files. Edit the app.component.html file to change the template used by the component in the Angular part of the project, as shown in Listing 3-23.

Listing 3-23. Editing the Template in the app.component.html File in the ClientApp/app Folder

```
<h1>
  Title: {{title}}
</h1>
```

As soon as you save the change, the Angular build process will start, and new modules will be created and used by the browser to update the client-side application without needing to reload the browser window, as illustrated by Figure 3-5.

Figure 3-5. *An update to an HTML template*

■ **Tip** The update process can take a while when the application is first started and can, on occasion, get bogged down even when everything has been running for a while. I like to keep the browser's JavaScript console open so that I can see the HMR messages that are displayed during the update. If an update takes too long, then reloading the browser will reload the JavaScript files and give the Angular application a fresh start.

Updating Razor Files

Razor view files are not updated as part of the HMR feature. When you make a change to a Razor view file, you must reload the browser window. The reload will send an HTTP request that will be received by ASP.NET Core, passed to the MVC framework, and used by a controller to select a view and render a new response.

Edit the Index.cshtml file in the Views/Home folder to apply the class shown in Listing 3-24.

Listing 3-24. Changing an Element Class in the Index.cshtml File in the Views/Home Folder

```
@section scripts {
  <script src="~/dist/inline.bundle.js" asp-append-version="true"></script>
  <script src="~/dist/polyfills.bundle.js" asp-append-version="true"></script>
  <script src="~/dist/vendor.bundle.js" asp-append-version="true"></script>
  <script src="~/dist/main.bundle.js" asp-append-version="true"></script>
}

<div class="navbar bg-inverse">
  <a class="navbar-brand text-white">@(ViewBag.Message ?? "SPORTS STORE")</a>
</div>
<div class="p-1 bg-info">
  <app-root></app-root>
</div>
```

Adding the div element to the bg-info class applies a Bootstrap CSS style that changes the background color. Nothing will happen when you save the change, but the updated view will be used if you reload the page using the browser, as shown in Figure 3-6.

Figure 3-6. *An update to a Razor view*

Updating C# Classes

The effect of changes to C# classes depends on which IDE you are using. To see how changes are handled, edit the Home controller to change the view selected by the Index action, as shown in Listing 3-25.

Listing 3-25. Selecting a Different View in the HomeController.cs File in the Controllers Folder

```csharp
using Microsoft.AspNetCore.Mvc;

namespace SportsStore.Controllers {
    public class HomeController : Controller {

        public IActionResult Index() {
            ViewBag.Message = "Sports Store App";
            return View();
        }
    }
}
```

The view bag property added to the listing will override the text displayed at the top of the view. If you are using Visual Studio and you started the application using IIS Express by selecting Debug ➤ Start Without Debugging, then you can trigger an update by reloading the web page in the browser. This will trigger an automatic project build and restart the application, as shown in Figure 3-7.

Figure 3-7. An update to an MVC controller in Visual Studio

If you are using Visual Studio Code, the dotnet run command used to start the application doesn't respond to changes. That means you must stop the application with Control+C and then start the application again using dotnet run. Once the application has started, reload the browser window to see the effect of the changes.

■ **Tip** Microsoft provides a NuGet package called DotNet Watcher, which can be used to watch the project folder for changes and trigger a rebuild and restart when a change is detected. See https://github.com/aspnet/DotNetTools for details.

Detecting TypeScript Errors

The hot module replacement feature will display any errors reported by the TypeScript compiler in the browser. To see an error message, add the statement shown in Listing 3-26 to the app.component.ts file in the ClientApp/app folder.

Listing 3-26. Forcing an Error in the app.component.ts File in the ClientApp/app Folder

```
import { Component } from '@angular/core';

@Component({
  selector: 'app-root',
  templateUrl: './app.component.html',
  styleUrls: ['./app.component.css']
})
export class AppComponent {
    title = 'Angular & ASP.NET Core MVC';

    title = no_such_object;
}
```

The statement added to the TypeScript component class creates two errors by assigning a nonexistent value to a property that has already been defined. As soon as you save the file, the Angular development tools will compile the class, regenerate the JavaScript modules, and try to do a hot replacement. But since the code can't be executed, you will see the error illustrated by Figure 3-8.

Figure 3-8. *A code error displayed in the browser*

The lines of text displayed by an error don't wrap onto multiple lines, so you will either need to work with a wide browser window or scroll to see the details.

For errors like the one introduced in Listing 3-26, you will also see a warning displayed by IntelliSense in Visual Studio or Visual Studio Code, as shown in Figure 3-9. (This shows Visual Studio Code but with the color scheme changed to Light to make the text easier to see on the page.)

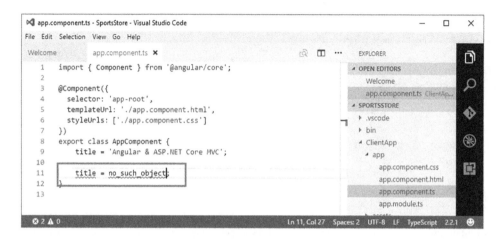

Figure 3-9. *A code error detected by the code editor*

Visual Studio and Visual Studio Code both compile TypeScript files automatically to detect and report errors in the code editor. This won't always display errors that are not simple code mistakes, so you must get used to handling errors displayed in the browser window, too.

If you are using Visual Studio, you can also select Build ➤ Build Solution, which will compile all of the files in the project, including TypeScript files, and problems are reported in the Error List window, as shown in Figure 3-10.

	Code	Description	Project	File	Line
❌	TS2300	Build:Duplicate identifier 'title'.	SportsStore	app.component.ts	11
❌	TS2304	Build:Cannot find name 'no_such_object'.	SportsStore	app.component.ts	11

Figure 3-10. *Build errors reported by Visual Studio*

To restore the application to its working statement, comment out the problem statement, as shown in Listing 3-27.

Listing 3-27. Commenting Out a Statement in the app.component.ts File in the ClientApp/app Folder

```
import { Component } from '@angular/core';

@Component({
  selector: 'app-root',
  templateUrl: './app.component.html',
  styleUrls: ['./app.component.css']
})
```

```
export class AppComponent {
    title = 'Angular & ASP.NET Core MVC';

    //title = no_such_object;
}
```

As soon as you save the change, the TypeScript file will be recompiled and used to create a module that will be used by the code running the browser to update the application, as shown in Figure 3-11.

Figure 3-11. *Correcting an error*

Visual Studio doesn't always manage to recover from errors automatically if you have selected Build ➤ Build Solution. Select Debug ➤ Start Without Debugging to restart the .NET Core runtime.

Summary

In this chapter, I showed you how to create a project that combines Angular and ASP.NET Core MVC. The process is a little complicated, but the result is a solid foundation that simplifies the development process and makes it easier to get the Angular and MVC parts of an application to work together. In the next chapter, I start work on the data model, which will underpin both the ASP.NET Core MVC and Angular parts of the SportsStore project.

CHAPTER 4

▨ ▨ ▨

Creating the Data Model

In this chapter, I start adding functionality to the ASP.NET Core MVC and Angular parts of the project to create a data model. I'll set up a SQL Server database to store the application data, and I'll define the model classes that Entity Framework Core will use to represent the data. On the Angular side, I'll define the TypeScript classes that will represent the data and define a repository that will make the data available throughout the application. Table 4-1 puts creating the data model into context.

Table 4-1. *Putting the Data Model in Context*

Question	Answer
What is it?	The data model describes the data in both parts of the application.
Why is it useful?	A consistent data model allows data to be consistently represented in Angular and ASP.NET Core MVC and to flow easily from one to the other.
How is it used?	The data model is defined as pairs of TypeScript and C# classes, with a repository in the Angular application and data context classes in the ASP.NET Core MVC application that allows the data to be stored using Entity Framework Core.
Are there any pitfalls or limitations?	The data model classes should be as simple as possible to ensure they can be represented consistently in TypeScript and C# and, for most applications, ensure they can be serialized as JSON.
Are there any alternatives?	No, if an application requires both Angular and ASP.NET Core MVC, then it almost certainly requires a data model.

Preparing for This Chapter

This chapter depends on the SportsStore project that I created in Chapter 3. No changes are required to prepare for this chapter. If you are using Visual Studio, then run the example application by selecting Debug ➤ Start Without Debugging. If you are using Visual Studio Code, then open a new command prompt and run the command shown in Listing 4-1 in the SportsStore folder.

▨ **Tip**   You can download the complete project for this chapter from `https://github.com/apress/esntl-angular-for-asp.net-core-mvc`. This is also where you will find updates and corrections for this book.

© Adam Freeman 2017
A. Freeman, *Essential Angular for ASP.NET Core MVC*, DOI 10.1007/978-1-4842-2916-3_4

Listing 4-1. Starting the Example Application

```
dotnet run
```

Use a browser to navigate to `http://localhost:5000` and you will see the result shown in Figure 4-1.

> ■ **Tip** You can download the complete project for every chapter without charge from the source code repository. See the Apress.com page for this book for a link.

Figure 4-1. *Running the example application*

Starting the Data Model

Just as with a stand-alone ASP.NET Core MVC project, the best place to start is with the data model. The biggest difference is that you need to describe data in both the Angular and MVC parts of the application.

Preparing the Database Server

I use Docker to run SQL Server throughout this book. Putting the database inside a container makes it easy to reset the examples between chapters and allows SQL Server to run on all the platforms that are supported by .NET Core without going through a complex configuration process. Add a file called `docker-compose.yml` to the `SportsStore` project and add the content shown in Listing 4-2.

> ■ **Note** This is an example of a Docker compose file, which simplifies the process of managing a Docker container. Docker compose files are written in the YAML format, which is sensitive to spaces and does not allow tab characters. It is important to copy the contents of this file exactly as shown. If you have problems, you can download the file from the source repository, `https://github.com/apress/esntl-angular-for-asp.net-core-mvc`.

Listing 4-2. The Contents of the docker-compose.yml File in the SportsStore Folder

```
version: "3"

services:
  database:
    image: "microsoft/mssql-server-linux:ctp2-0"
    ports:
      - 5100:1433
    environment:
      - ACCEPT_EULA=Y
      - SA_PASSWORD=mySecret123
```

This file configures SQL Server so that it will receive queries on port 5100, with the username SA and the password mySecret123.

USING THE PRERELEASE SQL SERVER VERSION

The image configuration property in Listing 4-2 specifies a prerelease of the Linux version of SQL Server, which can be used on all the platforms supported by .NET Core. This isn't ready for production, but it is stable and is acceptable for using the examples in the book. I'll provide an update in the GitHub repository for this book (https://github.com/apress/esntl-angular-for-asp.net-core-mvc) if there are any changes required when the final version is released.

Defining the Connection String

To provide Entity Framework Core with details of how to connect to the database, open the appsettings.json file and add the statements shown in Listing 4-3, taking care to enter the connection string on a single line.

■ **Tip** The appsettings files can be used to create environment-specific configurations, such that the settings in the appsettings.Development.json file override those in the main appsettings.json file when the application runs in the Development environment. I do not use this feature for the examples in this book, as explained in Chapter 12.

Listing 4-3. Adding a Connection String in the appsettings.json File in the SportsStore Folder

```
{
  "Logging": {
    "IncludeScopes": false,
    "LogLevel": {
      "Microsoft.EntityFrameworkCore": "Information",
      "Microsoft.AspNetCore.NodeServices": "Information",
      "Default": "Warning"
    }
  },
```

```
  "Data": {
    "Products": {
      "ConnectionString": "Server=localhost,5100;Database=SportsStore;User Id=sa;Password=my
Secret123;MultipleActiveResultSets=true"
    }
  }
}
```

Creating the ASP.NET Core MVC Data Model

The process of creating the data model for the MVC part of the application will be familiar to most MVC developers: a series of C# model classes is used to create a database schema, which is used to prepare a database to store the application's data.

An important difference from conventional ASP.NET Core development is that I do not create a repository interface and implementation class in the MVC part of the project. Instead, I create the repository in the Angular application, which is where the data is consumed. The structure of both applications will become clear as the application takes shape.

Defining the Model Data Types

Data types in a project that combines Angular and ASP.NET Core MVC should be as simple as possible so they can be described as C# and TypeScript classes. Simple classes can be readily represented as JSON data, allowing them to be sent between Angular and ASP.NET Core MVC using HTTP requests.

To get the data model started for the SportsStore application, I am going to define three classes, representing the products, the suppliers of those products, and customer feedback. Create a SportsStore/ Models folder, add a C# class file called Product.cs, and add the code shown in Listing 4-4.

Listing 4-4. The Contents of the Product.cs File in the Models Folder

```
using System.Collections.Generic;

namespace SportsStore.Models {
    public class Product {

        public long ProductId { get; set; }

        public string Name { get; set; }
        public string Category { get; set; }
        public string Description { get; set; }
        public decimal Price { get; set; }

        public Supplier Supplier { get; set; }
        public List<Rating> Ratings { get; set; }
    }
}
```

The ProductId property will be used as the primary key when storing Product objects in the database. The Name, Category, Description, and Price properties are regular properties that store simple data values.

The Supplier and Ratings properties are *navigation properties* that Entity Framework Core uses to associate a Product object with other data in the database. The objects accessed through a navigation property are referred to as *related data*. In this case, each Product object may be related to one Supplier object and multiple Rating objects.

■ **Tip** This is a more complex data model than I used in the SportsStore examples in the *Pro ASP.NET Core MVC* and *Pro Angular* books because there are some common problems with related data when Angular and ASP.NET Core MVC are used together, which I describe in later chapters.

Add a C# class file called Supplier.cs to the Models folder and add the code shown in Listing 4-5.

Listing 4-5. The Contents of the Supplier.cs File in the Models Folder

```
using System.Collections.Generic;

namespace SportsStore.Models {
    public class Supplier {

        public long SupplierId { get; set; }

        public string Name { get; set; }
        public string City { get; set; }
        public string State { get; set; }

        public IEnumerable<Product> Products { get; set; }
    }
}
```

The SupplierId property is used for the primary key when data is stored in the database, and the Name, City, and State properties are regular properties used to store simple data values. The Products property is a navigation property used to move through the related data in the database.

To complete the initial set of data model class files, add a C# class file called Rating.cs to the Models folder and add the statements shown in Listing 4-6.

Listing 4-6. The Contents of the Rating.cs File in the Models Folder

```
namespace SportsStore.Models {
    public class Rating {

        public long RatingId { get; set; }

        public int Stars { get; set; }

        public Product Product { get; set; }

    }
}
```

The RatingId property is used as the primary key when storing Rating objects in the database. The Stars property is a regular property used to store a rating from a customer. The Product property is a navigation property used to relate a Rating object to a Product object.

Creating the Database Context Class and the Seed Data

The next step is to create the database context class that provides access to the data through Entity Framework Core. Add a C# class file called `DataContext.cs` to the `Models` folder and add the statements shown in Listing 4-7.

Listing 4-7. The Contents of the DataContext.cs File in the Models Folder

```
using Microsoft.EntityFrameworkCore;

namespace SportsStore.Models {

    public class DataContext : DbContext {

        public DataContext(DbContextOptions<DataContext> opts)
            : base(opts) { }

        public DbSet<Product> Products { get; set; }
        public DbSet<Supplier> Suppliers { get; set; }
        public DbSet<Rating> Ratings { get; set; }
    }
}
```

The context class follows the standard pattern for Entity Framework Core and defines a constructor that accepts a `DbContextOptions<T>` object and that is configured during the ASP.NET Core startup sequence. The three `DbSet` properties provide access to the data in the database, allowing independent queries for each model type. You do not need to add `DbSet` properties for every model class, especially for related data types, but I find it convenient to do so.

The database is reset for every chapter to ensure you get the expected results from the examples in this book. This means it is useful to automatically populate the database with seed data so that the application always has data with which to work. Add a class file called `SeedData.cs` to the `Models` folder and add the statements shown in Listing 4-8.

Listing 4-8. The Contents of the SeedData.cs File in the Models Folder

```
using System.Collections.Generic;
using System.Linq;
using Microsoft.EntityFrameworkCore;
using SportsStore.Models;

namespace SportsStore {

    public class SeedData {

        public static void SeedDatabase(DataContext context) {
            context.Database.Migrate();
            if (context.Products.Count() == 0) {
                var s1 = new Supplier { Name = "Splash Dudes",
                    City = "San Jose", State = "CA"};
                var s2 = new Supplier { Name = "Soccer Town",
                    City = "Chicago", State = "IL"};
                var s3 = new Supplier { Name = "Chess Co",
                    City = "New York", State = "NY"};
```

```
            context.Products.AddRange(
                new Product { Name = "Kayak",
                    Description = "A boat for one person",
                    Category = "Watersports", Price = 275, Supplier = s1,
                    Ratings = new List<Rating> {
                        new Rating { Stars = 4 }, new Rating { Stars = 3 }}},
                 new Product { Name = "Lifejacket",
                    Description = "Protective and fashionable",
                    Category = "Watersports", Price = 48.95m, Supplier = s1,
                    Ratings = new List<Rating> {
                        new Rating { Stars = 2 }, new Rating { Stars = 5 }}},
                new Product {
                    Name = "Soccer Ball",
                    Description = "FIFA-approved size and weight",
                    Category = "Soccer", Price = 19.50m, Supplier = s2,
                    Ratings = new List<Rating> {
                        new Rating { Stars = 1 }, new Rating { Stars = 3 }}},
                new Product {
                    Name = "Corner Flags",
                    Description = "Give your pitch a professional touch",
                    Category = "Soccer", Price = 34.95m, Supplier = s2,
                    Ratings = new List<Rating> { new Rating { Stars = 3 }}},
                new Product {
                    Name = "Stadium",
                    Description = "Flat-packed 35,000-seat stadium",
                    Category = "Soccer", Price = 79500, Supplier = s2,
                    Ratings = new List<Rating> { new Rating { Stars = 1 },
                        new Rating { Stars = 4 }, new Rating { Stars = 3 }}},
                new Product {
                    Name = "Thinking Cap",
                    Description = "Improve brain efficiency by 75%",
                    Category = "Chess", Price = 16, Supplier = s3,
                    Ratings = new List<Rating> { new Rating { Stars = 5 },
                        new Rating { Stars = 4 }}},
                new Product {
                    Name = "Unsteady Chair",
                    Description = "Secretly give your opponent a disadvantage",
                    Category = "Chess", Price = 29.95m, Supplier = s3,
                    Ratings = new List<Rating> { new Rating { Stars = 3 }}},
                new Product {
                    Name = "Human Chess Board",
                    Description = "A fun game for the family",
                    Category = "Chess", Price = 75, Supplier = s3 },
                new Product {
                    Name = "Bling-Bling King",
                    Description = "Gold-plated, diamond-studded King",
                    Category = "Chess", Price = 1200, Supplier = s3 });
            context.SaveChanges();
        }
    }
  }
}
```

The SeedDatabase method starts by calling the DataContext.Database.Migrate method, which ensures that the schema in the database is up-to-date before the seed data is applied. Automatic migration is something that should be done with care in production applications because schema changes can result in data loss. The rest of the method creates a series of model objects, associates them with one another, and then saves them to the database using the DataContext.SaveChanges method.

To register the context class with Entity Framework Core and to ensure that the seed data is applied when ASP.NET Core starts, add the statements shown in Listing 4-9 to the Startup class.

Listing 4-9. Registering the Context Class in the Startup.cs File in the SportsStore Folder

```
using Microsoft.AspNetCore.Builder;
using Microsoft.AspNetCore.Hosting;
using Microsoft.Extensions.Configuration;
using Microsoft.Extensions.DependencyInjection;
using Microsoft.Extensions.Logging;
using Microsoft.AspNetCore.SpaServices.Webpack;
using SportsStore.Models;
using Microsoft.EntityFrameworkCore;

namespace SportsStore {
    public class Startup {
        public Startup(IHostingEnvironment env) {
            var builder = new ConfigurationBuilder()
                .SetBasePath(env.ContentRootPath)
                .AddJsonFile("appsettings.json", optional: false, reloadOnChange: true)
                .AddJsonFile($"appsettings.{env.EnvironmentName}.json", optional: true)
                .AddEnvironmentVariables();
            Configuration = builder.Build();
        }

        public IConfigurationRoot Configuration { get; }

        public void ConfigureServices(IServiceCollection services) {
            services.AddDbContext<DataContext>(options =>
                options.UseSqlServer(Configuration
                    ["Data:Products:ConnectionString"]));
            services.AddMvc();
        }

        public void Configure(IApplicationBuilder app,
                IHostingEnvironment env, ILoggerFactory loggerFactory) {
            loggerFactory.AddConsole(Configuration.GetSection("Logging"));
            loggerFactory.AddDebug();

            app.UseDeveloperExceptionPage();
            app.UseWebpackDevMiddleware(new WebpackDevMiddlewareOptions {
                HotModuleReplacement = true
            });
```

```
        app.UseStaticFiles();

        app.UseMvc(routes => {
            routes.MapRoute(
                name: "default",
                template: "{controller=Home}/{action=Index}/{id?}");
        });

        SeedData.SeedDatabase(app.ApplicationServices
            .GetRequiredService<DataContext>());
    }
  }
}
```

A database migration is required to create the database schema that will allow the database to store the application data. Use a command prompt to run the command shown in Listing 4-10 in the SportsStore folder.

■ **Tip**   If you are a long-term user of Entity Framework Core and Visual Studio, you may be accustomed to running the Add-Migration command in the Package Manager Console window, but I use the new dotnet ef commands throughout this book because they provide more useful error messages and work across platforms.

Listing 4-10. Creating the Database Migration

```
dotnet ef migrations add Initial
```

The result of running this command is that a Migrations folder is added to the project, containing C# class files that include statements that generate the database schema when the migration is applied to the database.

The files created for a migration start with a timestamp. If you examine the statements in the <timestamp>_Initial.cs file in the Migrations folder, you will see how Entity Framework Core is going to store the application's data. The database will contain three tables, called Products, Suppliers, and Ratings, corresponding to each of the three data model types. Each table has columns that correspond to the properties defined by the equivalent data model class, while the navigation properties are translated into foreign key relationships between the tables. Figure 4-2 shows a simplified representation of the database created by the migration and the seed data. (This is not a book about Entity Framework Core, but it helps to understand how the data is stored when it comes to querying the database to provide the application with its data.)

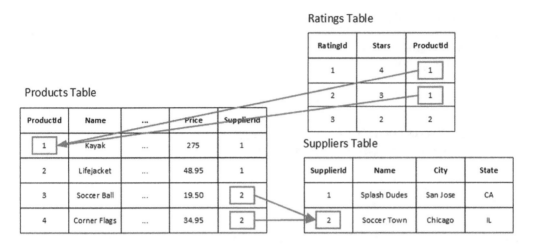

Figure 4-2. *The basic database structure*

The Products table is used to store Product objects and includes a SupplierId column that is used to capture the relationship to a Supplier object by storing the value of a SupplierId property from the Suppliers table. The Ratings table is used to store Rating objects and has a ProductId column that captures the relationship with the related Product object.

Testing the ASP.NET Core MVC Data Model

Before going further, it is worth taking a moment to make sure that Entity Framework Core can connect to the database and that the seed data is correctly applied. The simplest way to check the data model is to include some data in a view. Edit the Index action of the Home controller so that it receives a DataContext object through its constructor and passes on data to its view, as shown in Listing 4-11.

Listing 4-11. Working with Data in the HomeController.cs File in the Controllers Folder

```
using Microsoft.AspNetCore.Mvc;
using SportsStore.Models;
using System.Linq;

namespace SportsStore.Controllers {
    public class HomeController : Controller {
        private DataContext context;

        public HomeController(DataContext ctx) {
            context = ctx;
        }

        public IActionResult Index() {
            ViewBag.Message = "Sports Store App";
            return View(context.Products.First());
        }
    }
}
```

The data passed to the view is the first Product object stored in the database. To display the data, edit the Index.cshtml view to add the content shown in Listing 4-12.

Listing 4-12. Displaying Data in the Index.cshtml File in the Views/Home Folder

```
@section scripts {
  <script src="~/dist/inline.bundle.js" asp-append-version="true"></script>
  <script src="~/dist/polyfills.bundle.js" asp-append-version="true"></script>
  <script src="~/dist/vendor.bundle.js" asp-append-version="true"></script>
  <script src="~/dist/main.bundle.js" asp-append-version="true"></script>
}

<div class="navbar bg-inverse">
  <a class="navbar-brand text-white">@(ViewBag.Message ?? "SPORTS STORE")</a>
</div>

<div id="data" class="p-1 bg-warning">
  @Json.Serialize(Model)
</div>

<div class="p-1 bg-info">
  <app-root></app-root>
</div>
```

The @Json.Serialize method generates a JSON representation of the view model data provided by the action method. Save the changes to the controller and view and then start the database container by running the command shown in Listing 4-13 in the SportsStore folder.

Listing 4-13. Starting the Database Container

```
docker-compose up
```

When you first run this command, Docker downloads all the files it needs to create a container for SQL Server, which can take a while. Once the files are downloaded, Docker starts a new container, and the command prompt displays the output messages from the SQL Server startup.

■ **Tip**   If you see a message warning you that Docker does not have enough memory to start the container, then you may not have followed all of the setup instructions in Chapter 3. Return to that chapter for details of how to increase the amount of memory allocated to Docker.

Start the example application once the database has started. For Visual Studio users, this means selecting Debug ➤ Start Without Debugging. For Visual Studio Code users, this means opening a second command prompt, navigating to the SportsStore folder, and running the command shown in Listing 4-14.

Listing 4-14. Starting the Example Application

```
dotnet run
```

It can take a moment before you see any output from the dotnet run command. Be patient, and you will see details of the SQL statements sent to the database to apply the schema and from the Angular build tools.

Once the ASP.NET Core MVC part of the application is ready, open a new browser window and navigate to http://localhost:5000. The content shown by the browser contains a block of JSON data, as shown in Figure 4-3.

Figure 4-3. *Including JSON data in a view*

Here is the JSON data added to the HTML sent to the browser:

```
{
    "productId":1,"name":"Kayak","category":"Watersports",
    "description":"A boat for one person","price":275.00,
    "supplier":null,"ratings":null
}
```

The supplier and ratings properties are set to null because I did not tell Entity Framework Core to follow the navigation properties defined by the Product class to load the related Supplier and Rating data. I show you how to work with related data in Chapter 5.

■ **Caution** Do not continue until you see the JSON data in the view, as shown in Figure 4-3. Go back and make sure you have followed all the steps to prepare and populate the database. If you need to reset the database, then run docker-compose down in the SportsStore folder using a new command prompt, and finally run docker-compose up to create a fresh container and database.

Starting the Angular Data Model

Creating a data model in the Angular part of the project makes it easier to work with the data received from the MVC part. Create a ClientApp/app/models folder and add to it a TypeScript file called product.model. ts, with the code shown in Listing 4-15.

■ **Tip** The convention for Angular files is to include terms such as model and component in the file name to make the purpose of the file obvious. The name product.model.ts, for example, indicates that this is a TypeScript file that contains a model class called Product.

Listing 4-15. The Contents of the product.model.ts File in the ClientApp/app/models Folder

```
import { Supplier } from "./supplier.model";
import { Rating } from "./rating.model";

export class Product {
    constructor(
        public productId?: number,
        public name?: string,
        public category?: string,
        public description?: string,
        public price?: number,
        public supplier?: Supplier,
        public ratings?: Rating[] ) { }
}
```

Next, create a file called supplier.model.ts in the ClientApp/app/models folder and add the statements shown in Listing 4-16.

Listing 4-16. The Contents of the supplier.model.ts File in the ClientApp/app/models Folder

```
export class Supplier {

    constructor(
        public supplierId?: number,
        public name?: string,
        public city?: string,
        public state?: string) { }
}
```

Finally, create a file called rating.model.ts in the ClientApp/app/models folder and add the statements shown in Listing 4-17.

Listing 4-17. The Contents of the rating.model.ts File in the ClientApp/app/models Folder

```
import { Product } from "./product.model";

export class Rating {

    constructor(
        public ratingId?: number,
        public stars?: number,
        public product?: Product) { }

}
```

Understanding the TypeScript Data Model Classes

Since these are the first TypeScript classes that I create in this book, I am going to dig into some of the details and explain what they do and how they work.

TypeScript is a superset of JavaScript that adds a strong type system similar to the one you are already familiar with in C#. But TypeScript is not C#, and working on a project that combines Angular and ASP.NET Core MVC means writing code in two different languages, with two different sets of rules and features. There is a good deal of commonality between TypeScript and C#, as you might expect from two languages created by Microsoft, but there are some important differences, too.

If you are new to TypeScript, you might find some of this confusing, but don't worry, TypeScript starts to make sense as you get experience using it. Don't get bogged down in the detail if you get lost; just carry on reading and try to follow along as much as you can, even if not everything makes sense right away.

As you read through the sections that follow, bear in mind that the purpose of the Angular data model classes is to mirror the C# classes from the MVC part of the project so that data sent from the server can be represented in the client and displayed to the user.

JAVASCRIPT, ECMASCRIPT, AND TYPESCRIPT

JavaScript is a broad term that describes the language and runtime used to execute code in the browser. All modern browsers support JavaScript, which makes it possible to create Angular applications.

The name of the technology standard that describes the JavaScript language is *ECMAScript*, also known as ES. Each version of the standard is given a version number so that version 6 of ECMAScript is known as ES6, version 7 is known as ES7, and so on. To confuse matters, ES6 and ES7 are also known as ECMAScript 2015 and ECMAScript 2016.

Each new version of the language specification adds features, but it takes time for browsers to support them. It also takes time for browsers that don't support new features to fall out of use, which means you cannot rely on browsers to support a specific feature.

TypeScript is a language created and maintained by Microsoft. You do not have to use TypeScript to write Angular applications, but the alternative is more painful than learning TypeScript, requiring tortured JavaScript code that is difficult to read and maintain or learning languages that are much less like working with C#.

The good news is that TypeScript provides two useful features that help navigate through the mess of JavaScript standards and implementations. The first is that TypeScript provides a type system similar to the one used by C#, which makes it easier to detect common problems when compiling TypeScript code. (The TypeScript type system is applied only when your TypeScript code files are compiled and not at runtime. The TypeScript compiler has to remove details of the C#-style types and use the JavaScript type system to generate backward-compatible JavaScript code.)

The second feature is that TypeScript allows you to use the latest JavaScript language features in your project without having to worry about whether your users have browsers that support them. When the TypeScript compiler processes a TypeScript file, it generates backward-compatible JavaScript that runs in browsers that don't support ES6 or ES7. The version of JavaScript that is targeted by the TypeScript compiler is configured in the tsconfig.json file and defaults to ES5, which is the term used to refer to JavaScript support that predates the ES6 specification. (Don't worry if these terms do not make sense because the default settings used in the example application target the widest possible range of browsers and are suitable for most projects.)

Examining the Product Constructor

The best place to start is with the Product class. This class contains only a constructor, which is typical for a TypeScript data model class. Here is the Product class with the constructor highlighted:

```
import { Supplier } from "./supplier.model";
import { Rating } from "./rating.model";

export class Product {
    constructor(
        public productId?: number,
        public name?: string,
        public category?: string,
        public description?: string,
        public price?: number,
        public supplier?: Supplier,
        public ratings?: Rating[] ) { }
}
```

TypeScript constructors are denoted by the constructor keyword, rather than the name of the class, but they perform the same purpose as in C#, and each parameter receives a value that can be used to configure a new instance of the class.

Using the Right Name Capitalization Convention

JavaScript uses the camel case convention for its property names, which means that the first letter is lowercase and the first letter of each subsequent concatenated word is uppercase. This means that the C# property ProductId in the ASP.NET Core MVC part of the project becomes productId in Angular.

■ **Caution**   You might be tempted to pick one convention and use it in both parts of the application, but that will only cause problems later because the serialization process that creates JSON data automatically transforms names between the capitalization conventions.

Making the Parameters Optional

The question mark that follows a parameter name indicates that the parameter is optional.

```
...
public productId?: number,
...
```

Optional parameters are useful for model classes because you will not always have values for all the fields available when you create a new object. This can be because you are getting data from the user gradually through multiple HTML forms or because the data is built up over multiple HTTP requests to the server. Making all the constructor parameters optional gives you extra flexibility, allowing you to create new objects with all, some, or even no data values.

Unpacking the Properties

The reason that the Product class contains only a constructor is that TypeScript has a useful feature for avoiding a common coding pattern that is especially prevalent in model classes.

When you include an access modifier on a constructor parameter, such as public, TypeScript creates a property with the same name and access level as the parameter and assigns it the value received by the constructor. Table 4-2 shows the original Product class and a revised version that doesn't take advantage of this feature. It is easy to make a mistake when defining properties and copying values to them manually, either forgetting to assign a value to a property or assigning the wrong value. The TypeScript feature that automates this process produces identical results but in a more concise and less error-prone way.

Table 4-2. *The Effect of Constructor Parameter Unpacking*

Using Parameter Unpacking	Not Using Parameter Unpacking
``import { Supplier } from "./supplier.model";
import { Rating } from "./rating.model";

export class Product {
  constructor(
    public productId?: number,
    public name?: string,
    public category?: string,
    public description?: string,
    public price?: number,
    public supplier?: Supplier,
    public ratings?: Rating[]) { }
}``` | ```import { Supplier } from "./supplier.model";
import { Rating } from "./rating.model";

export class Product {

  constructor(
    productId?: number,
    name?: string,
    category?: string,
    description?: string,
    price?: number,
    supplier?: Supplier,
    ratings?: Rating[]) {

      this.productId = productId;
      this.name = name;
      this.category = category;
      this.description = description;
      this.price = price;
      this.supplier = supplier;
      this.ratings = ratings;
  }

  productId: number;
  name: string;
  category: string;
    description: string;
    price: number;
    supplier: Supplier
    ratings: Rating[];
}``` |

Understanding the Parameter Types

The type of each parameter is specified after its name, using one of the built-in JavaScript types or another TypeScript class defined in the project. The constructor parameters for the Product class rely on the built-in string and number types, which are used to represent character data and numbers, respectively. Table 4-3 lists the basic set of types supported by TypeScript.

Most of the properties defined by the Product class use types described in the table, but TypeScript also supports custom types. The supplier and rating properties are defined using the Supplier and Rating classes.

Table 4-3. *The Types Supported by TypeScript*

Type	Description
boolean	The boolean type can be assigned true or false and is equivalent to the C# bool type.
number	Unlike C#, there are no specific types for different types of numeric value. The number type can be used to represent integer or fractional numbers.
string	The string type is assigned text and is the counterpart to the C# string type.
array	TypeScript supports strongly typed arrays, which I demonstrate in later examples.
tuple	TypeScript tuples are similar to those in C# and are used to gather together a fixed-length collection of objects or values, whose types need not be the same.
enum	A TypeScript enum is similar to its C# counterpart and is used to assign friendly names to numeric values.
any	The any type is used as a placeholder when any type is acceptable.

Understanding JavaScript Modules

The most confusing term when you are new to Angular development is *module*, which is used to describe different parts of an application that are only loosely related. One use of this term is to describe a *JavaScript module*, which is a reusable piece of code that contains features that can be used elsewhere in the application.

JavaScript modules allow dependencies between the code in a JavaScript application to be determined, allowing the browser to load all the files it requires before executing the application. The webpack build process hides the details, but behind the scenes JavaScript modules are used to figure out which code files are required to run the application.

Each TypeScript file contains a separate JavaScript module, and the convention in an Angular application is to define each class in a separate file. The export keyword is used to make the class available outside of its file, like this:

```
...
export class Product {
...
```

Without the export keyword, the Product class would not be accessible outside of the file in which it is defined. The counterpart is the import keyword, which declares a dependency on classes exported from another JavaScript module. There are two import statements in the product.module.ts file, and they declare dependencies on two other classes, like this:

```
...
import { Supplier } from "./supplier.model";
import { Rating } from "./rating.model";
...
```

A TypeScript import statement specifies the type that is required and its location. These statements import Supplier from the supplier.model JavaScript module and Rating from the rating.model JavaScript module.

There are two ways to specify the location of a JavaScript module. The import statements in the product.model.ts file are *relative* imports, which means they specify a file path relative to the current file. This type of location begins with a period and includes the path to the target file but omits the file extension so that the .ts of the TypeScript file or the .js of the JavaScript file that it is compiled into is not included.

The other type of import omits the period from the target location and declares a dependency on an NPM package, such as the JavaScript modules that provide the Angular functionality. As an example, here is an import statement from the app.component.ts file from the ClientApp/app folder that declares a dependency on the @angular/core module:

```
...
import { Component } from '@angular/core';
...
```

This statement declares a dependency on the Component class defined in a package called @angular/core. (The @ character is part of the JavaScript module name used by Google for Angular modules.) The TypeScript compiler and the webpack tools resolve this kind of dependency by searching in the node_modules folder in the project.

Understanding TypeScript Access Control

TypeScript supports three levels of access control: public, private, and protected. The default access level is public, which means a method or property can be accessed from anywhere in the application. The private keyword means that a method or property can be accessed only within its defining class. The protected keyword means that a method or property can be accessed only within its defining class or a derived class.

For most Angular development, you can ignore the access control keywords. The exception is when you want to take care of the constructor parameter unpacking feature, which works only when an access control keyword is applied to a parameter. It is for this reason that all the constructor parameters in the Product class are decorated with the public keyword, and the result is that TypeScript automatically generates public properties that are accessible elsewhere in the application.

Integrating the Angular Data Model

It is not enough to simply define the classes that represent the data in the application. To complete the data model, I need to integrate those classes into the rest of the application, which I do in the sections that follow.

Defining the Repository

The repository pattern isolates the code that manages the data from the rest of the application and makes it easy to provide access to data to any part of the application that requires it. To create a repository, add a new TypeScript file called repository.ts in the ClientApp/app/models folder and add the code shown in Listing 4-18.

WHY ANGULAR REPOSITORIES ARE JUST CLASSES

If you have implemented the repository pattern in an ASP.NET Core MVC application, you may be surprised by how basic the Angular equivalent is. In .NET, the repository typically consists of a C# interface and one or more implementation classes. The mapping between the interface and the implementation class that provides the detail is configured using the ASP.NET Core dependency injection system and hidden away from data-consuming classes, which declare their dependency on the interface.

TypeScript does support interfaces, but the Angular dependency injection system does not support them, which means that the repository is defined as a simple class, undermining some of the benefits of the repository pattern.

Listing 4-18. The Contents of the repository.ts File in the ClientApp/app/models Folder

```
import { Product } from "./product.model";

export class Repository {

    constructor() {
        this.product = JSON.parse(document.getElementById("data").textContent);
    }

    product: Product;
}
```

The Repository class defines one property, called product, which returns a Product object. I add more features to the Angular repository later, but this is enough to get started.

The constructor for the Repository class sets the value of the product property by doing something that is helpful for a book example but that should be considered carefully in a real project, which is to interact directly with the Document Object Model (DOM) API. The DOM API is a set of JavaScript objects and functions provided by the browser that allows the HTML document to be managed programmatically. It is this API that lets frameworks such as Angular present content to the user and to respond to interactions. The Repository constructor uses the DOM API to locate the element that contains the JSON data and get its content. This content is then converted from a JSON string to a JavaScript object using the JSON.parse method and assigned to the product property.

```
...
this.product = JSON.parse(document.getElementById("data").textContent);
...
```

Using the DOM allows me to access the data included in the Razor view, but it is not how data is usually provided to an Angular application. I replace the DOM code in Chapter 5 when I introduce an HTTP web service.

■ **Note**   Working directly with the DOM API means that your application can run only in browsers and may not work properly on other platforms that don't implement the DOM API. This may not be an issue for your projects, but it is important to understand the effect.

Defining the Angular Feature Module

I mentioned earlier that the term *module* has multiple meanings in an Angular application and explained that each TypeScript file contains a JavaScript module, managed using the import and export keywords.

The next type of module is the Angular *feature module*, which is used to group related functionality together, such as the data repository classes in the data model. Using feature modules makes Angular applications easier to manage and maintain, although the real benefits are available when working with Angular building blocks such as components, which I start working with in detail in Chapter 7.

For this chapter, I am going to create a feature module so that the data model can be easily integrated into the rest of the Angular application. Add a file called model.module.ts in the ClientApp/app/models folder and add the statements shown in Listing 4-19.

Listing 4-19. The Contents of the model.module.ts File in the ClientApp/app/models Folder

```
import { NgModule } from "@angular/core";
import { Repository } from "./repository";

@NgModule({
    providers: [Repository]
})
export class ModelModule { }
```

The code in the listing defines a TypeScript class called ModelModule. The class has no properties or methods and is just a vehicle for the *decorator*, which is used to provide Angular with metadata about a building block, performing a role loosely similar to a C# attribute. This is the decorator:

```
...
@NgModule({
    providers: [Repository]
})
...
```

The decorator begins with the @ character followed by the decorator type. The type of this decorator is NgModule, which tells Angular that the ModelModule class is an Angular module. The decorator type is followed by the (and { characters and one or more configuration properties, followed by the } and) characters. There is only one configuration property in this decorator, called providers, which is used to register classes for dependency injection.

Just like ASP.NET Core MVC, Angular allows application building blocks to specify the services they need using their class constructors. These dependencies are resolved via dependency injection, using the classes that are registered in Angular module's providers properties. In this case, other parts of the application will be able to receive a Repository object using dependency injection.

```
...
@NgModule({
    providers: [Repository]
})
...
```

Decorators must be imported like any other TypeScript type, which is why the listing includes this statement:

```
...
import { NgModule } from "@angular/core";
...
```

The @angular/core JavaScript module includes the types that provide the most important Angular features, including decorators.

Configuring the Angular Root Module

The *root module* is a special Angular module that configures the entire application. One of its roles is to give Angular details of the feature modules that the application requires. To edit the root module, open the app.module.ts file in the ClientApp/app folder and make the changes shown in Listing 4-20.

Listing 4-20. Configuring the Root Module in the app.module.ts File in the ClientApp/app Folder

```
import { BrowserModule } from '@angular/platform-browser';
import { NgModule } from '@angular/core';
import { FormsModule } from '@angular/forms';
import { HttpModule } from '@angular/http';
import { AppComponent } from './app.component';
import { ModelModule } from "./models/model.module";

@NgModule({
    declarations: [AppComponent],
    imports: [BrowserModule, FormsModule, HttpModule, ModelModule],
    providers: [],
    bootstrap: [AppComponent]
})
export class AppModule { }
```

The root module is defined by applying the @NgModule decorator to a class, called AppModule by convention, and provides the configuration of the application using four properties, which are described in Table 4-4.

Table 4-4. *The Angular Module Configuration Properties*

Name	Description
imports	This property is used to specify the Angular modules that the application requires. The BrowserModule, FormsModule, and HttpModule modules provide core Angular functionality. The ModelModule is the custom feature module that contains the data model for the example application.
providers	This property is used to specify services for the dependency injection feature. This property is empty in the root module because the only service currently in the Angular application is defined in the model feature module.
declarations	This property is used to provide Angular with a list of the building blocks used in the application. For the root module, this property specifies AppComponent, which is the only building block in the application at the moment.
bootstrap	This property specifies the root component for the application, which will be used to start the application. For the example application, this property is set to AppComponent, which is the only component in the Angular application currently.

Displaying the Data

The basic plumbing for the Angular data model is complete. There is a repository that has been configured for use with the Angular dependency injection feature. The repository obtains its data from an element in the HTML sent to the browser, which is represented using TypeScript classes that correspond to the server-side ones defined using C#.

The next step is to use the repository to get the data and display it to the user. In an Angular application, the key building block is a *component*, which provides the logic and data required to display HTML content to the user. In loose terms, an Angular component is equivalent to an ASP.NET Core MVC controller, while an Angular component's template is equivalent to a Razor view. The key difference is that the MVC controllers and views are used to generate a response to an HTTP request, after which they have finished their job, but an Angular component and its template have an ongoing responsibility to manage the HTML displayed to the user and respond to user interaction and changes to the data model.

You will learn more about how components work in later examples. For the moment all I am going to do is update the existing component in the application, which was created during the project setup so that it declares a dependency on the Repository class and provides its template with the data it contains. Edit the app.component.ts file and make the changes shown in Listing 4-21.

■ **Tip**   Visual Studio users will have to expand the app.component.html item in the Solution Explorer to reveal the app.component.ts file.

Listing 4-21. Working with the Repository Class in the app.component.ts File in the ClientApp/app Folder

```
import { Component } from '@angular/core';
import { Repository } from "./models/repository";
import { Product } from "./models/product.model";

@Component({
  selector: 'app-root',
  templateUrl: './app.component.html',
  styleUrls: ['./app.component.css']
})
export class AppComponent {

    constructor(private repo: Repository) { }

    get product(): Product {
        return this.repo.product;
    }
}
```

The app.component.ts file defines a class called AppComponent. You can tell that this is a component because it has been decorated with the @Component decorator, which provides Angular with the configuration settings that are required to make the component work, as described in Table 4-5.

Table 4-5. *The Component Configuration Properties in Listing 4-21*

Name	Description
selector	This property is used to specify the HTML element that the component will be responsible for managing. For this component, the selector property tells Angular that the component will manage the app-root element that can be found in the HTML generated by the Index.cshtml Razor view.
templateUrl	This property is used to specify the component's template, which is the HTML content that will be displayed to the user.
styleUrls	This property is used to specify one or more CSS stylesheets that will be applied to the component's template content. I do not use this feature in this book and rely on the Bootstrap CSS framework for styling all the content in the examples.

The goal is to provide the component's template with access to the data in the repository so that it can be displayed to the user, which is achieved by making two additions to the AppComponent class.

The first addition is a constructor. The constructor has a Repository parameter called repo, which is how dependencies are declared in an Angular application. The parameter tells Angular that the AppComponent class needs a Repository object and provides it when a new AppComponent object is created. The private keyword has been applied to the repo parameter, which means that a property with the same name will be defined and assigned the value of the constructor parameter and that can be accessed only within the AppComponent class.

■ **Tip**   You must register classes as services using the providers property of an Angular module before they can be used for dependency injection. The Repository class was registered as a service in Listing 4-19.

The second addition in Listing 4-21 is a read-only property called product that returns the value of the Repository object's product property. Notice that the this keyword is used to access the repo property, like this:

```
...
return this.repo.product;
...
```

The this keyword must be used to access TypeScript instance methods and properties. If you forget to use this, which is easy to do if you are used to the way that C# works, then you will see an error telling you that the compiler "cannot find name <name>."

To display the data to the user, edit the app.component.html file and replace the contents with those shown in Listing 4-22.

Listing 4-22. The Contents of the app.component.html File in the ClientApp/app Folder

```
<table class="table table-sm table-striped">
    <tr><th>Name</th><td>{{product?.name}}</td></tr>
    <tr><th>Category</th><td>{{product?.category}}</td></tr>
    <tr><th>Description</th><td>{{product?.description}}</td></tr>
    <tr><th>Price</th><td>{{product?.price}}</td></tr>
</table>
```

This fragment of HTML relies on an important Angular feature: the *data binding*. Data bindings incorporate data provided by a controller into a template and, in this case, display the value of properties defined by the Product object returned by the component's product property.

I have used the most basic type of data binding in this example, which is denoted by the double brace characters ({{ and }}). I demonstrate more complex bindings in later chapters, but this type of binding evaluates its contents to produce a value that is inserted into an element. This binding, for example, displays the value of the name property of the Product object provided by the component:

```
...
<tr><th>Name</th><td>{{product?.name}}</td></tr>
...
```

The question mark is the TypeScript safe navigation operator, and it has the same purpose as the C# equivalent, preventing the name property from being read when the product property has not been initialized.

Save the changes to the TypeScript files, and the browser will display the static JSON data and the table that has been generated dynamically using that data, as shown in Figure 4-4.

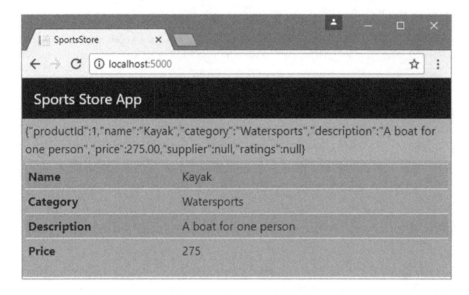

Figure 4-4. *Generating content dynamically using Angular*

Reviewing the Application Structure

The example application is taking shape. There is a data model in both the MVC and Angular parts of the project, and data is passed between them, albeit through the awkward mechanism of including JSON in a Razor view. I remove the static JSON data in the next chapter and replace it with an HTTP web service, but using Razor to pass data from the server to the client is a useful technique for getting the data model working in both parts of the project. Before moving on, it is worth taking a moment to consider the emerging structure of the SportsStore application and understand how the different features on the server and client sides have started to mesh together.

Reviewing the ASP.NET Core MVC Application Structure

When you use the browser to navigate to http://localhost:5000, the HTTP request is passed to the MVC framework, which routes it to the Index action method defined by the Home controller. This action method uses Entity Framework Core to read the Product data from the SQL Server database using Entity Framework Core and uses it as the view model data for the Index.cshtml view.

Razor processes the Index.cshtml view and generates an HTML response for the browser that includes a JSON representation of the Product data from the database, script elements that load the JavaScript files required by the Angular application, and an app-root element to which the Angular application will be applied. The browser follows the URLs in the script element to load the JavaScript files, which are provided by the static files feature of the ASP.NET Core runtime from the wwwroot folder. The JavaScript files are generated automatically from the TypeScript files using webpack, which has been integrated into the ASP. NET Core request pipeline (and is the reason that it takes the application a while to start up). Figure 4-5 shows the structure of the ASP.NET Core MVC part of the application.

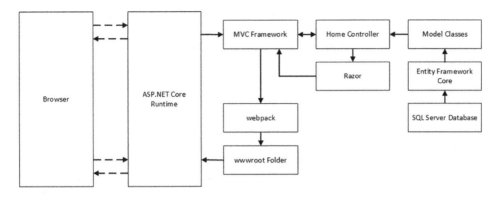

Figure 4-5. *The structure of the ASP.NET Core MVC part of the application*

The ASP.NET Core MVC part of the application is made up of familiar building blocks. A controller, action method, and Razor view work together with Entity Framework Core to generate responses for HTTP requests. The responses sent to the client contain HTML elements that provide everything the browser needs to run the Angular application, but the ASP.NET Core components do not have any knowledge of the Angular application.

Reviewing the Angular Application Structure

The Angular part of the application is rudimentary, but there is enough functionality to generate a table that displays data to the user. The HTML document received by the browser contains the app-root element into which the dynamic content produced by the Angular application is inserted, and it also contains the script elements for JavaScript files that contain the Angular framework and the custom application and data model classes. The HTML document also contains the JSON data used to populate the data table, although I replace this in Chapter 5 with a web service, which is a more conventional method for delivering data to an Angular application. Figure 4-6 shows the structure of the Angular part of the application.

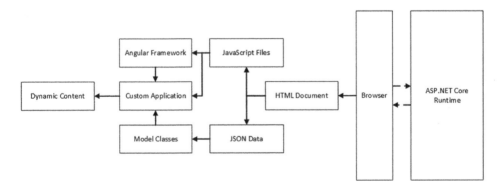

Figure 4-6. *The structure of the Angular part of the application*

The Angular part of the application has no insights into ASP.NET Core MVC. It does not know (or care) how the data is stored or represented by ASP.NET Core and Entity Framework Core. The two parts of the application work together to deliver the application and the data to the user, but they exist and run independently.

Summary

In this chapter, I started to add functionality to both the ASP.NET Core MVC and Angular parts of the application, focusing on the data model. I created a SQL Server database, populated it with seed data, and created C# data model classes so that the default MVC controller and view were able to send JSON data to the application. On the client side, I defined the TypeScript classes that represent the application data, along with a repository that is available to the rest of the Angular application through the dependency injection feature. I finished this chapter by updating the default component and template to generate tables in a row based on the JSON data. In the next chapter, I start the process of creating an HTTP web service and integrating it into the application.

CHAPTER 5

■ ■ ■

Creating a Web Service

In this chapter, I start the process of creating an HTTP web service that the Angular application can use to request data from ASP.NET Core MVC. This process is not as simple as it might be because of the way that different features interact, both in the MVC and Angular parts of the application, but the result is a solid foundation for accessing data that I build on in Chapter 6 to support a complete set of data operations.

My focus on this chapter is starting the web service and checking that each new addition works as expected. This means I request and display data in the Angular part of the project without building the final features that will present the data to the user. I start building the Angular features in earnest in Chapter 8. But for this chapter, I write just enough code to get the data and display it in the browser. Table 5-1 puts the chapter in context.

Table 5-1. *Putting the Web Service in Context*

Question	Answer
What is it?	An HTTP web service provides Angular with access to the data managed by ASP.NET Core MVC and Entity Framework Core.
Why is it useful?	The web service exposes the data in a format that is easily requested and consumed by the Angular application.
How is it used?	The Angular application sends HTTP requests to the ASP.NET Core MVC application and receives data responses in return. The responses typically represent data using the JSON data format, which is easy to create in ASP.NET Core MVC and easy to consume in Angular.
Are there any pitfalls or limitations?	Getting Entity Framework Core, ASP.NET Core MVC, and Angular to work together requires careful development and lots of testing to get the right results. There are many pitfalls for the unwary, especially when handling GET requests.
Are there any alternatives?	You don't have to use a web service, but doing so makes it difficult to send data between the Angular and ASP.NET Core MVC parts of the project.

■ **Note** The web service features in this chapter and Chapter 6 are unsecured, which means that any client can access the data and make changes. I show you how to add authentication and authorization to the web service in Chapter 11 and how to protect your application from cross-site request forgery (CSRF) attacks.

© Adam Freeman 2017
A. Freeman, *Essential Angular for ASP.NET Core MVC*, DOI 10.1007/978-1-4842-2916-3_5

Preparing for This Chapter

This chapter uses the SportsStore project that I created in Chapter 3 and modified in Chapter 4. To ensure that the contents of the database are reset, open a command prompt, navigate to the SportsStore folder, and run the commands shown in Listing 5-1.

■ **Tip**   You can download the complete project for this chapter from `https://github.com/apress/esntl-angular-for-asp.net-core-mvc`. This is also where you will find updates and corrections for this book.

Listing 5-1. Resetting the Database

```
docker-compose down
docker-compose up
```

The first command removes the Docker database container from the previous chapter. The second command creates and starts a fresh container.

Start the application to apply the database schema and add the seed data. If you are using Visual Studio, you can do this by selecting Debug ➤ Start Without Debugging. If you are using Visual Studio Code or just prefer working with the command line, then open a command prompt, navigate to the SportsStore folder, and run the command shown in Listing 5-2.

Listing 5-2. Starting the Application

```
dotnet run
```

Use a browser to navigate to `http://localhost:5000`, and you will see the content shown in Figure 5-1.

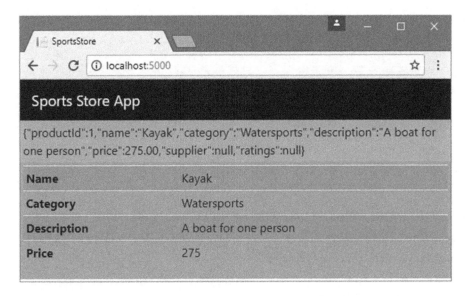

Figure 5-1. *Running the example application*

Introducing a Web Service

The Angular part of the project is getting data from the MVC framework through the HTML response sent by the Home controller. This was helpful when putting the plumbing for the data model into place because it let me focus on the database, model classes, and repository, but including JSON data in HTML documents has some shortcomings. The first, and most obvious, is that users don't typically expect to have to see the application data alongside the regular content. The second shortcoming is that getting that data into Angular required using the browser's DOM API, which restricts the application to running in browsers, even though Angular has the potential to work on a range of different platforms.

To improve the application, I am going to introduce an HTTP web service. In this arrangement, the Angular application will start without any data and immediately make an HTTP request back to the ASP.NET Core MVC application. The HTTP request will be made asynchronously and is known as an *Ajax request*, which used to stand for Asynchronous JavaScript and XML but has become a term in its own right, not least because XML is rarely used and has been largely replaced by JSON as the standard data format for HTTP data requests. In the sections that follow, I show you how to plan and create a web service using ASP.NET Core MVC and integrate it into Angular.

Understanding RESTful Web Services

There are no hard-and-fast rules for how web services should work, but the most common approach is to adopt the Representational State Transfer (REST) pattern. There is no authoritative specification for REST, and there is no consensus about what constitutes a RESTful web service, but there are some common themes that are widely used for web services.

The lack of a detailed specification leads to endless disagreement about what REST means and how RESTful web service should be created, all of which can be safely ignored just as long as the web services you create work for your projects.

The core premise of REST—and the only aspect for which there is broad agreement—is that a web service defines an API through a combination of the URLs and HTTP methods such as GET and POST, which are also known as the HTTP verbs. The verb specifies the type of operation, while the URL specifies the data object or objects that the operation applies to.

71

As an example, here is a URL that might identify a `Product` object in the example application:

```
/api/products/1
```

This URL may identify the `Product` object that has a value of 1 for its `ProductId` property. The URL identifies the `Product`, but it is the HTTP method that specifies what should be done with it. Table 5-2 lists the HTTP methods that are commonly used in web services and the operations they conventionally represent.

Table 5-2. *HTTP Methods and Operations*

HTTP Method	Description
GET	This method is used to retrieve one or more data objects.
POST	This method is used to create a new object.
PUT	This method is used to update an existing object.
PATCH	This method is used to update part of an existing object.
DELETE	This method is used to delete an object.

It is a good idea to give some thought to the API you are going to present through your web service before starting development. It is worth paying special attention to the operations that can be performed with the GET method because they can be more complicated than you might expect.

Creating the Web Service

Once you become experienced in designing and implementing web services, you will reach the point where you can write all the C# code first and only then add the code to the Angular application to consume the services you have created. For this book, I am going to take a more iterative approach, integrating each new feature in both parts of the application to emphasize how the different parts of the application work together and to check that everything functions as expected. In the sections that follow, I set up a web service and integrate it into the Angular application.

Creating the Web Service Controller

ASP.NET Core MVC makes it easy to add web services to an application using standard controller features. Create a C# class file called `ProductValuesController.cs` in the `Controllers` folder and add the code shown in Listing 5-3.

Listing 5-3. The Contents of the ProductValuesController.cs File in the Controllers Folder

```
using Microsoft.AspNetCore.Mvc;
using SportsStore.Models;

namespace SportsStore.Controllers {

    [Route("api/products")]
    public class ProductValuesController : Controller {
        private DataContext context;
```

```
        public ProductValuesController(DataContext ctx) {
            context = ctx;
        }

        [HttpGet("{id}")]
        public Product GetProduct(long id) {
            return context.Products.Find(id);
        }
    }
}
```

This is a regular ASP.NET Core MVC controller, derived from the `Controller` class in the `Microsoft.AspNetCore.Mvc` namespace, just like the existing `Home` controller that has been rendering Razor views for the examples so far. The name of this new controller class is `ProductValuesController`, which follows the convention of including the word `Values` in the name to indicate that the controller will return data to its clients rather than HTML.

Another convention for web service controllers is to create a separate part of the routing schema dedicated to handling requests for data. The most common way to do this is to create URLs for web services that start with `/api`, followed by the plural form of the name of the data type that the web service handles. For a web service handling `Product` objects, this means that HTTP requests should be sent to the `/api/products` URL, which I have configured using the `Route` attribute, like this:

```
...
[Route("api/products")]
...
```

The only action defined by the controller is the `GetProduct` method, which returns a single `Product` object based on its primary key, which is the value assigned to its `ProductId` property. The action method is decorated with the `HttpGet` method, which will allow ASP.NET Core MVC to use this action to handle HTTP GET requests:

```
...
[HttpGet("{id}")]
public Product GetProduct(long id) {
...
```

The attribute's argument extends the URL schema defined by the `Route` attribute so that the `GetProduct` method can be reached by a URL in the form `/api/products/{id}`.

Action methods for web services can return .NET objects, which are automatically serialized and sent to the client. In the case of the `GetProduct` method, the result is a `Product` object.

Testing the Web Service

To test the new web service, restart the ASP.NET Core MVC application, open a web browser, and request the URL shown in Listing 5-4.

Listing 5-4. Testing the Web Service

```
http://localhost:5000/api/products/1
```

The HTTP request from the browser is received by ASP.NET Core, which passes it on to the MVC framework. The combination of the Route and HttpGet attributes indicates that the GetProduct method in the ProductValues controller can handle the request. The GetProduct method uses the Find method defined by the database context's DbSet property to retrieve a Product object from the database and return it as the result. The Product object is serialized and returned to the browser, which will display the data it receives.

```
{
  "productId":1,"name":"Kayak","category":"Watersports",
  "description":"A boat for one person","price":275.00,
  "supplier":null,"ratings":null
}
```

The Product object is serialized into JSON, which is the standard data format used for web services. Each property is automatically converted from the C# capitalization convention (ProductId) to the JavaScript convention (productId).

Notice that the navigation properties for the related Supplier and Rating objects have been included in the JSON data but set to null. This is because Entity Framework Core doesn't load related data unless specifically asked to, so no objects were assigned to the Supplier and Ratings products of the Product objects that Entity Framework Core created when it read the data from the database. I show you how to work with related data later in this chapter.

Using the Web Service in the Angular Application

The web service doesn't do much at the moment, but it is enough to get started with, and there is just enough functionality to integrate it into the Angular application, which I demonstrate in the sections that follow.

Removing the Static Data from the Razor View

The first step is to remove the static data from the Razor view, which is no longer required now that the web service will provide data directly to the Angular application. Comment out the statements that generated the JSON data in the Index.cshtml view, as shown in Listing 5-5. (I have also taken the opportunity to remove a Bootstrap class from the div element, which I added in Chapter 4 to highlight the Angular application content.)

Listing 5-5. Removing the Static Data from the Index.cshtml File in the Views/Home Folder

```
@section scripts {
  <script src="~/dist/inline.bundle.js" asp-append-version="true"></script>
  <script src="~/dist/polyfills.bundle.js" asp-append-version="true"></script>
  <script src="~/dist/vendor.bundle.js" asp-append-version="true"></script>
  <script src="~/dist/main.bundle.js" asp-append-version="true"></script>
}

<div class="navbar bg-inverse">
  <a class="navbar-brand text-white">@(ViewBag.Message ?? "SPORTS STORE")</a>
</div>

@*<div id="data" class="p-1 bg-warning">*@
@*  @Json.Serialize(Model)*@
@*</div>*@
```

```
<div class="p-1">
  <app-root></app-root>
</div>
```

Consuming the Web Service Data in the Repository

The final step is to update the Angular Repository class so that it gets its data from the web service, as shown in Listing 5-6.

Listing 5-6. Getting Web Service Data in the repository.ts File in the ClientApp/app/models Folder

```
import { Product } from "./product.model";
import { Injectable } from "@angular/core";
import { Http } from "@angular/http";

@Injectable()
export class Repository {

    constructor(private http: Http) {
        this.getProduct(1);
    }

    getProduct(id: number) {
        this.http.get("/api/products/" + id)
            .subscribe(response => this.product = response.json());
    }

    product: Product;
}
```

Understanding the Http Class

Support for making HTTP requests in Angular applications is provided by the Http class, which is defined in the @angular/http module. The new constructor for the Repository class declares a dependency on the Http class like this:

```
...
constructor(private http: Http) {}
...
```

Angular will provide an Http object as the constructor argument when a new Repository object is created, which will be assigned to a private instance variable called http. The Http class provides methods for making HTTP requests, including the get method, which sends an HTTP GET request and which the getProduct method uses, like this:

```
...
getProduct(id: number) {
    this.http.get("/api/products/" + id)
        .subscribe(response => this.product = response.json());
}
...
```

The get method accepts a URL as its argument. The URL specified in the listing is a relative URL, which will be requested from the same location that the application was loaded from. This means the request will be sent to `http://localhost:5000/api/products/1`, which is the same URL used to test the web service in Listing 5-4.

Understanding Observables

The result of the `Http.get` method is an `Observable<Response>` object, which is an example of an *observable*. Observables are part of a library called Reactive Extensions, produced by Microsoft, which is used by Angular to connect different parts of the application. For the most part, you don't work directly with observables in an Angular application because they are used behind the scenes, but one exception is when you need to introduce data into the application, such as from a web service.

An observable represents an item of work that will be performed asynchronously and produce a result at some point in the future, loosely equivalent to a .NET `Task`. The `Observable<Response>` result returned by the `Http.get` method, for example, represents an asynchronous activity that will produce a `Response` object when it is complete. The `Response` class is defined in the `@angular/http` module and is used by Angular to represent a response from an HTTP server.

The `subscribe` method is used to invoke a function when the work represented by the `Observable` has completed. The function receives the `Observable` result, which is a `Response` object in this case, and I use the `Response.json` method to parse the JSON data sent by the web service and assign it to the `product` property, like this:

```
...
getProduct(id: number) {
    this.http.get("/api/products/" + id)
        .subscribe(response => this.product = response.json());
}
...
```

The overall effect is that when a new instance of the `Repository` class is created, the constructor calls the getProduct method, which sends an HTTP request to the web service and uses the JSON data received in response to set the `product` property, which can be accessed by the rest of the application.

■ **Tip**   You only need to understand enough about how observables work to get data into the Angular application, but if you want to know more about the features that are available, then you can consult the Reactive Extensions project web site at `https://github.com/Reactive-Extensions/RxJS`.

Understanding the @Injectable Decorator

You must apply the `@Injectable` decorator if you are defining a class that will be instantiated using the Angular dependency injection feature and that class's constructor has its own dependencies. I didn't need to apply this decorator to the `Repository` class in Chapter 4 because there was no constructor, but now that there is a dependency on an `Http` object, the `@Injector` decorator must be applied.

```
...
@Injectable()
export class Repository {
...
```

As Angular resolves the dependencies to create a new object, the @Injectable decorator indicates that it needs to resolve the constructor parameters. If you forget to apply the @Injectable decorator, the application will compile but won't run, and you will see an error like this in the browser's JavaScript console:

```
Error: Can't resolve all parameters for MyClass
```

When you save the changes to the file and navigate to http://localhost:5000, the Angular application will display the data, as shown in Figure 5-2.

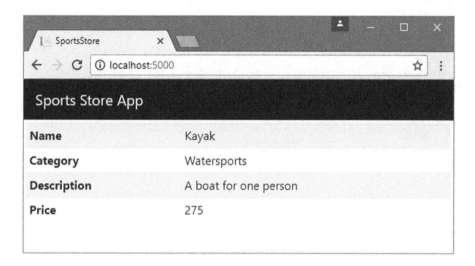

Figure 5-2. *Getting the data from the web service*

Understanding Live Data and Asynchronous Responses

The way that the Repository class handles its data may seem odd: the constructor calls the getProduct method, and the data that is received is assigned to a property.

You might be tempted to simplify the structure of the Repository class so that the HTTP request is sent when the value of the product property is read, but if you do, you will end up sending repeated HTTP requests to the web service, all of which ask for the same data. To understand why this is the case, add the statements shown in Listing 5-7 to the Repository class.

Listing 5-7. Adding Logging Statements in the repository.ts File in the ClientApp/app/models Folder

```
import { Product } from "./product.model";
import { Injectable } from "@angular/core";
import { Http } from "@angular/http";

@Injectable()
export class Repository {
    private productData: Product;

    constructor(private http: Http) {
        this.getProduct(1);
    }
}
```

77

```
    getProduct(id: number) {
        this.http.get("/api/products/" + id)
            .subscribe(response => {
                this.productData = response.json();
                console.log("Product Data Received");
            });
    }

    get product(): Product {
        console.log("Product Data Requested");
        return this.productData;
    }
}
```

The console.log statements write messages to the browser's JavaScript console, indicating when the HTTP request delivers data to the application and when Angular reads the value of the product property to get the data it needs to display in the application's data bindings.

When you save the changes, the browser will reload, and you will see a sequence of messages like this displayed in the browser JavaScript console:

```
...
Product Data Requested
Product Data Requested
Product Data Received
Product Data Requested
Product Data Requested
...
```

The data model in an Angular application is *live*, meaning that changes to the data model are automatically reflected in the content displayed to the user. This is a powerful feature, as you will see as features are added to the example in later chapters, but the process by which Angular deals with changes means that data bindings are evaluated repeatedly, which is why there are so many Product Data Requested messages shown in the JavaScript console.

If I had placed the code that leads to the HTTP request in the getter of the product property, then a new HTTP request would have been sent to the web service each time that Angular evaluated its data bindings, each of which would request the same data.

Notice also that some of the Product Data Requested messages appear before the Product Data Received message, showing that Angular starts evaluating its data bindings before the HTTP response from the web service is received and processed.

Consolidating the HTTP Request Code

Although the Http class provides methods to create different types of HTTP request (the get method for HTTP GET requests, the post method for HTTP post requests, and so on), it generally makes sense to use the Http.request method, which allows the HTTP method to be specified as an argument. This will allow all the methods that are defined by the Repository class to be consolidated, which will make it easier to deal with common tasks such as processing the data in a response without repeating code. In preparation for the features that are to follow, revise the Repository class as shown in Listing 5-8.

Listing 5-8. Using Common Request Code in the repository.ts File in the ClientApp/app/models Folder

```
import { Product } from "./product.model";
import { Injectable } from "@angular/core";
import { Http, RequestMethod, Request, Response } from "@angular/http";
import { Observable } from "rxjs/Observable";
import "rxjs/add/operator/map";

const productsUrl = "/api/products";

@Injectable()
export class Repository {
    private productData: Product;

    constructor(private http: Http) {
        this.getProduct(1);
    }

    getProduct(id: number) {
        this.sendRequest(RequestMethod.Get, productsUrl + "/" + id)
            .subscribe(response => { this.productData = response; });
    }

    private sendRequest(verb: RequestMethod, url: string,
        data?: any): Observable<any> {

        return this.http.request(new Request({
            method: verb, url: url, body: data
        })).map(response => response.json());
    }

    get product(): Product {
        console.log("Product Data Requested");
        return this.productData;
    }
}
```

The request method defined by the Http class accepts a Request object that describes the request, which is configured using method, url, and body properties. The method property specifies the HTTP method for the request using a RequestMethod value. The result of the request method is an Observable<Response> that will produce a Response object when the request is complete. The map method is provided by the Reactive Extensions library and allows an observable to be transformed, in this case by parsing the JSON from the HTTP response. The code in Listing 5-8 works in the same way as the previous example but will allow all the HTTP requests to be originated in a single method.

■ **Tip** Notice that an import statement is required to access the map method. Each operator that Reactive Extensions provides for working with observables is defined in its own file that must be imported before it can be used.

Adding Placeholder Content

A consequence of using asynchronous requests to get data is that there is a period where there is no data to display to the user. You may not have noticed this interval because the response from the web service is immediate when the browser and the ASP.NET Core runtime are on the same machine. But once an application is deployed and clients connect to the server over public networks, the effect can be obvious to the user. To simulate a substantial delay, add the statement shown in Listing 5-9 to the web service controller to introduce a five-second delay to handling data requests.

Listing 5-9. Introducing a Delay in the ProductValuesController.cs File in the Controllers Folder

```
using Microsoft.AspNetCore.Mvc;
using SportsStore.Models;

namespace SportsStore.Controllers {

    [Route("api/products")]
    public class ProductValuesController : Controller {
        private DataContext context;

        public ProductValuesController(DataContext ctx) {
            context = ctx;
        }

        [HttpGet("{id}")]
        public Product GetProduct(long id) {
            System.Threading.Thread.Sleep(5000);
            return context.Products.Find(id);
        }
    }
}
```

Restart the application and use the browser to navigate to http://localhost:5000. The Angular application will load and, as part of that process, an HTTP request will be sent to the web service to get the data that will be displayed to the user. You will see that the table is displayed without content for a few seconds and then populated, as shown in Figure 5-3.

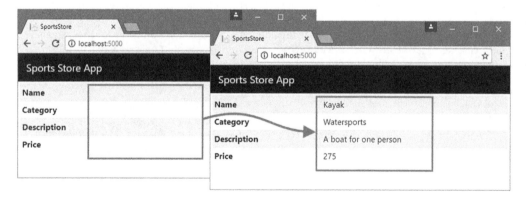

Figure 5-3. *The effect of a delay in receiving the web service data*

Introducing a delay emphasizes the dynamic nature of data in Angular. When the HTTP request completed and the data was introduced into the application, Angular automatically updates the content it displays to the user, reflecting the change without needing any explicit instruction. But a delay in receiving the data leaves the user looking at an empty table, and it is good practice to introduce some placeholder content to display to the user while waiting for data to load.

To make it obvious to the user that the application is waiting for data, make the changes to the HTML template shown in Listing 5-10.

Listing 5-10. Displaying Placeholder Content in the app.component.html File in the ClientApp/app Folder

```
<table class="table table-sm table-striped">
    <tr><th>Name</th><td>{{product?.name || 'Loading Data...'}}</td></tr>
    <tr><th>Category</th><td>{{product?.category || 'Loading Data...'}}</td></tr>
    <tr><th>Description</th>
        <td>{{product?.description || 'Loading Data...'}}</td>
    </tr>
    <tr><th>Price</th><td>{{product?.price  || 'Loading Data...'}}</td></tr>
</table>
```

The expressions in data bindings, which appears between the {{ and }} characters, are not just references for data values. Instead, they are fragments of JavaScript code that are evaluated to produce the content that will be presented to the user. This listing uses the JavaScript logical OR operator (||) in a way that is loosely equivalent to the C# null coalescing operator, like this:

```
...
<td>{{product?.name || 'Loading Data...'}}</td>
...
```

This effect is to display the value of the name property if the product property has been assigned and the Loading Data message when it hasn't. The product property is assigned only when the HTTP request has completed, which has the effect of displaying the loading message until the data is available, as shown in Figure 5-4.

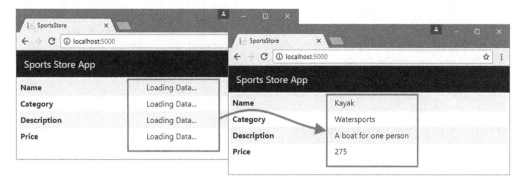

Figure 5-4. *Displaying a loading message*

Loading Related Data

To avoid loading data that may not be needed, Entity Framework Core doesn't load related data unless specifically instructed to do so. To include the Supplier and Rating objects that are associated with a Product object, change the query performed by the web service controller, as shown in Listing 5-11.

Listing 5-11. Including Related Data in the ProductValuesController.cs File in the Controllers Folder

```
using Microsoft.AspNetCore.Mvc;
using SportsStore.Models;
using Microsoft.EntityFrameworkCore;
using System.Linq;

namespace SportsStore.Controllers {

    [Route("api/products")]
    public class ProductValuesController : Controller {
        private DataContext context;

        public ProductValuesController(DataContext ctx) {
            context = ctx;
        }

        [HttpGet("{id}")]
        public Product GetProduct(long id) {
            //System.Threading.Thread.Sleep(5000);
            return context.Products
                        .Include(p => p.Supplier)
                        .Include(p => p.Ratings)
                        .FirstOrDefault(p => p.ProductId == id);
        }
    }
}
```

The Include method tells Entity Framework Core to follow a navigation property and load the related data. In the listing, the Include method is used to select the Product.Supplier and Product.Ratings properties and load the related Supplier and Rating objects.

The Include method is called on the IQueryable<T> interface, which is implemented by the DbSet properties defined by the database context class. The IQueryable<T> interface is derived from IEnumerable<T> but represents a database query that will be evaluated by the Entity Framework Core database provider to minimize the amount of data that will be read from the database. The Include method can be chained together to select multiple navigation properties but cannot be used with the Find method. As a consequence, selecting the Product object with the specified key must be done with the FirstOrDefault method, which selects the first object that matches the query and returns null if there are no matches in the database.

Understanding the Circular Reference Problem

The code in Listing 5-11 contains a problem that causes so much confusion that it is worth exploring in detail. To see the problem, restart the ASP.NET Core MVC application and use a browser to request the URL http://localhost:5000/api/products/1. The application will report the following exception:

```
...
Newtonsoft.Json.JsonSerializationException: Self referencing loop detected with
type   'SportsStore.Models.Product'. Path 'supplier.products'.
...
```

The Newtonsoft.Json namespace contains the excellent Json.NET package that Microsoft uses for JSON serialization in ASP.NET Core. Json.NET keeps track of the objects it serializes to avoid circular references that would lead to the same data being endlessly serialized. For example, in a situation where object A has a reference object B and object B has a reference to object A, there is a risk that the serializer will get stuck in a loop endlessly following the references between the objects. To avoid this situation, the serializer throws an exception when it follows a reference to an object that it has already serialized.

Looking at the code in Listing 5-11, you might struggle to see why using the Include method has created a circular reference. The problem is caused by a well-intentioned Entity Framework Core feature that attempts to minimize the amount of data read from the database but that causes problems in ASP.NET Core MVC applications. To see what is happening, change the configuration of the JSON serializer in the Startup class so that it doesn't report an exception when it detects a circular reference, as shown in Listing 5-12.

Listing 5-12. Configuring the JSON Serializer in the Startup.cs File in the SportsStore Folder

```
using Microsoft.AspNetCore.Builder;
using Microsoft.AspNetCore.Hosting;
using Microsoft.Extensions.Configuration;
using Microsoft.Extensions.DependencyInjection;
using Microsoft.Extensions.Logging;
using Microsoft.AspNetCore.SpaServices.Webpack;
using SportsStore.Models;
using Microsoft.EntityFrameworkCore;
using Newtonsoft.Json;

namespace SportsStore {
    public class Startup {
        public Startup(IHostingEnvironment env) {
            var builder = new ConfigurationBuilder()
                .SetBasePath(env.ContentRootPath)
                .AddJsonFile("appsettings.json", optional: false, reloadOnChange: true)
                .AddJsonFile($"appsettings.{env.EnvironmentName}.json", optional: true)
                .AddEnvironmentVariables();
            Configuration = builder.Build();
        }

        public IConfigurationRoot Configuration { get; }

        public void ConfigureServices(IServiceCollection services) {
            services.AddDbContext<DataContext>(options =>
                options.UseSqlServer(Configuration
                    ["Data:Products:ConnectionString"]));
            services.AddMvc().AddJsonOptions(opts =>
                opts.SerializerSettings.ReferenceLoopHandling
                    = ReferenceLoopHandling.Serialize);
        }

        public void Configure(IApplicationBuilder app,
                IHostingEnvironment env, ILoggerFactory loggerFactory) {
            loggerFactory.AddConsole(Configuration.GetSection("Logging"));
            loggerFactory.AddDebug();
```

```
            app.UseDeveloperExceptionPage();
            app.UseWebpackDevMiddleware(new WebpackDevMiddlewareOptions {
                HotModuleReplacement = true
            });

            app.UseStaticFiles();

            app.UseMvc(routes => {
                routes.MapRoute(
                    name: "default",
                    template: "{controller=Home}/{action=Index}/{id?}");
            });

            SeedData.SeedDatabase(app.ApplicationServices
                .GetRequiredService<DataContext>());
        }
    }
}
```

This doesn't fix the problem, but it does reveal what is causing it, albeit by allowing a circular reference to create a terminal stack overflow. Restart the ASP.NET Core MVC application and use a browser to request the http://localhost:5000/api/products/1 URL. Instead of the exception shown earlier, the application will terminate with this error:

```
...
Process is terminated due to StackOverflowException
...
```

This is the situation that the JSON serializer tries to avoid. You can see what caused the problem by examining the JSON content that was displayed by the browser before the application stopped, which is easier to understand if you format the data like this:

```
...
{ "productId":1, "name":"Kayak", "category":"Watersports",
  "description":"A boat for one person", "price":275.00,
  "supplier":{
    "supplierId":1, "name":"Splash Dudes", "city":"San Jose",
    "state":"CA",
    "products":[
      { "productId":1, "name":"Kayak", "category":"Watersports",
        "description":"A boat for one person", "price":275.00,
        "supplier":{
          "supplierId":1,"name":"Splash Dudes", "city":"San Jose",
          "state":"CA",
          "products":[
            { "productId":1, "name":"Kayak", "category":"Watersports",
...
```

When Entity Framework Core creates objects, it tries to populate navigation properties with objects that have already been created by the same database context. This can be a useful feature in some kinds of application, such as desktop apps, where a database context object has a long life and is used to make many requests over time. It isn't useful for ASP.NET Core MVC applications where a new context object is created for each HTTP request. In the example application, the only objects that Entity Framework Core creates are the ones for the current query, which starts with a Product object and includes the related Supplier and Rating objects.

When Entity Framework Core creates the Supplier object, it looks at the objects it has already created to see whether any of them can be used to populate the Products navigation property. There is one such object, which is the Product object that has already been created, so Entity Framework Core adds this to the collection assigned to the Supplier.Products property. This creates the circular reference, which isn't a problem when the references are between objects in the .NET Core runtime but cause problems when they are serialized to JSON, which doesn't have any way to represent references between objects.

The application terminates with a StackOverflowException because the JSON serializer follows these the references and writes out each object it encounters. The Product object has a reference to the Supplier object through its Supplier property, which has a reference to the Product object through its Products property, which has a reference to the Supplier object, and so on.

Breaking the Circular References

There is no way to stop Entity Framework Core from using existing objects for navigation properties. Preventing the problem means breaking the references between objects after they have been created by Entity Framework Core and before they are processed by the JSON serializer, as shown in Listing 5-13.

Listing 5-13. Breaking References in the ProductValuesController.cs File in the Controllers Folder

```
using Microsoft.AspNetCore.Mvc;
using SportsStore.Models;
using Microsoft.EntityFrameworkCore;
using System.Linq;

namespace SportsStore.Controllers {

    [Route("api/products")]
    public class ProductValuesController : Controller {
        private DataContext context;

        public ProductValuesController(DataContext ctx) {
            context = ctx;
        }

        [HttpGet("{id}")]
        public Product GetProduct(long id) {
            Product result = context.Products
                        .Include(p => p.Supplier)
                        .Include(p => p.Ratings)
                        .First(p => p.ProductId == id);

            if (result != null) {
                if (result.Supplier != null) {
                    result.Supplier.Products = null;
                }

                if (result.Ratings != null) {
                    foreach (Rating r in result.Ratings) {
                        r.Product = null;
```

```
                }
            }
        }
        return result;
    }
  }
}
```

To break the relationships, the listing sets the Supplier.Products property to null. There is also a circular reference between the Product and Rating objects, so the listing enumerates the Rating objects returned by the Product object's Ratings property to set their Product property to null. To see the result, restart the ASP.NET Core MVC application and use a browser to request the http://localhost:5000/api/products/1 URL, which will produce the following data:

```
{
  "productId":1,"name":"Kayak","category":"Watersports",
  "description":"A boat for one person","price":275.00,
  "supplier":{
    "supplierId":1,"name":"Splash Dudes","city":"San Jose",
    "state":"CA","products":null},
  "ratings":[{"ratingId":1,"stars":4,"product":null},
             {"ratingId":2,"stars":3,"product":null}]
}
```

AVOIDING PROBLEMATIC SOLUTIONS

There are two other ways to prevent the JSON serializer from throwing exceptions about circular references, both of which will show up if you search online for the error text, but neither of which really solves the problem.

The most common advice is to change the configuration of the serializer so that it simply ignores any object that it has already serialized, using a configuration statement like this in the Startup class:

```
...
services.AddMvc().AddJsonOptions(opts =>
  opts.SerializerSettings.ReferenceLoopHandling = ReferenceLoopHandling.Ignore);
...
```

The Ignore setting prevents exceptions, but it doesn't stop extraneous data from being returned by the web service, which can be a problem when you are handling requests for multiple objects. Each object retrieved from the database gives Entity Framework Core more scope to populate navigation properties, adding to the data sent to the client.

The other approach is to add the JsonIgnore attribute to navigation properties in the model classes to stop the serializer following them when creating JSON data. This solves the problem in the short term but prevents you from being able to create useful web services that deal with the model classes directly, rather than as related data.

Breaking Circular References in Additional Related Data

One of the odd effects of the way that Entity Framework Core populates navigation properties is that the related data is often incomplete. In the previous example, the only Product object that Entity Framework Core had to work with was the one that was being queried, which meant that all the other Product objects associated with that Supplier were simply not available and so were not included in the result.

If you want to include additional related data, you can load it using the ThenInclude method, which will ensure that all the data in the database will be used and not just whatever has been loaded so far. For example, to include all the Product objects associated with a Supplier, add the ThenInclude method to the web service query, as shown in Listing 5-14.

Listing 5-14. Including Additional Data in the ProductValuesController.cs File in the Controllers Folder

```
using Microsoft.AspNetCore.Mvc;
using SportsStore.Models;
using Microsoft.EntityFrameworkCore;
using System.Linq;

namespace SportsStore.Controllers {

    [Route("api/products")]
    public class ProductValuesController : Controller {
        private DataContext context;

        public ProductValuesController(DataContext ctx) {
            context = ctx;
        }

        [HttpGet("{id}")]
        public Product GetProduct(long id) {
            Product result = context.Products
                        .Include(p => p.Supplier).ThenInclude(s => s.Products)
                        .Include(p => p.Ratings)
                        .First(p => p.ProductId == id);

            if (result != null) {
                if (result.Supplier != null) {
                    result.Supplier.Products = result.Supplier.Products.Select(p =>
                        new Product {
                            ProductId = p.ProductId,
                            Name = p.Name,
                            Category = p.Category,
                            Description = p.Description,
                            Price = p.Price,
                    });
                }

                if (result.Ratings != null) {
                    foreach (Rating r in result.Ratings) {
                        r.Product = null;
                    }
                }
            }
        }
```

```
            return result;
        }
    }
}
```

This example requires a different technique for dealing with circular references. Rather than set a property to null, new Product objects without the circular reference to the Supplier are created using the LINQ Select method.

To understand why this is important, restart the ASP.NET Core MVC application and use a browser to navigate to the http://localhost:5000/api/products/1 URL. The JSON data returned by the web service includes the Product object, the Product object's related Supplier, and the Supplier object's related Product objects (and the Rating objects, but they are not important for this example).

```
{
  "productId":1,"name":"Kayak","category":"Watersports",
  "description":"A boat for one person","price":275.00,
  "supplier":{"supplierId":1,"name":"Splash Dudes","city":"San Jose",
  "state":"CA",
  "products":[
    { "productId":1,"name":"Kayak","category":"Watersports",
      "description":"A boat for one person", "price":275.00,
      "supplier":null,"ratings":null},
    { "productId":2,"name":"Lifejacket","category":"Watersports",
      "description":"Protective and fashionable","price":48.95,
      "supplier":null,"ratings":null}]},
  "ratings":[{"ratingId":1,"stars":4,"product":null},
            {"ratingId":2,"stars":3,"product":null}]
}
```

The highlighting shows that the same Product objects appear twice in the JSON data, which is typical when the Include and ThenInclude methods are used to get data on both ends of a navigation property.

Entity Framework Core creates only one Product object for the Kayak product, and this means that setting its Supplier property to null wouldn't just break the relationship for the nested related data; it would also break the relationship between the main Product object that has been queried and its Supplier, which would exclude all of the related data.

Omitting Null Properties

A consequence of using navigation properties, whether they are followed or not, is that the JSON data sent to the client contains properties whose values are null. This doesn't often cause problems, but it does consume bandwidth, and it is good practice to omit them. Add the configuration statement shown in Listing 5-15 to the Startup class to tell the JSON serializer to omit properties that are null.

Listing 5-15. Configuring the JSON Serializer in the Startup.cs File in the SportsStore Folder

```
...
public void ConfigureServices(IServiceCollection services) {
    services.AddDbContext<DataContext>(options =>
        options.UseSqlServer(Configuration
            ["Data:Products:ConnectionString"]));
```

```
services.AddMvc().AddJsonOptions(opts => {
    opts.SerializerSettings.ReferenceLoopHandling
        = ReferenceLoopHandling.Serialize;
    opts.SerializerSettings.NullValueHandling = NullValueHandling.Ignore;
});
}
...
```

Restart the ASP.NET Core MVC application and use a browser to request http://localhost:5000/api/products/1 and you see that the null properties are no longer included in the JSON returned by the web service, like this:

```
{
  "productId":1,"name":"Kayak","category":"Watersports",
  "description":"A boat for one person","price":275.00,
  "supplier":{
    "supplierId":1,"name":"Splash Dudes","city":"San Jose","state":"CA",
    "products":[{"productId":1,"name":"Kayak","category":"Watersports",
                "description":"A boat for one person","price":275.00},
               {"productId":2,"name":"Lifejacket","category":"Watersports",
                "description":"Protective and fashionable","price":48.95}]},
  "ratings":[{"ratingId":1,"stars":4},{"ratingId":2,"stars":3}]
}
```

Displaying Related Data

No special steps are required to display the related data in the Angular part of the project, which is handled automatically when the JSON data is processed. To display the related data, add the elements shown in Listing 5-16 to the Angular component's template.

Listing 5-16. Displaying Related Data in the app.component.html File in the ClientApp/app Folder

```
<table class="table table-sm table-striped">
    <tr><th colspan="2" class="bg-info">Product</th></tr>
    <tr><th>Name</th><td>{{product?.name || 'Loading Data...'}}</td></tr>
    <tr><th>Category</th><td>{{product?.category || 'Loading Data...'}}</td></tr>
    <tr>
        <th>Description</th>
        <td>{{product?.description || 'Loading Data...'}}</td>
    </tr>
    <tr><th>Price</th><td>{{product?.price || 'Loading Data...'}}</td></tr>
    <tr><th colspan="2" class="bg-info">Supplier</th></tr>
    <tr><th>Name</th><td>{{product?.supplier?.name}}</td></tr>
    <tr><th>City</th><td>{{product?.supplier?.city}}</td></tr>
    <tr><th>State</th><td>{{product?.supplier?.state}}</td></tr>
    <tr><th>Products</th><td>{{product?.supplier?.products?.length}}</td></tr>
</table>
```

The new elements use data bindings with expressions that use the safe navigation operator to select properties from the related Supplier object. When you save the change to the template and navigate to http://localhost:5000, the browser will display the content shown in Figure 5-5.

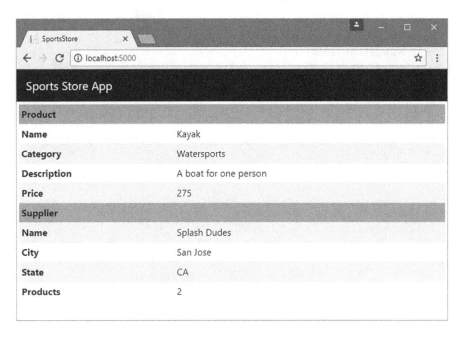

Figure 5-5. *Displaying related data in the Angular application*

Implementing the GET Method for Multiple Objects

In a RESTful web service, the HTTP GET method typically does double duty and is used to denote queries for one object and queries for multiple objects, with the request URL being used to specify the purpose of the query. In this section, I demonstrate how to support queries for multiple objects and how to display the data in an Angular application. The result will be to expand the API provided by the web service, as shown in Table 5-3.

Table 5-3. *The Web Service API with GET for Multiple Objects*

Method	URL	Description
GET	/api/products/<id>	Retrieves a single Product object
GET	/api/products	Retrieves multiple Product objects

Implementing the Web Service Action Method

It took a long time to explain how to implement the GET method for single objects because of the complexities of serializing related data. But once you understand how to deal with circular references, the process for dealing with multiple objects is simpler. To add support for querying for multiple objects, add the action method shown in Listing 5-17 to the ProductValues controller.

Listing 5-17. Adding an Action in the ProductValuesController.cs File in the Controllers Folder

```
using Microsoft.AspNetCore.Mvc;
using SportsStore.Models;
using Microsoft.EntityFrameworkCore;
using System.Linq;
using System.Collections.Generic;

namespace SportsStore.Controllers {

    [Route("api/products")]
    public class ProductValuesController : Controller {
        private DataContext context;

        public ProductValuesController(DataContext ctx) {
            context = ctx;
        }

        [HttpGet("{id}")]
        public Product GetProduct(long id) {

          // ...statements omitted for brevity...

        }

        [HttpGet]
        public IEnumerable<Product> GetProducts(bool related = false) {
            IQueryable<Product> query = context.Products;
            if (related) {
                query = query.Include(p => p.Supplier).Include(p => p.Ratings);
                List<Product> data = query.ToList();
                data.ForEach(p => {
                    if (p.Supplier != null) {
                        p.Supplier.Products = null;
                    }
                    if (p.Ratings != null) {
                        p.Ratings.ForEach(r => r.Product = null);
                    }
                });
                return data;
            } else {
                return query;
            }
        }
    }
}
```

The GetProducts method is decorated with the HttpGet attribute, which tells the MVC framework that it can be used to handle GET requests. The action method defines a related parameter that is used to indicate whether related data should be included in the response, which defaults to false.

Within the action method, if the related data is not required, then the result is the IQueryable<Product> object obtained by reading the database context object's Product property. If related data is required, then I use the ToList method to force execution of the query and create a List<Product> on which I can use the ForEach method to break the circular references before the data is serialized.

To test the new action, restart the ASP.NET Core MVC application and use a browser to request http://localhost:5000/api/products. This URL requests the products without related data and will produce a result with data like this (I have shown just two Product objects for brevity):

```
...
[{"productId":1,"name":"Kayak","category":"Watersports",
  "description":"A boat for one person","price":275.00},
 {"productId":2,"name":"Lifejacket","category":"Watersports",
  "description":"Protective and fashionable","price":48.95},
...
```

To include related data in the request, use a browser to request http://localhost:5000/api/products?related=true, which will produce data like this:

```
...
[{"productId":1,"name":"Kayak","category":"Watersports",
  "description":"A boat for one person","price":275.00,
  "supplier":{"supplierId":1,"name":"Splash Dudes",
              "city":"San Jose","state":"CA"},
  "ratings":[{"ratingId":1,"stars":4},{"ratingId":2,"stars":3}]},
 {"productId":2,"name":"Lifejacket","category":"Watersports",
  "description":"Protective and fashionable","price":48.95,
  "supplier":{"supplierId":1,"name":"Splash Dudes",
  "city":"San Jose","state":"CA"},
  "ratings":[{"ratingId":3,"stars":2},{"ratingId":4,"stars":5}]},
...
```

■ **Tip**   You can extend the ASP.NET Core MVC routing configuration so that you don't have to use query parameters in your URLs. I have not done so because I add some additional features to this action method that would make for a complicated routing configuration. In my projects, especially if the Angular application is the only client of the web service, then I tend to use query parameters for simplicity.

Querying Multiple Objects in the Angular Application

The process of sending a request from the Angular application to get multiple objects follows the same basic pattern as for a single object. The first step is to define a new method in the Repository class to send the request and process the response, as shown in Listing 5-18. (I have also taken the opportunity to remove the console.log statements that I used to demonstrate the odd design of the Repository class in the previous section.)

Listing 5-18. Adding a Method in the repository.ts File in the ClientApp/app/model Folder

```
import { Product } from "./product.model";
import { Injectable } from "@angular/core";
import { Http, RequestMethod, Request, Response } from "@angular/http";
import { Observable } from "rxjs/Observable";
import "rxjs/add/operator/map";

const productsUrl = "/api/products";

@Injectable()
export class Repository {

    constructor(private http: Http) {
        this.getProducts(true);
    }

    getProduct(id: number) {
        this.sendRequest(RequestMethod.Get, productsUrl + "/" + id)
            .subscribe(response => {
                this.product = response.json();
            });
    }

    getProducts(related = false) {
        this.sendRequest(RequestMethod.Get, productsUrl + "?related=" + related)
            .subscribe(response => this.products = response);
    }

    private sendRequest(verb: RequestMethod, url: string, data?: any)
        : Observable<any> {

        return this.http.request(new Request({
            method: verb, url: url, body: data
        })).map(response => response.json());
    }

    product: Product;
    products: Product[];
}
```

The getProducts method sends an HTTP request to the /api/products URL, which gets all the Product data that is available. The method defines an optional parameter that is used to set the related query string parameter in the request URL to specify whether the response should include related data.

Updating the Component

The next step is to update the component so that it defines a property that the template can use to access the product data, as shown in Listing 5-19. Templates can only access data through their component, which is why these mapping properties are required.

Listing 5-19. Defining a Property in the app.component.ts File in the ClientApp/app Folder

```
import { Component } from '@angular/core';
import { Repository } from "./models/repository";
import { Product } from "./models/product.model";

@Component({
    selector: 'app-root',
    templateUrl: './app.component.html',
    styleUrls: ['./app.component.css']
})
export class AppComponent {

    constructor(private repo: Repository) { }

    get product(): Product {
        return this.repo.product;
    }

    get products(): Product[] {
        return this.repo.products;
    }
}
```

Updating the Component's Template

To display the data obtained from the web service, replace the contents of the `app.component.html` file with those shown in Listing 5-20.

Listing 5-20. Displaying Data in the app.component.html File in the ClientApp/app Folder

```
<table class="table table-sm table-striped">
    <tr>
        <th>Name</th><th>Category</th><th>Price</th>
        <th>Supplier</th><th>Ratings</th>
    </tr>
    <tr *ngFor="let product of products">
        <td>{{product.name}}</td>
        <td>{{product.category}}</td>
        <td>{{product.price}}</td>
        <td>{{product.supplier?.name || 'None'}}</td>
        <td>{{product.ratings?.length || 0}}</td>
    </tr>
</table>
```

The important part of the template is an Angular *directive*, which is used to change the HTML that is presented to the user based on the data in the model. Here is the element that this directive has been applied to, with the directive itself shown in bold:

```
...
<tr *ngFor="let product of products">
...
```

This is an example of a structural directive, which alters the structure or content of an HTML element. In this case, the directive, which is called ngFor, is responsible for repeating the HTML element it is applied to for each object in an array. The directive's expression specifies the array and tells Angular to assign, in turn, each object in the collection returned by the component's products property to a variable called product that can be used in data bindings in the element's content, like this:

```
...
<td>{{product.name}}</td>
...
```

The effect is similar to a Razor @foreach expression, but the ngFor expression is applied as an attribute of the HTML element that will be duplicated.

Some of the data binding expressions in Listing 5-20 use the || operator, which produces useful results even when there is no data available to display. This does loosely the same thing as the C# ?? operator but has some wrinkles, as explained in the "Understanding JavaScript Truth" sidebar.

UNDERSTANDING JAVASCRIPT TRUTH

JavaScript has an unusual approach to evaluating expressions as true or false, which you need to understand to create effective Angular data binding expressions. All expressions can be *truthy* or *falsy*, which means they will evaluate as either true or false. This can lead to some unexpected results. The following expressions are always falsy and will always evaluate to false in an Angular data binding expression:

- The false (boolean) value

- The 0 (number) value

- The empty string ("")

- null

- undefined

- NaN (a special number value)

All other values are truthy and will evaluate to true, which can be confusing. For example, "false" (a string whose content is the word false) is truthy.

In Listing 5-20, one of the data binding expressions relies on the fact that the product.supplier.name property may be null, which will be falsy, in which case placeholder content should be shown.

```
...
<td>{{product.supplier?.name || 'None'}}</td>
...
```

The || operator performs an OR comparison to coalesce null values. If the value of the product.supplier.name value isn't falsy, then it will be used as the result of the data binding expression. If it is falsy, typically because it is null, then the None string literal value will be used as the expression result.

The result is that a tr element is created, along with the td elements it contains, for each of the objects obtained from the web service, which you can see by navigating to http://localhost:5000, as shown in Figure 5-6.

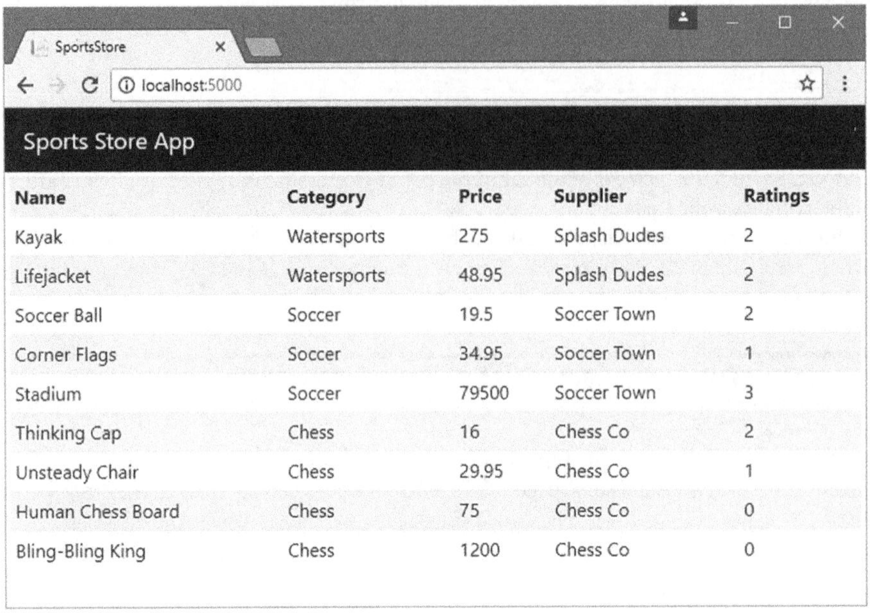

Figure 5-6. *Displaying multiple objects*

Filtering the Data

The web service responds to GET requests sent to the /api/products URL by sending all the Product objects that have been stored in the database. That's fine for an example application that has nine items, but most real applications store enough data that it doesn't make sense to send it all to the client for every request.

To finish this chapter, I am going to add support for allowing the client to provide the web service with instructions for filtering the data it receives. I am going to define three different ways for the client to select Product objects: filtering by category, searching by name, or searching by description. The client will be able to specify a category by adding a query string to the base URL, like this:

/api/products**?category=soccer**

This URL will return only those Product objects whose Category property equals soccer.

For the second filter, the client will be able to perform a search by adding a search term to the query string, like this:

/api/products?category=soccer&**search=stadium**

This URL will return only those Product objects that are in the soccer category and whose Name or Description properties contain stadium.

Applying Filtering in the Web Service

Not all the filters will be applied to every request, which means that the web service must carefully build up the query for Entity Framework Core to execute. To add support for the three data filters, add the code shown in Listing 5-21 to the GetProducts method in the ProductValues controller.

Listing 5-21. Filtering Data in the ProductValuesController.cs File in the Controllers Folder

```
...
[HttpGet]
public IEnumerable<Product> GetProducts(string category, string search,
        bool related = false) {
    IQueryable<Product> query = context.Products;

    if (!string.IsNullOrWhiteSpace(category)) {
        string catLower = category.ToLower();
        query = query.Where(p => p.Category.ToLower().Contains(catLower));
    }
    if (!string.IsNullOrWhiteSpace(search)) {
        string searchLower = search.ToLower();
        query = query.Where(p => p.Name.ToLower().Contains(searchLower)
            || p.Description.ToLower().Contains(searchLower));
    }

    if (related) {
        query = query.Include(p => p.Supplier).Include(p => p.Ratings);
        List<Product> data = query.ToList();
        data.ForEach(p => {
            if (p.Supplier != null) {
                p.Supplier.Products = null;
            }
            if (p.Ratings != null) {
                p.Ratings.ForEach(r => r.Product = null);
            }
        });
        return data;
    } else {
        return query;
    }
}
...
```

The IQueryable<T> interface is especially useful for filtering data because it allows the query to be constructed step by step and will be executed only when the results are enumerated. In the listing, I inspect the parameter values and use them to build up the query using LINQ.

To test the ability to filter data, restart the ASP.NET Core MVC application and use a browser to request http://localhost:5000/api/products?category=soccer. This URL requests the Product objects in the Soccer category and will produce the following result:

```
[{"productId":3,"name":"Soccer Ball","category":"Soccer",
  "description":"FIFA-approved size and weight","price":19.50},
{ "productId":4,"name":"Corner Flags","category":"Soccer",
```

```
    "description":"Give your pitch a professional touch","price":34.95},
{ "productId":5,"name":"Stadium","category":"Soccer",
  "description":"Flat-packed 35,000-seat stadium","price":79500.00}]
```

Applying Filtering in the Angular Application

A corresponding set of changes are required in the Angular repository to support data filtering. First, add a TypeScript file called configClasses.repository.ts to the models folder and use it to define the class shown in Listing 5-22.

Listing 5-22. The Content of the configClasses.repository.ts File in the ClientApp/app/models Folder

```
export class Filter {
    category?: string;
    search?: string;
    related: boolean = false;

    reset() {
        this.category = this.search = null;
        this.related = false;
    }
}
```

This class will be used to specify the filtering that will be applied to product data. To update the repository to use this class and implement the filtering, make the changes shown in Listing 5-23.

Listing 5-23. Filtering Data in the repository.ts File in the ClientApp/app/models Folder

```
import { Product } from "./product.model";
import { Injectable } from "@angular/core";
import { Http, RequestMethod, Request, Response } from "@angular/http";
import { Observable } from "rxjs/Observable";
import "rxjs/add/operator/map";
import { Filter } from "./configClasses.repository";

const productsUrl = "/api/products";

@Injectable()
export class Repository {
    private filterObject = new Filter();

    constructor(private http: Http) {
        this.filter.category = "soccer";
        this.filter.related = true;
        this.getProducts();
    }

    getProduct(id: number) {
        this.sendRequest(RequestMethod.Get, productsUrl + "/" + id)
            .subscribe(response => this.product = response);
    }
```

```
getProducts() {
    let url = productsUrl +  "?related=" + this.filter.related;

    if (this.filter.category) {
        url += "&category=" + this.filter.category;
    }
    if (this.filter.search) {
        url += "&search=" + this.filter.search;
    }

    this.sendRequest(RequestMethod.Get, url)
        .subscribe(response => this.products = response);
}

private sendRequest(verb: RequestMethod, url: string, data?: any)
    : Observable<any> {

    return this.http.request(new Request({
        method: verb, url: url, body: data
    })).map(response => response.json());
}

product: Product;
products: Product[];

get filter(): Filter {
    return this.filterObject;
}
}
```

The listing defines a TypeScript class called Filter that has properties that correspond to the query string parameters that the web service supports. The Repository class defines a filter property that provides read-only access to a Filter object that is used in the getProducts method to compose the URL for the HTTP request. For testing, the constructor has also been updated to use the filter so that the web service will be asked to select the Product objects that are in the Soccer category. When you save the changes to the TypeScript file and navigate to http://localhost:5000, the browser will show the filtered data, as illustrated in Figure 5-7.

Name	Category	Price	Supplier	Ratings
Soccer Ball	Soccer	19.5	Soccer Town	2
Corner Flags	Soccer	34.95	Soccer Town	1
Stadium	Soccer	79500	Soccer Town	3

Figure 5-7. Filtering data in the Angular application

Understanding the Structure of the Web Service

The web service isn't complete, but its basic structure has been defined, allowing the client to send a request for single and multiple product objects. The structure of the MVC part of the application will be familiar to most ASP.NET Core MVC developers because it follows the same basic approach that it used for round-trip applications, except that the action methods return data that is serialized into JSON, as shown in Figure 5-8.

Figure 5-8. The structure of the ASP.NET Core MVC web service

The Angular application is more complex than the ASP.NET Core MVC application. In particular, the way that Angular responds immediately to changes in the data that is displayed through its data bindings means that there is a separation between the methods by which data is requested and the properties that are used to make that data available to the rest of the application, as shown in Figure 5-9.

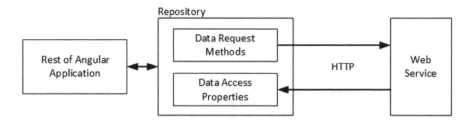

Figure 5-9. The structure of the repository in the Angular application

This indirection will start to make sense in Chapter 7, where I explain how the structure of an Angular application allows features to cooperate with one another and how the data model becomes the heart of the application.

Summary

In this chapter, I replaced the static JSON data in the Razor view with an HTTP web service that follows the basic principles of REST. I created a new MVC controller for handling data requests and explained the interactions between related data and the JSON serializer. I created a repository in the Angular application, used it to demonstrate how Angular provides support for making asynchronous HTTP requests, and explained how the responses are represented using observables. In the next chapter, I continue to work on the web service providing the features that are required to create, modify, and delete data objects.

CHAPTER 6

Completing the Web Service

In Chapter 5, I created the web service and added support for handling HTTP GET requests. In this chapter, I complete the implementation by adding support for the POST, PUT, PATCH, and DELETE methods, which allows the client to create, update, and delete data.

■ **Note** The web service features in this chapter and Chapter 5 are unsecured, which means that any client can access the data and make changes. I show you how to add authentication and authorization to the web service in Chapters 11 and 12.

Preparing for This Chapter

This chapter uses the SportsStore project that I created in Chapter 3 and modified in the chapters since. To ensure that the contents of the database are reset, open a command prompt, navigate to the SportsStore folder, and run the commands shown in Listing 6-1.

■ **Tip** You can download the complete project for this chapter from https://github.com/apress/esntl-angular-for-asp.net-core-mvc. This is also where you will find updates and corrections for this book.

Listing 6-1. Resetting the Database

```
docker-compose down
docker-compose up
```

The first command removes the Docker database container from the previous chapter. The second command creates and starts a fresh container.

Start the application to apply the database schema and add the seed data. If you are using Visual Studio, you can do this by selecting Debug ➤ Start Without Debugging. If you are using Visual Studio Code or just prefer working with the command line, then open a command prompt, navigate to the SportsStore folder, and run the command shown in Listing 6-2.

Listing 6-2. Starting the Application

```
dotnet run
```

Use a browser to navigate to `http://localhost:5000`, and you will see the content shown in Figure 6-1.

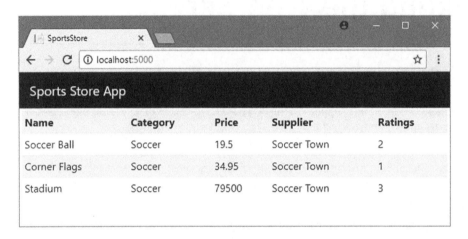

Figure 6-1. *Running the example application*

Implementing the POST Method

The HTTP POST method is used to store new data objects in the database. As noted in Chapter 5, getting Angular, ASP.NET Core MVC, and Entity Framework Core to work together requires some care, especially when it comes to related data, and implementing POST requests has its share of pitfalls. In the sections that follow, I show you how to add support for creating data while avoiding the most common problems.

Understanding the API Enhancements

Adding support for the POST method will expand the API provided by the web service, as shown in Table 6-1.

Table 6-1. *The Web Service API with POST Support for Storing New Objects*

Method	URL	Description
GET	/api/products/<id>	Retrieves a single Product object
GET	/api/products	Retrieves multiple Product objects
POST	/api/products	Stores a new Product object
POST	/api/suppliers	Stores a new Supplier object

The additions to Table 6-1 provide URLs for both the Product and Supplier classes in the data model. It can be tempting to allow clients to supply new related data in a request so that a Product object is received along with a new Supplier object and both are stored in the database. This is an approach that works well at first but quickly becomes complex; ultimately it produces a client that requires deep knowledge of how the web service works internally and produces a web service that requires constant tinkering and that responds badly to changes elsewhere in the application.

A more robust approach is to handle the creation of each type of data separately. This requires more work initially but produces a better result that more easily responds to changes.

AVOIDING KEY VALUES IN URLS

Notice that the POST URLs in Table 6-1 do not include an ID, such as /api/products/100, for example, to tell the web service to create a new Product object with a ProductId value of 100, mirroring the URL format for querying single objects with the GET method.

Storing application data in a relational database creates restrictions on the values that can be used for a Product object's ProductId property because the value is used as a primary key in the database. ProductId values must be numeric, and they must not exceed the maximum value of the SQL data type that has been assigned to store ProductId values in the database table. Most critically, values must be unique. The client must know about all of these restrictions and be updated if they change, and the activity of clients must be coordinated in some way to avoid selecting duplicate values. All of this is possible, but it is much simpler to leave the database server to generate the values automatically when it stores data, which is how Entity Framework Core configures the database by default. This ensures that only valid values will be used and avoids any need to deal with multiple clients trying to store data using the same key at the same time.

Creating the Data Binding Classes

I am going to define a separate class that will be used by the MVC model binder to get details for the Product object that should be created from a POST request. Create a Models/BindingTargets folder and add to it a C# class file called ProductData.cs with the code shown in Listing 6-3.

Listing 6-3. The Contents of the ProductData.cs File in the Models/BindingTargets Folder

```
using System.ComponentModel.DataAnnotations;

namespace SportsStore.Models.BindingTargets {

    public class ProductData {

        [Required]
        public string Name { get; set; }

        [Required]
        public string Category { get; set; }

        [Required]
        public string Description { get; set; }

        [Range(1, int.MaxValue, ErrorMessage = "Price must be at least 1")]
```

```
    public decimal Price { get; set; }

    public long Supplier { get; set; }

    public Product Product => new Product {
        Name = Name, Category = Category,
        Description = Description, Price = Price,
        Supplier = Supplier == 0 ? null : new Supplier { SupplierId = Supplier }
    };
    }
}
```

In the next section, I will use the `ProductData` class as the parameter for the action method that will receive POST requests. This will allow me to receive JSON data from the client that looks like this:

```
{ "name": "X-Ray Scuba Mask", "category": "Watersports",
  "description": "See what the fish are hiding", "price": 49.99,
  "supplier": 1 }
```

The `Product` property defined by the `ProductData` class creates a `Product` object and a `Supplier` object that I will use to perform the database operation, as shown in the next section.

USING DATA BINDING CLASSES

You don't have to use a separate class like the one in Listing 6-3, but there comes a point where using the original data model class, which is `Product` in this case, becomes too complex to manage.

I could get the data I required using the `Product` class, but it would be complicated trying to get the right result from the MVC model binder while avoiding problems with Entity Framework Core and the JSON serializer.

To start, I don't want the client to provide a `ProductId` value or to include a `Supplier` object as related data, preferring instead to receive details of the `Supplier` that a `Product` should be associated with by specifying its key. To allow the client to send the data as I want, I would have to add a property to the `Product` class. But this isn't straightforward; I can't add a property called `Supplier`, for example, because it is already used as a navigation property. I could add a property called `SupplierId`, but that would be detected by Entity Framework Core and used to update the database schema to prevent `Product` objects from being stored without a relationship with a `Supplier`. And the value of this property would be set by Entity Framework Core when it reads data and then included in the responses for GET requests by the JSON serializer. If I add use a different property name, Entity Framework Core will add a new column to the `Products` table in the database.

The validation attributes used by the MVC model binder, which includes the `Required` and `Range` attributes used in Listing 6-3, are also used by Entity Framework Core to apply constraints to the database schema. Applying these attributes to the `Product` class will change the schema the next time that a database migration is created and applied, causing unexpected effects and even data loss in some cases.

All of these problems can be solved using attributes. The JSON serializer supports an attribute that tells it to ignore a property. Entity Framework Core supports an attribute that tells it not to create a new column in the database table. The MVC framework supports attributes that prevent the model binder from populating a property from the request data and for specifying a buddy class to provide the validation metadata so that it isn't detected by Entity Framework Core.

But the result is that the Product class festooned in attributes that are trying to manage the interactions of the serializer, the model binder, and the data layer. As the application gets more complex, managing the model classes and their behavior gets difficult. Adding a class specifically for data binding lets me partition up the functionality so that I can get the data I want from the client in a reasonable format without worrying about causing unexpected side effects.

A similar class is required to handle data when creating Supplier objects. Add a C# class file called SupplierData.cs to the Models/BindingTargets folder with the statements shown in Listing 6-4.

Listing 6-4. The Contents of the SupplierData.cs File in the Models/BindingTargets Folder

```
using System.ComponentModel.DataAnnotations;

namespace SportsStore.Models.BindingTargets {

    public class SupplierData {

        [Required]
        public string Name { get; set; }

        [Required]
        public string City { get; set; }

        [Required]
        [StringLength(2, MinimumLength = 2)]
        public string State { get; set; }

        public Supplier Supplier => new Supplier {
            Name = Name, City = City, State = State
        };
    }
}
```

Implementing the Web Service Action Methods

The implementation of the action method to handle POST requests is simpler than the GET actions from Chapter 5. To add support for creating objects, add the method shown in Listing 6-5 to the ProductValues controller.

Listing 6-5. Adding an Action Method in the ProductValuesController.cs File in the Controllers Folder

```
using Microsoft.AspNetCore.Mvc;
using SportsStore.Models;
using Microsoft.EntityFrameworkCore;
using System.Linq;
using System.Collections.Generic;
using SportsStore.Models.BindingTargets;
```

```
namespace SportsStore.Controllers {

    [Route("api/products")]
    public class ProductValuesController : Controller {
        private DataContext context;

        public ProductValuesController(DataContext ctx) {
            context = ctx;
        }

        // ..other action methods omitted for brevity...

        [HttpPost]
        public IActionResult CreateProduct([FromBody] ProductData pdata) {
            if (ModelState.IsValid) {
                Product p = pdata.Product;
                if (p.Supplier != null && p.Supplier.SupplierId != 0) {
                    context.Attach(p.Supplier);
                }
                context.Add(p);
                context.SaveChanges();
                return Ok(p.ProductId);
            } else {
                return BadRequest(ModelState);
            }
        }
    }
}
```

The CreateProduct method has a ProductData parameter, which will be populated by the MVC model binder with the data sent by the client. This parameter is decorated with the FromBody attribute, which tells the model binder to get data values from the request body (and without which the JSON data sent by the client will be ignored).

The result of the CreateProduct method is an IActionResult method, which provides flexibility for returning an error if the data sent by the client doesn't pass the validation checks applied using the Required and Range attributes from Listing 6-4. If the data doesn't perform validation, then a 400 Bad Request response is sent to the client, along with JSON data containing a list of the validation errors.

```
...
return BadRequest(ModelState);
...
```

If the data does pass validation, then I get the Product object by calling the ProductData.Product property. To work out whether the Product will be related to a Supplier, I check the value of the Product. Suppler.SupplierId property, and if it is defined and isn't zero, I call the database context object's Attach method, like this:

```
...
if (p.Supplier != null && p.Supplier.SupplierId != 0) {
    context.Attach(p.Supplier);
}
...
```

By default, Entity Framework Core will create related objects automatically, which means it will try to create a new Supplier object as well as a new Product object. This is because Entity Framework Core doesn't know anything about the Product and Supplier objects and just assumes that both are new and must be stored in the database. This presents a problem because the database won't allow Supplier objects to be created when the SupplierId value is specified and because there should already be a Supplier with that SupplierId value. The Attach method makes Entity Framework Core aware of an object and tells it that only subsequent changes to it should be written to the database.

■ **Tip**   Notice that the Supplier object has only a SupplierId value. Since the purpose of the POST operation is to create a Product object, only the data required for the new row in the Products table is required. This means that Entity Framework Core only needs to know the value of the SupplierId property so that it can create the foreign key relationship and will ignore the rest of the Supplier properties, which means that there is no need for the client to send values for them to the web service.

The database context's Add method tells Entity Framework Core that the Product object should be stored in the database and the operation is performed when the SaveChanges method is called.

```
...
context.Add(p);
context.SaveChanges();
...
```

When the data is stored, the database will generate a value for the ProductId property and will automatically update the Product object with that value. To provide the client with the value, I pass it to the Ok method so that it can be included in the 200 OK response.

```
...
return Ok(p.ProductId);
...
```

Creating the Web Service Controller for Supplier Objects

The MVC framework is flexible enough to support multiple data types and URLs in a single web service controller, but defining one controller for each data type produces code that is easier to understand and manage. Add a new C# class file called SupplierValuesController.cs to the Controllers folder and add the code shown in Listing 6-6.

Listing 6-6. The Contents of the SupplierValuesController.cs File in the Controllers Folder

```
using Microsoft.AspNetCore.Mvc;
using SportsStore.Models;
using SportsStore.Models.BindingTargets;
using System.Collections.Generic;

namespace SportsStore.Controllers {

    [Route("api/suppliers")]
    public class SupplierValuesController : Controller {
        private DataContext context;
```

```
    public SupplierValuesController(DataContext ctx) {
        context = ctx;
    }

    [HttpGet]
    public IEnumerable<Supplier> GetSuppliers() {
        return context.Suppliers;
    }

    [HttpPost]
    public IActionResult CreateSupplier([FromBody]SupplierData sdata) {
        if (ModelState.IsValid) {
            Supplier s = sdata.Supplier;
            context.Add(s);
            context.SaveChanges();
            return Ok(s.SupplierId);
        } else {
            return BadRequest(ModelState);
        }
    }
  }
}
```

This controller uses the Route attribute so that it can handle requests sent to the /api/suppliers URL. There are action methods for GET and POST requests, following the same pattern for querying and creating Supplier objects.

Creating Data Objects in the Angular Application

To add support for creating new Product and Supplier objects in the Angular application, add the method shown in Listing 6-7 to the Repository class so that it can send POST requests to the web service.

Listing 6-7. Sending POST Requests in the repository.ts File in the ClientApp/app Folder

```
import { Product } from "./product.model";
import { Injectable } from "@angular/core";
import { Http, RequestMethod, Request, Response } from "@angular/http";
import { Observable } from "rxjs/Observable";
import "rxjs/add/operator/map";
import { Filter } from "./configClasses.repository";
import { Supplier } from "./supplier.model";

const productsUrl = "/api/products";
const suppliersUrl = "/api/suppliers";

@Injectable()
export class Repository {
    private filterObject = new Filter();

    constructor(private http: Http) {
        //this.filter.category = "soccer";
        this.filter.related = true;
```

```
        this.getProducts();
}

getProduct(id: number) {
    this.sendRequest(RequestMethod.Get, productsUrl + "/" + id)
        .subscribe(response => this.product = response);
}

getProducts() {
    let url = productsUrl + "?related=" + this.filter.related;

    if (this.filter.category) {
        url += "&category=" + this.filter.category;
    }
    if (this.filter.search) {
        url += "&search=" + this.filter.search;
    }

    this.sendRequest(RequestMethod.Get, url)
        .subscribe(response => this.products = response);
}

getSuppliers() {
    this.sendRequest(RequestMethod.Get, suppliersUrl)
        .subscribe(response => this.suppliers = response);
}

createProduct(prod: Product) {
    let data = {
        name: prod.name, category: prod.category,
        description: prod.description, price: prod.price,
        supplier: prod.supplier ? prod.supplier.supplierId : 0
    };

    this.sendRequest(RequestMethod.Post, productsUrl, data)
        .subscribe(response => {
            prod.productId = response;
            this.products.push(prod);
        });
}

createProductAndSupplier(prod: Product, supp: Supplier) {
    let data = {
        name: supp.name, city: supp.city, state: supp.state
    };

    this.sendRequest(RequestMethod.Post, suppliersUrl, data)
        .subscribe(response => {
            supp.supplierId = response;
            prod.supplier = supp;
            this.suppliers.push(supp);
            if (prod != null) {
```

```
                        this.createProduct(prod);
                    }
                });
        }

        private sendRequest(verb: RequestMethod, url: string, data?: any)
            : Observable<any> {

            return this.http.request(new Request({
                method: verb, url: url, body: data
            })).map(response => response.json());
        }

        product: Product;
        products: Product[];
        suppliers: Supplier[] = [];

        get filter(): Filter {
            return this.filterObject;
        }
}
```

The createProduct method accepts a Product object, uses it to create an object in the format that the web service requires, and sends it using a POST request. The subscribe method is used on the Observable to receive the response, which is parsed to get the value for the productId property. The Product object received through the parameter is updated and added to the end of the products array using the JavaScript push method. The createProductAndSupplier method builds on the createProduct method to create a Supplier and then create a related Product.

Adding Support for Creating an Object in the Component

The next step is to define methods in the Angular component that can be called when the user wants to create a new product or supplier, as shown in Listing 6-8.

Listing 6-8. Adding Methods in the app.component.ts File in the ClientApp/app Folder

```
import { Component } from '@angular/core';
import { Repository } from "./models/repository";
import { Product } from "./models/product.model";
import { Supplier } from "./models/supplier.model";

@Component({
    selector: 'app-root',
    templateUrl: './app.component.html',
    styleUrls: ['./app.component.css']
})
export class AppComponent {

    constructor(private repo: Repository) { }

    get product(): Product {
        return this.repo.product;
    }
```

```
get products(): Product[] {
    return this.repo.products;
}

createProduct() {
    this.repo.createProduct(new Product(0, "X-Ray Scuba Mask", "Watersports",
        "See what the fish are hiding", 49.99, this.repo.products[0].supplier));
}

createProductAndSupplier() {
    let s = new Supplier(0, "Rocket Shoe Corp", "Boston", "MA");
    let p = new Product(0, "Rocket-Powered Shoes", "Running",
        "Set a new record", 100, s);
    this.repo.createProductAndSupplier(p, s);
}
}
```

The createProduct method creates a new Product object and asks the repository to send it to the web service. The Supplier that will be associated with the Product is taken from the first element in the products array, just so that the web service can be tested. The createProductAndSupplier creates both Product and Supplier objects and passes them to the corresponding repository method.

Updating the Component Template

The final step is to add a new element to the HTML template in the Angular application that will allow the user to trigger the creation of a new object by calling the createProduct in the component, as shown in Listing 6-9.

Listing 6-9. Adding Elements in the app.component.html File in the ClientApp/app Folder

```
<table class="table table-sm table-striped">
    <tr>
        <th>Name</th><th>Category</th><th>Price</th>
        <th>Supplier</th><th>Ratings</th>
    </tr>
    <tr *ngFor="let product of products">
        <td>{{product.name}}</td>
        <td>{{product.category}}</td>
        <td>{{product.price}}</td>
        <td>{{product.supplier?.name || 'None'}}</td>
        <td>{{product.ratings?.length || 0}}</td>
    </tr>
</table>
<button class="btn btn-primary m-1" (click)="createProduct()">
    Create Product
</button>
<button class="btn btn-primary m-1" (click)="createProductAndSupplier()">
    Create Product and Supplier
</button>
```

113

The `button` elements have been configured using the Angular *event binding* feature, which responds to events generated by an HTML element by evaluating an expression. The highlighted part of this element is the event binding.

```
...
<button class="btn btn-primary m-1" (click)="createProduct()">
...
```

The parentheses (the (and) characters) denote an event binding and surround the name of the event, which is `click`. The `click` event is triggered when the user clicks the button, at which point Angular evaluates the expression and invokes the component's `createProduct` method, defined in Listing 6-8. Event binding expressions can only access methods and properties defined by the component. The result is that clicking the buttons will create new products.

Restart the ASP.NET Core MVC application, reload the browser, and click the Create Product button. A new item will appear in the table, associated with the existing Splash Dudes supplier. Click the Create Product And Supplier button, and a new item will appear, associated with a new Rocker Shoe Corp supplier. Figure 6-2 shows the effect of both buttons.

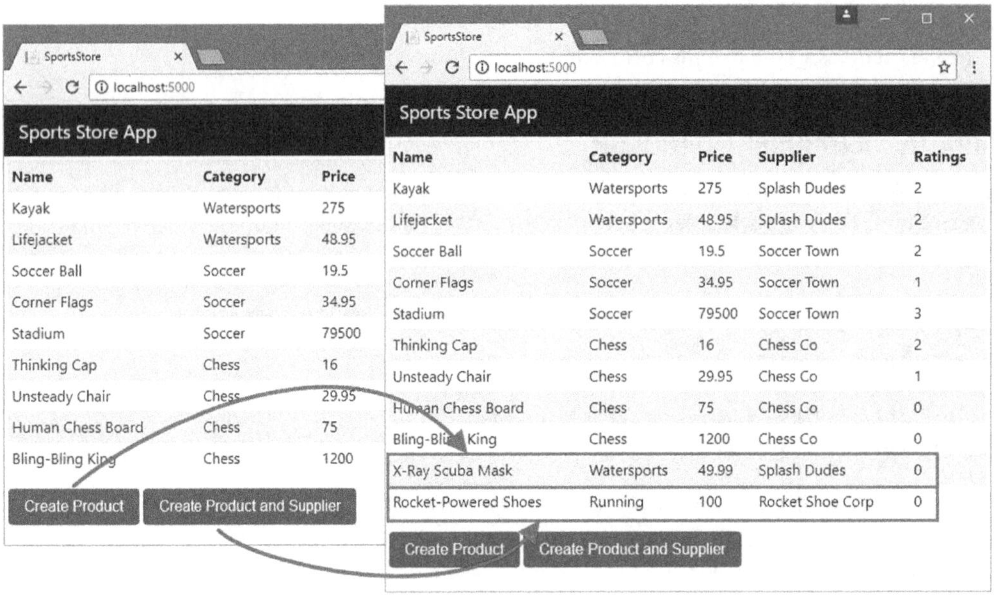

Figure 6-2. *Creating new products*

■ **Note** The structure of the Angular application separates the process of creating the new objects from displaying them. The object that is returned by the web service is added to the data model and automatically displayed by Angular through the `ngFor` directive, which adds a new row to the table. You may find this approach convoluted, but it simplifies the process of creating application features because any change to the data model is displayed to the user.

■ **Tip**   If you click the buttons repeatedly, multiple objects will be created, but each will have different `ProductId` or `SupplierId` property value, which will be assigned by the database server.

Implementing the PUT Method

The HTTP PUT method is used to replace an existing data object with a new one and requires an approach similar to the one required by the POST method in the previous section. Supporting the PUT method leads to the expansion of the web service API, as described in Table 6-2. For all the new URLs, the object that is being updated will be identified using the id segment of the request URL.

■ **Tip**   When using the PUT method, the client must provide values for all the new object's properties. If you want to perform more selective updates, then see the section called "Implementing the PATCH method."

Table 6-2.   *The Web Service API with PUT Support for Updating Objects*

Method	URL	Description
GET	/api/products/<id>	Retrieves a single Product object
GET	/api/products	Retrieves multiple Product objects
POST	/api/products	Stores a new Product object
POST	/api/suppliers	Stores a new Supplier object
PUT	/api/products/<id>	Replaces an existing Product object
PUT	/api/suppliers/<id>	Replaces an existing Supplier object

Implementing the Web Service Action Methods

To add support for updating Product data, add the action method shown in Listing 6-10 to the ProductValues controller.

Listing 6-10.   Adding an Action Method in the ProductValuesController.cs File in the Controllers Folder

```
using Microsoft.AspNetCore.Mvc;
using SportsStore.Models;
using Microsoft.EntityFrameworkCore;
using System.Linq;
using System.Collections.Generic;
using SportsStore.Models.BindingTargets;

namespace SportsStore.Controllers {

    [Route("api/products")]
    public class ProductValuesController : Controller {
        private DataContext context;
```

```
        public ProductValuesController(DataContext ctx) {
            context = ctx;
        }

        // ...other methods omitted for brevity...

        [HttpPut("{id}")]
        public IActionResult ReplaceProduct(long id, [FromBody] ProductData pdata) {
            if (ModelState.IsValid) {
                Product p = pdata.Product;
                p.ProductId = id;
                if (p.Supplier != null && p.Supplier.SupplierId != 0) {
                    context.Attach(p.Supplier);
                }
                context.Update(p);
                context.SaveChanges();
                return Ok();
            } else {
                return BadRequest(ModelState);
            }
        }
    }
}
```

The MVC model binder will create the ProductData object from the request data, which is then used to create a Product, whose ProductId property is set from the id parameter so that Entity Framework Core knows which existing object is to be updated.

The data context object's Attach method is used to prevent Entity Framework Core from trying to store a new Supplier object, while the Update method is used to register the Product object with Entity Framework Core so that it will replace the existing data.

The database is updated by calling the SaveChanges method, and the Ok method is used to return a 200 OK response to the client. If the request data doesn't pass validation, a 400 Bad Request response will be sent, and no update will be performed.

Similar code is required to replace Supplier objects. Add the action method shown in Listing 6-11 to the SupplierValues controller.

Listing 6-11. Adding an Action Method in the SupplierValuesController.cs File in the Controllers Folder

```
using Microsoft.AspNetCore.Mvc;
using SportsStore.Models;
using SportsStore.Models.BindingTargets;
using System.Collections.Generic;

namespace SportsStore.Controllers {

    [Route("api/suppliers")]
    public class SupplierValuesController : Controller {
        private DataContext context;

        public SupplierValuesController(DataContext ctx) {
            context = ctx;
        }
```

```
// ...other methods omitted for brevity...

[HttpPut("{id}")]
public IActionResult ReplaceSupplier(long id,
        [FromBody] SupplierData sdata) {
    if (ModelState.IsValid) {
        Supplier s = sdata.Supplier;
        s.SupplierId = id;
        context.Update(s);
        context.SaveChanges();
        return Ok();
    } else {
        return BadRequest(ModelState);
    }
}
}
}
```

No special measures are required to replace Supplier objects, and the context object's Update method is used to tell Entity Framework Core to replace a Supplier that is obtained from the SupplierData parameter.

Replacing Products in the Angular Application

By now the process of taking advantage of new web service features will be familiar, even if not all of the details about how Angular works are clear. First, add new methods to the Angular Repository class that will accept Product or Supplier objects and send a PUT request to the web service, as shown in Listing 6-12.

Listing 6-12. Adding Methods in the repository.ts File in the ClientApp/app Folder

```
import { Product } from "./product.model";
import { Injectable } from "@angular/core";
import { Http, RequestMethod, Request, Response } from "@angular/http";
import { Observable } from "rxjs/Observable";
import "rxjs/add/operator/map";
import { Filter } from "./configClasses.repository";
import { Supplier } from "./supplier.model";

const productsUrl = "/api/products";
const suppliersUrl = "/api/suppliers";

@Injectable()
export class Repository {
    private filterObject = new Filter();

    constructor(private http: Http) {
        //this.filter.category = "soccer";
        this.filter.related = true;
        this.getProducts();
    }
```

```
// ...other methods omitted for brevity...

replaceProduct(prod: Product) {
    let data = {
        name: prod.name, category: prod.category,
        description: prod.description, price: prod.price,
        supplier: prod.supplier ? prod.supplier.supplierId : 0
    };
    this.sendRequest(RequestMethod.Put, productsUrl + "/" + prod.productId, data)
        .subscribe(response => this.getProducts());
}

replaceSupplier(supp: Supplier) {
    let data = {
        name: supp.name, city: supp.city, state: supp.state
    };
    this.sendRequest(RequestMethod.Put,
        suppliersUrl + "/" + supp.supplierId, data)
        .subscribe(response => this.getProducts());
}

private sendRequest(verb: RequestMethod, url: string, data?: any)
    : Observable<any> {

    return this.http.request(new Request({
        method: verb, url: url, body: data
    })).map(response => {
        return response.headers.get("Content-Length") != "0"
            ? response.json() : null;
    });
}

product: Product;
products: Product[];
suppliers: Supplier[] = [];

get filter(): Filter {
    return this.filterObject;
}
}
```

I send the HTTP PUT request and then use the subscribe method to refresh the Product data. This is an inefficient approach, but it demonstrates that you can handle the response from one HTTP request by starting another.

Notice that the sendRequest method has changed in this listing. The web service will now return responses that contain no JSON data to parse, so the code in the map method checks the response's Content-Length header to determine whether to call the json method.

Adding Support for Replacing Objects in the Component

The next step is to add methods to the Angular component that can be invoked using event bindings in the component's template, as shown in Listing 6-13.

Listing 6-13. Adding Methods in the app.component.ts File in the ClientApp/app Folder

```
import { Component } from '@angular/core';
import { Repository } from "./models/repository";
import { Product } from "./models/product.model";
import { Supplier } from "./models/supplier.model";

@Component({
    selector: 'app-root',
    templateUrl: './app.component.html',
    styleUrls: ['./app.component.css']
})
export class AppComponent {

    constructor(private repo: Repository) { }

    // ...other methods omitted for brevity...

    replaceProduct() {
        let p = this.repo.products[0];
        p.name = "Modified Product";
        p.category = "Modified Category";
        this.repo.replaceProduct(p);
    }

    replaceSupplier() {
        let s = new Supplier(3, "Modified Supplier", "New York", "NY");
        this.repo.replaceSupplier(s);
    }
}
```

The new methods, replaceProduct and replaceSupplier, create replacement objects and use the repository to send them to the web service. Add the elements shown in Listing 6-14 to the component's template so that the new component methods can be invoked.

Listing 6-14. Adding Elements in the app.component.html File in the ClientApp/app Folder

```
<table class="table table-sm table-striped">
    <tr>
        <th>Name</th><th>Category</th><th>Price</th>
        <th>Supplier</th><th>Ratings</th>
    </tr>
    <tr *ngFor="let product of products">
        <td>{{product.name}}</td>
        <td>{{product.category}}</td>
        <td>{{product.price}}</td>
        <td>{{product.supplier?.name || 'None'}}</td>
```

```
        <td>{{product.ratings?.length || 0}}</td>
    </tr>
</table>
<button class="btn btn-primary m-1" (click)="createProduct()">
    Create Product
</button>
<button class="btn btn-primary m-1" (click)="createProductAndSupplier()">
    Create Product and Supplier
</button>
<button class="btn btn-primary m-1" (click)="replaceProduct()">
    Replace Product
</button>
<button class="btn btn-primary m-1" (click)="replaceSupplier()">
    Replace Supplier
</button>
```

The new button elements use the click event binding with expressions that invoke the component methods. Restart the application, use a browser to navigate to http://localhost:5000, and click the Replace Product and Replace Supplier buttons, the effect of which are shown in Figure 6-3.

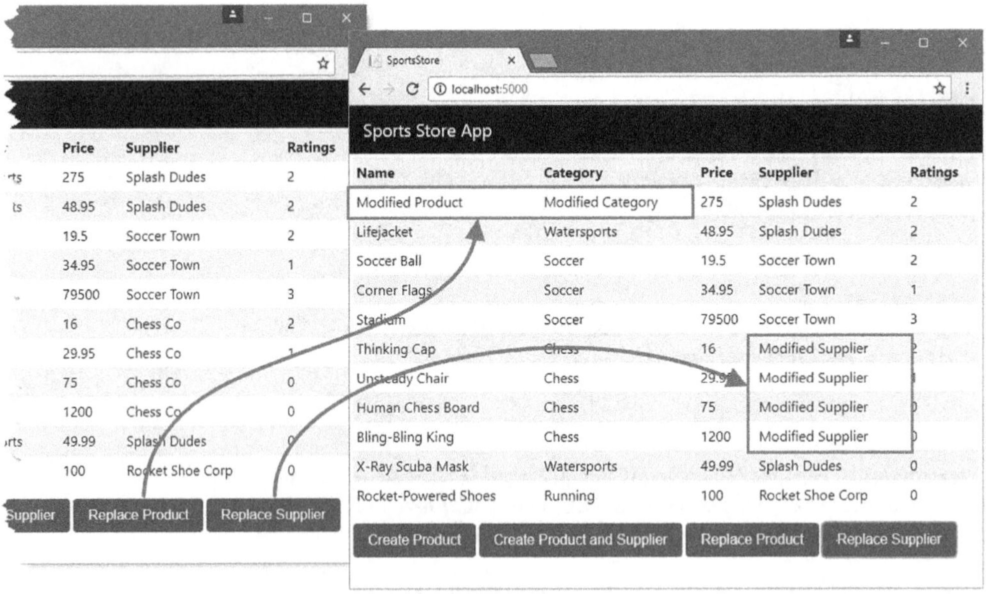

Figure 6-3. *Replacing objects*

When you click the Replace Product button, the first Product in the table is replaced. When you click the Replace Supplier button, the Supplier related to the Chess products is replaced.

Implementing the PATCH Method

For simple data types, edit operations can be handled by replacing the existing object using the PUT method. Even if you need to change only a single property value in the Product class, for example, it isn't too much trouble to use a PUT method and include the values for all the other Product properties, too.

But not all data types are as easy to work with, either because they define many more properties or because the client doesn't have access to all of them for security reasons. The solution is to use a PATCH request, which sends just the changes to the web service rather than a complete replacement object. Supporting the PATCH method leads to the expansion of the web service API, as described in Table 6-3.

■ **Tip**   You can be selective about the data types for which you implement the PATCH method. For the SportsStore application, I am going to provide support only for `Product` objects, which means that changes to `Supplier` objects can be performed only using PUT requests.

Table 6-3. *The Web Service API with PUT Support for Updating Objects*

Method	URL	Description
GET	/api/products/<id>	Retrieves a single `Product` object
GET	/api/products	Retrieves multiple `Product` objects
POST	/api/products	Stores a new `Product` object
POST	/api/suppliers	Stores a new `Supplier` object
PUT	/api/products/<id>	Replaces an existing `Product` object
PUT	/api/suppliers/<id>	Replaces an existing `Supplier` object
PATCH	/api/products/<id>	Updates a `Product` object

Understanding JSON Patch

ASP.NET Core MVC has support for working with the JSON Patch standard, which allows changes to be specified in a uniform way. The JSON Patch standard allows for a complex set of changes to be described, but for the SportsStore application, I need to deal with only two kinds of change for the `Product` object: altering the value of a property and removing a property. Changing property values will allow the client to selectively edit existing data, while removing a property will allow the client to break the relationship between a `Product` and its `Supplier`.

I am not going to go into the details of the JSON Patch standard, which you can read at `https://tools.ietf.org/html/rfc6902`, but the client is going to send the web service JSON data like this in its HTTP PATCH requests:

```
[
{ "op": "replace", "path": "name", "value": "Green Kayak"},
{ "op": "replace", "path": "price", "value": 200},
{ "op": "replace", "path": "supplier", "value": null}
]
```

A JSON Patch document is expressed as an array of operations. Each operation has an `op` property, which specifies the type of operation, and a `path` property, which specifies where the operation will be applied.

For the SportsStore application (and, in fact, for most applications) only the `replace` operation is required, which is used to change the value of a property. This JSON Patch document sets new values for the `name`, `price`, and `supplier` properties. (The effect of setting the `supplier` property to `null` will be to break the relationship with a supplier.) The properties defined by the `Product` class not included in the JSON Patch document will not be modified.

Enhancing the Product Binding Target

I need to enhance the model binding target for Product objects to get JSON Patch documents working seamlessly with ASP.NET Core MVC and Entity Framework Core to ensure that only the values affected by a PATCH request will be modified. To that end, make the changes shown in Listing 6-15 to the ProductData class.

Listing 6-15. Adding a Product Object in the ProductData.cs File in the Models/BindingTargets Folder

```
using System.ComponentModel.DataAnnotations;

namespace SportsStore.Models.BindingTargets {

    public class ProductData {

        [Required]
        public string Name {
            get => Product.Name; set => Product.Name = value;
        }

        [Required]
        public string Category {
            get => Product.Category; set => Product.Category = value;
        }

        [Required]
        public string Description {
            get => Product.Description; set => Product.Description = value;
        }

        [Range(1, int.MaxValue, ErrorMessage = "Price must be at least 1")]
        public decimal Price {
            get => Product.Price; set => Product.Price = value;
        }

        public long? Supplier {
            get => Product.Supplier?.SupplierId ?? null;
            set {
                if (!value.HasValue) {
                    Product.Supplier = null;
                } else {
                    if (Product.Supplier == null) {
                        Product.Supplier = new Supplier();
                    }
                    Product.Supplier.SupplierId = value.Value;
                }
            }
        }

        public Product Product { get; set; } = new Product();
    }
}
```

These changes map the properties defined by the ProductData class onto a Product object. This allows me to take advantage of the Entity Framework Core change-tracking feature on the Product object, which ensures that only values that are changed by the operations in the JSON Patch document are updated in the database.

Implementing the Web Service Action Method

To add support for handling PATCH requests for Product objects, add the action method shown in Listing 6-16 to the ProductValues controller.

Listing 6-16. Adding an Action Method in the ProductValuesController.cs File in the Controllers Folder

```
using Microsoft.AspNetCore.Mvc;
using SportsStore.Models;
using Microsoft.EntityFrameworkCore;
using System.Linq;
using System.Collections.Generic;
using SportsStore.Models.BindingTargets;
using Microsoft.AspNetCore.JsonPatch;

namespace SportsStore.Controllers {

    [Route("api/products")]
    public class ProductValuesController : Controller {
        private DataContext context;

        public ProductValuesController(DataContext ctx) {
            context = ctx;
        }

        // ...other methods omitted for brevity...

        [HttpPatch("{id}")]
        public IActionResult UpdateProduct(long id,
                [FromBody]JsonPatchDocument<ProductData> patch) {

            Product product = context.Products
                            .Include(p => p.Supplier)
                            .First(p => p.ProductId == id);
            ProductData pdata = new ProductData { Product = product };
            patch.ApplyTo(pdata, ModelState);

            if (ModelState.IsValid && TryValidateModel(pdata)) {

                if (product.Supplier != null && product.Supplier.SupplierId != 0) {
                    context.Attach(product.Supplier);
                }
                context.SaveChanges();
                return Ok();
            } else {
                return BadRequest(ModelState);
            }
```

```
       }
     }
}
```

The UpdateProduct method is decorated with the HttpPatch attribute and defines a long parameter that will identify the Product that is being modified and a JsonPatchDocument<ProductData> parameter that represents the JSON Patch document (this parameter must be decorated with the FromBody attribute).

To get the current data, I retrieve the Product object identified by the id parameter and use it to create a ProductData object.

```
...
Product product = context.Products
                    .Include(p => p.Supplier)
                    .First(p => p.ProductId == id);
ProductData pdata = new ProductData { Product = product };
...
```

Entity Framework Core performs change tracking on the objects it creates, which means that only modifications to the Product objects will be written to the database. The next step is to apply the operations in the JSON Patch document to the ProductData object, which will pass on those changes to the Product object.

```
...
patch.ApplyTo(pdata, ModelState);
...
```

The ApplyTo method updates the controller's model state to record any errors in the JSON Patch document, such as an operation on a property that isn't defined by the ProductData class. Before storing the changes in the database, I check the ModelState.IsValid property and explicitly validate the ProductData object to make sure that the changes have not created an invalid outcome.

```
...
if (ModelState.IsValid && TryValidateModel(pdata)) {
...
```

If there are no validation errors, the changes are written to the database by calling the context object's SaveChanges method, and the modified Product object is returned to the client.

Updating Objects in the Angular Application

To add support for sending PATCH requests to the web service, add the method shown in Listing 6-17 to the Repository class in the Angular application.

Listing 6-17. Adding a Method in the repository.ts File in the ClientApp/app/models Folder

```
import { Product } from "./product.model";
import { Injectable } from "@angular/core";
import { Http, RequestMethod, Request, Response } from "@angular/http";
import { Observable } from "rxjs/Observable";
import "rxjs/add/operator/map";
import { Filter } from "./configClasses.repository";
import { Supplier } from "./supplier.model";
```

124

```
const productsUrl = "/api/products";
const suppliersUrl = "/api/suppliers";

@Injectable()
export class Repository {
    private filterObject = new Filter();

    constructor(private http: Http) {
        //this.filter.category = "soccer";
        this.filter.related = true;
        this.getProducts();
    }

    // ...other methods omitted for brevity...

    updateProduct(id: number, changes: Map<string, any>) {
        let patch = [];
        changes.forEach((value, key) =>
            patch.push({ op: "replace", path: key, value: value }));

        this.sendRequest(RequestMethod.Patch, productsUrl + "/" + id, patch)
            .subscribe(response => this.getProducts());
    }
}
```

The updateProduct method receives a number parameter that identifies the Product to be modified and a Map object whose keys are the names of the properties that have changed. A simple JSON Patch document is created using the replace operation for each of the entries in the Map, which is then sent to the web service using an HTTP PATCH request. The subscribe method is used to reload the data from the web service.

Adding Support for Updating Objects in the Component

The next step is to add a method to the Angular component that can be invoked using event bindings in the component's template, which will respond by calling the new method in the repository, as shown in Listing 6-18.

Listing 6-18. Adding a Method in the app.component.ts File in the ClientApp/app Folder

```
import { Component } from '@angular/core';
import { Repository } from "./models/repository";
import { Product } from "./models/product.model";
import { Supplier } from "./models/supplier.model";

@Component({
    selector: 'app-root',
    templateUrl: './app.component.html',
    styleUrls: ['./app.component.css']
})
export class AppComponent {

    constructor(private repo: Repository) { }
```

```
// ...other methods omitted for brevity...

updateProduct() {
    let changes = new Map<string, any>();
    changes.set("name", "Green Kayak");
    changes.set("supplier", null);
    this.repo.updateProduct(1, changes);
}
}
```

The new method, updateproduct, changes the name property and sets the supplier property to null. Add the elements shown in Listing 6-19 to the component's template so that the new component method can be invoked.

Listing 6-19. Adding an Element in the app.component.html File in the ClientApp/app Folder

```
<table class="table table-sm table-striped">
    <tr>
        <th>Name</th><th>Category</th><th>Price</th>
        <th>Supplier</th><th>Ratings</th>
    </tr>
    <tr *ngFor="let product of products">
        <td>{{product.name}}</td>
        <td>{{product.category}}</td>
        <td>{{product.price}}</td>
        <td>{{product.supplier?.name || 'None'}}</td>
        <td>{{product.ratings?.length || 0}}</td>
    </tr>
</table>

<button class="btn btn-primary m-1" (click)="createProduct()">
    Create Product
</button>
<button class="btn btn-primary m-1" (click)="createProductAndSupplier()">
    Create Product and Supplier
</button>
<button class="btn btn-primary m-1" (click)="replaceProduct()">
    Replace Product
</button>
<button class="btn btn-primary m-1" (click)="replaceSupplier()">
    Replace Supplier
</button>
<button class="btn btn-primary m-1" (click)="updateProduct()">
    Update Product
</button>
```

The new button element uses the click event binding with an expression that invokes the component's updateProduct method. Restart the application, use a browser to navigate to http://localhost:5000, and click the Update Product button, the effect of which is shown in Figure 6-4.

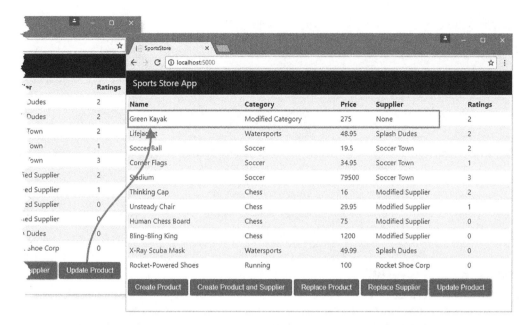

Figure 6-4. *Updating objects*

───

■ **Tip** The code for the update operation is just to check that the feature is working. If you want to repeat the update, then run the commands in Listing 6-1 to reset the database, restart the ASP.NET Core MVC part of the application, and then reload the web browser to see the original, unmodified data.

───

Implementing the DELETE Method

The last HTTP method that the web service must support is DELETE, which is used to remove data. Supporting the DELETE method leads to the expansion of the web service API as described in Table 6-4. The object to delete will be identified by the last segment in the request URL.

Table 6-4. *The Web Service API with PUT Support for Updating Objects*

Method	URL	Description
GET	/api/products/<id>	Retrieves a single Product object
GET	/api/products	Retrieves multiple Product objects
POST	/api/products	Stores a new Product object
POST	/api/suppliers	Stores a new Supplier object
PUT	/api/products/<id>	Replaces an existing Product object
PUT	/api/suppliers/<id>	Replaces an existing Supplier object
PATCH	/api/products/<id>	Updates a Product object
DELETE	/api/products/<id>	Deletes a Product object
DELETE	/api/suppliers/<id>	Deletes a Supplier object

Configuring the Database

Databases won't allow data to be deleted if doing so creates an inconsistency. For the SportsStore application, an inconsistency would be to delete a Product but leave its related Rating objects in the database, resulting in table rows that have a foreign key relationship to nonexistent data. Avoiding inconsistencies means either removing related data or updating it so that it refers to another object.

The easiest way to avoid inconsistencies is to have the database handle related data for you automatically. To change the configuration of the database, add the method shown in Listing 6-20 to the database context class.

Listing 6-20. Configuring Delete Operations in the DataContext.cs File in the Models Folder

```
using Microsoft.EntityFrameworkCore;
using Microsoft.EntityFrameworkCore.Metadata;

namespace SportsStore.Models {

    public class DataContext : DbContext {

        public DataContext(DbContextOptions<DataContext> opts)
            : base(opts) { }

        public DbSet<Product> Products { get; set; }
        public DbSet<Supplier> Suppliers { get; set; }
        public DbSet<Rating> Ratings { get; set; }

        protected override void OnModelCreating(ModelBuilder modelBuilder) {
            modelBuilder.Entity<Product>().HasMany<Rating>(p => p.Ratings)
                .WithOne(r => r.Product).OnDelete(DeleteBehavior.Cascade);
            modelBuilder.Entity<Product>().HasOne<Supplier>(p => p.Supplier)
                .WithMany(s => s.Products).OnDelete(DeleteBehavior.SetNull);
        }
    }
}
```

When you create a database migration, Entity Framework Core builds up the schema that will be applied to the database by looking at the data model classes and following a set of conventions for deciding how to store instances of those classes and how to represent relationships between them. For the most part, this process is invisible to the ASP.NET Core developer, who just uses the context class to store and retrieve data as .NET objects.

The DbContext class, from which context classes are derived, provides the OnModelCreating method, which can be used to override the conventions used to create the database schema. The OnModelCreating method receives a ModelBuilder object, which is used to configure the schema using a feature known as the Entity Framework Core fluent API, through which it is possible to describe the schema programmatically.

In Listing 6-20, I used the fluent API to describe the relationship between the Product and Rating classes, like this:

```
...
modelBuilder.Entity<Product>().HasMany<Rating>(p => p.Ratings)
    .WithOne(r => r.Product).OnDelete(DeleteBehavior.Cascade);
...
```

The Entity method tells Entity Framework Core which data model class I want to configure, and the HasMany and WithOne methods are used to describe both sides of the one-to-many relationship between the Product and Rating classes. These three methods simply describe the relationship that Entity Framework Core had already determined by following its usual conventions, and it is only the OnDelete method that introduces a new change. This method is used to specify how the database should act when an object is deleted using one of the three values of the DeleteBehavior enumeration described in Table 6-5.

Table 6-5. *The Values Defined by the DeleteBehavior Enumeration*

Name	Description
Restrict	This value prevents an object from being deleted unless there is no related data.
Cascade	This value automatically deletes related data when an object is deleted.
SetNull	This value sets the foreign key column in the related data to NULL when an object is deleted.

The Restrict value is the one that Entity Framework Core used by default when I created the database migration in Chapter 4. In Listing 6-20, I specified the Cascade behavior for the relationship between Product and Rating objects and specified the SetNull behavior for the relationship between the Product and Supplier objects. This means deleting Product data will automatically delete the related Rating data, while deleting a Supplier will leave the related Product data in the database but cause the Supplier property for those objects to be set to NULL.

To create a migration that will apply the new behaviors to the database schema, open a new command prompt and run the command shown in Listing 6-21 in the SportsStore folder. This migration will change the delete behavior in the database and will be applied automatically when the application is started.

Listing 6-21. Creating a New Database Migration

```
dotnet ef migrations add ChangeDeleteBehavior
```

Implementing the Web Service Action Method

Performing the delete operation is simple once the database configuration has been changed. To add support for deleting Product objects, add the method shown in Listing 6-22 to the ProductValues controller.

Listing 6-22. Adding a Method in the ProductValuesController.cs File in the Controllers Folder

```
using Microsoft.AspNetCore.Mvc;
using SportsStore.Models;
using Microsoft.EntityFrameworkCore;
using System.Linq;
using System.Collections.Generic;
using SportsStore.Models.BindingTargets;
using Microsoft.AspNetCore.JsonPatch;

namespace SportsStore.Controllers {

    [Route("api/products")]
    public class ProductValuesController : Controller {
        private DataContext context;

        public ProductValuesController(DataContext ctx) {
            context = ctx;
        }

        // ...other methods omitted for brevity...

        [HttpDelete("{id}")]
        public void DeleteProduct(long id) {
            context.Products.Remove(new Product { ProductId = id });
            context.SaveChanges();
        }
    }
}
```

The DeleteProduct method creates a new Product object that has the ID value provided by the client and passes it to the database context's Remove method. This gives Entity Framework Core enough information to perform the delete operation when the SaveChanges method is called.

The same technique can be used to delete Supplier objects, even though the behavior of the database will be different. To add support for removing Supplier data from the database, add the action shown in Listing 6-23 to the SupplierValues controller.

Listing 6-23. Deleting Data in the SupplierValuesController.cs File in the Controllers Folder

```
using Microsoft.AspNetCore.Mvc;
using SportsStore.Models;
using SportsStore.Models.BindingTargets;
using System.Collections.Generic;

namespace SportsStore.Controllers {

    [Route("api/suppliers")]
    public class SupplierValuesController : Controller {
        private DataContext context;
```

```
        public SupplierValuesController(DataContext ctx) {
            context = ctx;
        }

        // ...other methods omitted for brevity...

        [HttpDelete("{id}")]
        public void DeleteSupplier(long id) {
            context.Remove(new Supplier { SupplierId = id });
            context.SaveChanges();
        }
    }
}
```

Deleting Objects in the Angular Application

To add support for sending DELETE requests to the web service, add the methods shown in Listing 6-24 to the Repository class in the Angular application.

Listing 6-24. Adding a Method in the repository.ts File in the ClientApp/app/models Folder

```
import { Product } from "./product.model";
import { Injectable } from "@angular/core";
import { Http, RequestMethod, Request, Response } from "@angular/http";
import { Observable } from "rxjs/Observable";
import "rxjs/add/operator/map";
import { Filter } from "./configClasses.repository";
import { Supplier } from "./supplier.model";

const productsUrl = "/api/products";
const suppliersUrl = "/api/suppliers";

@Injectable()
export class Repository {
    private filterObject = new Filter();

    constructor(private http: Http) {
        //this.filter.category = "soccer";
        this.filter.related = true;
        this.getProducts();
    }

    // ...other methods omitted for brevity...

    deleteProduct(id: number) {
        this.sendRequest(RequestMethod.Delete, productsUrl + "/" + id)
            .subscribe(response => this.getProducts());
    }

    deleteSupplier(id: number) {
        this.sendRequest(RequestMethod.Delete, suppliersUrl + "/" + id)
            .subscribe(response => {
```

```
                this.getProducts();
                this.getSuppliers();
            });
    }
}
```

The HTTP requests are sent using the Http class, and both methods refresh the application's data when the request completes.

Adding Support for Deleting Objects in the Component

The next step is to add methods to the component that will act as a bridge between the buttons that the user will click and the repository, as shown in Listing 6-25.

Listing 6-25. Adding Methods in the app.component.ts File in the ClientApp/app Folder

```
import { Component } from '@angular/core';
import { Repository } from "./models/repository";
import { Product } from "./models/product.model";
import { Supplier } from "./models/supplier.model";

@Component({
    selector: 'app-root',
    templateUrl: './app.component.html',
    styleUrls: ['./app.component.css']
})
export class AppComponent {

    constructor(private repo: Repository) { }

    // ...other methods omitted for brevity...

    deleteProduct() {
        this.repo.deleteProduct(1);
    }

    deleteSupplier() {
        this.repo.deleteSupplier(2);
    }
}
```

To use these methods, add the elements shown in Listing 6-26 to the component's template. These button elements use the Angular event binding to invoke the deleteProduct or deleteSupplier method when they are clicked.

Listing 6-26. Adding Elements in the app.component.html File in the ClientApp/app Folder

```
<table class="table table-sm table-striped">
    <tr>
        <th>Name</th><th>Category</th><th>Price</th>
        <th>Supplier</th><th>Ratings</th>
    </tr>
    <tr *ngFor="let product of products">
        <td>{{product.name}}</td>
        <td>{{product.category}}</td>
        <td>{{product.price}}</td>
        <td>{{product.supplier?.name || 'None'}}</td>
        <td>{{product.ratings?.length || 0}}</td>
    </tr>
</table>

<button class="btn btn-primary m-1" (click)="createProduct()">
    Create Product
</button>
<button class="btn btn-primary m-1" (click)="createProductAndSupplier()">
    Create Product and Supplier
</button>
<button class="btn btn-primary m-1" (click)="replaceProduct()">
    Replace Product
</button>
<button class="btn btn-primary m-1" (click)="replaceSupplier()">
    Replace Supplier
</button>
<button class="btn btn-primary m-1" (click)="updateProduct()">
    Update Product
</button>
<button class="btn btn-primary m-1" (click)="deleteProduct()">
    Delete Product
</button>
<button class="btn btn-primary m-1" (click)="deleteSupplier()">
    Delete Supplier
</button>
```

Restart the ASP.NET Core MVC application and use a browser to navigate to http://localhost:5000.
Clicking the Delete Product button will delete the Product object whose ProductId value is 1 (the Kayak product), and clicking the Delete Supplier button will delete the Supplier object whose SupplierId value is 2 (the Soccer Town supplier), as shown in Figure 6-5.

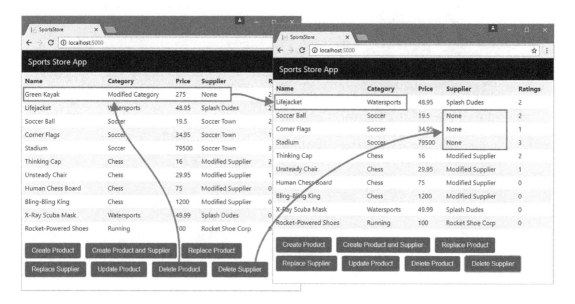

Figure 6-5. *Deleting products and suppliers*

■ **Tip**   The code for the delete operation is just to check that the feature is working. If you want to repeat the deletions, then run the commands in Listing 6-1 to reset the database, restart the ASP.NET Core MVC part of the application, and then reload the web browser to see the original, unmodified data.

Summary

In this chapter, I showed you how to add support to the web service for the HTTP methods that allow the client to modify the application data. I showed you how to use the POST method to store new objects, how to use the PUT and PATCH methods to replace or modify existing data, and how to use the DELETE method to remove data. In the next chapter, I show you how to structure an Angular application, building functionality around the data model and the HTTP web service.

CHAPTER 7

■ ■ ■

Structuring an Angular Application

One of the biggest causes of confusion is the way that an Angular application is structured. The building blocks of an Angular application seem, at first glance, to be direct counterparts to those in an ASP.NET Core MVC application. But if you treat the Angular building blocks in the same way as their ASP.NET counterparts, you will end up with a client-side application that doesn't work or becomes impossible to modify.

In this chapter, I explain the two key features that shape the structure of an Angular application and demonstrate how they are used to allow features to work together. The first Angular feature is the live data model, which is the beating heart of an Angular application and reflects data changes in the content that is displayed to the user. The second feature is URL routing, which is used to decide which content the user sees. The ASP.NET Core MVC part of the application also uses a data model and URL routing, but, as you will see, there are some important differences both in how they work and in how they are used. Table 7-1 puts these features in context.

Table 7-1. *Putting Angular Application Structure in Context*

Question	Answer
What is it?	Angular applications are built using small features. The structure of the application lets these features work together to deliver complex functionality to the user.
Why is it useful?	Features work together make it easier to write and maintain Angular applications.
How is it used?	Features can cooperate using the data model or using the Angular URL routing system.
Are there any pitfalls or limitations?	The idea of collaborating using the data model can be confusing if you are new to Angular development and can require a lot of iterative development until you get everything working the way you want.
Are there any alternatives?	You can build monolithic Angular applications. These don't require as much planning or structural development but are harder to enhance and maintain.

© Adam Freeman 2017
A. Freeman, *Essential Angular for ASP.NET Core MVC*, DOI 10.1007/978-1-4842-2916-3_7

Preparing for This Chapter

This chapter uses the SportsStore project I created in Chapter 3 and modified in the chapters since. To ensure that the contents of the database are reset, open a command prompt, navigate to the SportsStore folder, and run the commands shown in Listing 7-1.

■ **Tip**　You can download the complete project for this chapter from https://github.com/apress/esntl-angular-for-asp.net-core-mvc. This is where you will also find updates and corrections for this book.

Listing 7-1. Resetting the Database

```
docker-compose down
docker-compose up
```

The first command removes the Docker database container from the previous chapter. The second command creates and starts a fresh container.

Start the application to apply the database schema and add the seed data. If you are using Visual Studio, you can do this by selecting Debug ➤ Start Without Debugging. If you are using Visual Studio Code or just prefer working with the command line, then open a command prompt, navigate to the SportsStore folder, and run the command shown in Listing 7-2.

Listing 7-2. Starting the Application

```
dotnet run
```

Use a browser to navigate to http://localhost:5000 and you will see the content shown in Figure 7-1.

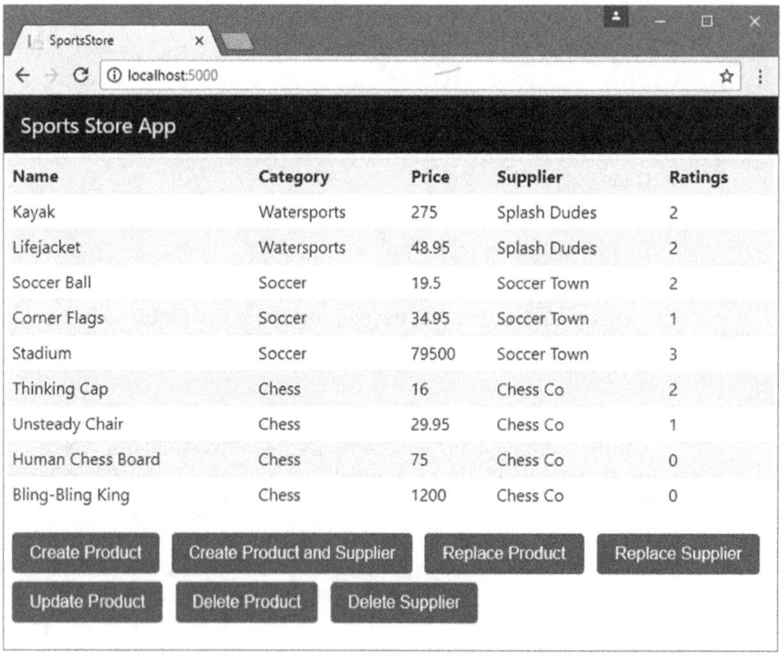

Figure 7-1. Running the example application

Using the Data Model for Component Cooperation

Components are the building blocks for an Angular application. Each component is a TypeScript class that provides the methods and properties required to support an HTML template that contains directives and data bindings. Every feature in an Angular application usually has its own component, which can be combined to create more functionality. The key to getting components to work together is the application's data model.

In Chapters 5 and 6, the Angular Repository class that provides access to the application data had an unusual design, which is split into two parts. In the first part of the Repository, the application data is available through three properties: the product property provides access to a single Product object, the products property provides access to a collection of Product objects, and the suppliers property provides access to a collection of Supplier objects. The second part of the Repository is the set of methods that send HTTP requests to the web service and use the results to update the product, products, and suppliers properties.

This two-part design makes it easier for components to cooperate without being tightly coupled, producing a flexible way to build applications. This isn't the only way that components can cooperate, but it is the simplest and most effective because it takes advantage of the way that Angular automatically responds to data changes. In the sections that follow, I create some new Angular components and use them to demonstrate how they can cooperate through the data model.

Creating the Display Component

To keep this example simple, the first component will only display data from the data model, which it will obtain through the products property defined by the Repository class.

Creating the Component Class

Create a folder called structure and add to it a TypeScript file called productTable.component.ts. The convention is to use descriptive file names in Angular projects, and this name tells you that this is the TypeScript class for a component called productTable, which gives you a hint of what the component is for. Once you have created the file, add the code shown in Listing 7-3.

Listing 7-3. The Contents of the productTable.component.ts File in the ClientApp/app/structure Folder

```
import { Component } from '@angular/core';
import { Repository } from "../models/repository";
import { Product } from "../models/product.model";

@Component({
    selector: "product-table",
    templateUrl: "./productTable.component.html"
})
export class ProductTableComponent {

    constructor(private repo: Repository) { }

    get products(): Product[] {
        return this.repo.products;
    }
}
```

137

Most components start like the one shown in the listing and grow as features are added to the application. Since this is the first new component that I have added to the SportsStore project, I will go through each statement and explain its purpose.

Understanding the Import Statements

The first three statements use the import keyword to declare dependencies on the types that the component relies on.

```
...
import { Component } from '@angular/core';
import { Repository } from "../models/repository";
import { Product } from "../models/product.model";
...
```

In any component, the import statements will be a mix of Angular classes, which are found in modules whose name starts with @angular, and custom classes that are specific to the application, which are specified using a relative file path. In this case, the component depends on Component in the @angular/core module, which is used to tell Angular when a class is a component, and the Repository and Product files, which are defined in the models folder.

■ **Tip** The paths used in import statements never include file extensions. That means if you want to declare a dependency on the Product class, for example, you use the path "../models/product.model" and not "../models/product.model.ts" or "../models.product.model.js".

Understanding the Class

Components are TypeScript classes that provide the methods and properties required to support a template. The convention is to include the term Component in the class name, which is why the class in Listing 7-3 is called ProductTableComponent. You don't have to follow this convention, but it helps keep the files in a project organized.

```
...
export class ProductTableComponent {

    constructor(private repo: Repository) { }

    get products(): Product[] {
        return this.repo.products;
    }
}
...
```

The constructor is used to declare a dependency on the Repository class, which will be resolved using the dependency injection feature when a new instance of the component is created. (The Repository class was configured for dependency injection in Chapter 4).

The other feature in the component class is a read-only property called `products`, which returns the value of the `products` property defined by the `Repository` class. The directives and bindings in an HTML template can only access the methods and properties defined by its component. This means that most components start out just providing access to the data in the model and start defining more complex logic as the application develops.

Understanding the Decorator

The `@Component` decorator is what brings the component to life and provides Angular with the information it needs to apply the component in the application.

```
...
@Component({
    selector: "product-table",
    templateUrl: "productTable.component.html"
})
export class ProductTableComponent {
...
```

The configuration properties of the `@Component` decorator tell Angular how the component should be used. The `selector` property tells Angular that it should apply the component when it encounters a `product-table` element in an HTML template. (You will see how I create this element shortly). The `templateUrl` property specifies the component's HTML template file, which provides the content that will be displayed by the component.

Creating the HTML Template

A component's template provides the HTML content that will be displayed to the user, as well as the directives and data bindings that will bring that content to life. Create an HTML file called `productTable.component.html` in the `ClientApp/app/structure` folder and add the content shown in Listing 7-4. (It is important that the name of the template file exactly matches the value of the `templateUrl` property in the component's decorator).

Listing 7-4. The Contents of the productTable.component.html File in the ClientApp/app/structure Folder

```
<table class="table table-striped">
    <tr><th>Name</th><th>Category</th><th>Price</th></tr>
    <tr *ngFor="let product of products">
        <td>{{product.name}}</td>
        <td>{{product.category}}</td>
        <td>{{product.price}}</td>
    </tr>
</table>
```

This template uses features shown in earlier chapters. The `ngFor` directive is used to read the value of the component's `products` property and generate a `tr` element for each `Product` in the array that returns. Each object is assigned to a temporary variable called `product`, which is then used in data bindings to set the content of `td` elements. The result is a table that contains a row for each `Product` in the repository, showing the value of the `name`, `category`, and `price` properties.

Creating the Filter Component

The next component will present the user with a selection of buttons that will be used to filter the Product objects in the repository. Add a TypeScript file called categoryFilter.component.ts in the ClientApp/app/ structure folder and add the code shown in Listing 7-5.

Listing 7-5. The Contents of the categoryFilter.component.ts File in the ClientApp/app/structure Folder

```
import { Component } from '@angular/core';
import { Repository } from "../models/repository";

@Component({
    selector: "category-filter",
    templateUrl: "categoryFilter.component.html"
})
export class CategoryFilterComponent {
    public chessCategory = "chess";

    constructor(private repo: Repository) { }

    setCategory(category: string) {
        this.repo.filter.category = category;
        this.repo.getProducts();
    }
}
```

This file defines the CategoryFilterComponent class, to which the @Component decorator has been applied. The decorator tells Angular to use this component when it encounters a category-filter HTML element and to use a template file called categoryFilter.component.html. The component class defines a constructor that allows it to receive a Repository object through dependency injection. The setCategory method accepts a category, which is used to configure the Repository object's filter and refresh the application's data.

Creating the HTML Template

To create the template for the filter component, add a file called categoryFilter.component.html to the ClientApp/app/structure folder and add the markup shown in Listing 7-6.

Listing 7-6. The Contents of the categoryFilter.component.html File in the ClientApp/app/structure Folder

```
<div class="m-1">
    <button class="btn btn-primary" (click)="setCategory('soccer')">Soccer</button>
    <button class="btn btn-primary" (click)="setCategory(chessCategory)">
        Chess
    </button>
    <button class="btn btn-primary"
        (click)="setCategory('Water' + 'Sports')">Watersports</button>
    <button class="btn btn-primary" (click)="setCategory(null)">All</button>
</div>
```

The event binding feature tells Angular to evaluate an expression when an event is triggered. The event bindings in this template are for the click event, and the expressions invoke the component's setCategory method. Notice the different ways that the argument to the setCategory method is specified by the event bindings. The first binding specifies the category in the expression.

```
...
<button class="btn btn-primary" (click)="setCategory('soccer')">
...
```

The value soccer is a literal string and must be quoted. JavaScript supports both double and single quotes (the " and ' characters), and I have used double quotes to denote the expression and single quotes for the literal value.

No quotes are required in the second event binding, which specifies a property defined by the component as the argument.

```
...
<button class="btn btn-primary" (click)="setCategory(chessCategory)">
...
```

This binding will use the value of the chessCategory property as the value to the setCategory method. The third binding shows that Angular will evaluate the expression, allowing operations to be performed in expressions.

```
...
<button class="btn btn-primary"  (click)="setCategory('Water' + 'Sports')">
...
```

When this button is clicked, Angular will evaluate the expression, which concatenates two literal string values and passes the result to the setCategory method.

Applying the New Components

Angular must be configured to use new components, which is in contrast to the convention-over-configuration philosophy of ASP.NET Core MVC. In most applications, a new Angular module is created for each major area of functionality in the application, such as the model module created in Chapter 4, but to keep things simple, register the new components in the Angular application's root module, as shown in Listing 7-7.

Listing 7-7. Registering Components in the app.module.ts File in the ClientApp/app Folder

```
import { BrowserModule } from '@angular/platform-browser';
import { NgModule } from '@angular/core';
import { FormsModule } from '@angular/forms';
import { HttpModule } from '@angular/http';
import { AppComponent } from './app.component';
import { ModelModule } from "./models/model.module";
import { ProductTableComponent } from "./structure/productTable.component"
import { CategoryFilterComponent } from "./structure/categoryFilter.component"
```

```
@NgModule({
    declarations: [AppComponent, ProductTableComponent, CategoryFilterComponent],
    imports: [BrowserModule, FormsModule, HttpModule, ModelModule],
    providers: [],
    bootstrap: [AppComponent]
})
export class AppModule { }
```

The component classes are registered in the declarations property of the NgModule decorator, which makes Angular aware they exist and can be applied to HTML elements.

The next step is to add the HTML elements that are specified by the new component's selector properties. Replace the contents of the app.component.html file, which is the template for the component specified by the root component's bootstrap property in Listing 7-7, with the elements shown in Listing 7-8.

Listing 7-8. Replacing the Contents of the app.component.html File in the ClientApp/app Folder

```
<category-filter></category-filter>
<product-table></product-table>
```

These elements replace the content that was previously displayed by the user. When the application starts, Angular will process the template, discover the category-filter and product-table elements, and look at the list of components that have been registered to see which ones should be applied. Figure 7-2 shows the result, although you may need to reload the browser for the changes to take effect.

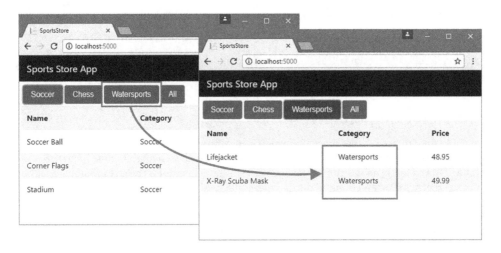

Figure 7-2. *Adding components to the Angular application*

Clicking one of the buttons changes the filter that is applied to the data. The figure shows the effect of clicking the Watersports button, which has the effect of selecting only those products in the Watersports category.

Understanding the Application Structure

The two new components have no direct knowledge of one another, but the actions performed using one component (clicking a button) are reflected in the other (filtering data). This works because the components take advantage of the two parts of the data repository that I described at the start of this section, as illustrated in Figure 7-3.

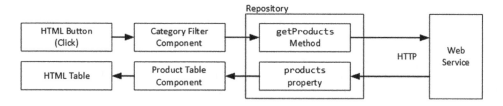

Figure 7-3. *Understanding collaborating components*

When the user clicks a button, the event binding invokes the category filter component's `setCategory` method, which updates the repository filter and reloads the data. At this point, the category filter component's job is done.

The repository sends the HTTP request to the ASP.NET Core MVC web service and receives the filtered `Product` data, which is assigned to the `products` property. This is the property used in the `ngFor` directive's expression in the product table component's template, and Angular updates the content that is displayed by that template to reflect the change.

Adding Another Component

The two new components may leave you with the impression that some components only read data from the model, while others only make changes. In fact, components are more flexible and can be used to create complex sets of relationships, while still relying on the data model to aid coordination. To see how this works, create a file called the `productDetail.component.ts` file in the `ClientApp/app/structure` folder and add the code shown in Listing 7-9.

Listing 7-9. The Contents of the productDetail.component.ts File in the ClientApp/app/structure Folder

```
import { Component } from '@angular/core';
import { Repository } from "../models/repository";
import { Product } from "../models/product.model";

@Component({
    selector: "product-detail",
    templateUrl: "productDetail.component.html"
})
export class ProductDetailComponent {

    constructor(private repo: Repository) { }

    get product(): Product {
        return this.repo.product;
    }
}
```

The `ProductDetailComponent` class has a constructor that receives a `Repository` object, which will be provided through the dependency injection feature, and a `product` property that returns the value of the property with the same name in the `Repository`.

The `Component` decorator tells Angular to apply this component when it encounters the `product-detail` element and provides the location of the component's template. To create the template, add a file called `productDetail.component.html` in the `ClientApp/app/structure` folder and add the HTML elements shown in Listing 7-10.

Listing 7-10. The Contents of the productDetail.component.html File in the ClientApp/app/structure Folder

```
<table class="table table-striped">
    <tr><th colspan="2" class="bg-info">Product</th></tr>
    <tr><th>Name</th><td>{{product?.name || 'No Data'}}</td></tr>
    <tr><th>Category</th><td>{{product?.category || 'No Data'}}</td></tr>
    <tr>
        <th>Description</th>
        <td>{{product?.description || 'No Data'}}</td>
    </tr>
    <tr><th>Price</th><td>{{product?.price  || 'No Data'}}</td></tr>
    <tr><th colspan="2" class="bg-info">Supplier</th></tr>
    <tr><th>Name</th><td>{{product?.supplier?.name}}</td></tr>
    <tr><th>City</th><td>{{product?.supplier?.city}}</td></tr>
    <tr><th>State</th><td>{{product?.supplier?.state}}</td></tr>

<tr><th>Products</th><td>{{product?.supplier?.products?.length}}</td></tr>
</table>
```

To register the component so that it can be used by Angular, change the configuration of the root module, as shown in Listing 7-11.

Listing 7-11. Registering a Component in the app.module.ts File in the ClientApp Folder

```
import { BrowserModule } from '@angular/platform-browser';
import { NgModule } from '@angular/core';
import { FormsModule } from '@angular/forms';
import { HttpModule } from '@angular/http';
import { AppComponent } from './app.component';
import { ModelModule } from "./models/model.module";
import { ProductTableComponent } from "./structure/productTable.component"
import { CategoryFilterComponent } from "./structure/categoryFilter.component"
import { ProductDetailComponent } from "./structure/productDetail.component";

@NgModule({
    declarations: [AppComponent, ProductTableComponent,
        CategoryFilterComponent, ProductDetailComponent],
    imports: [BrowserModule, FormsModule, HttpModule, ModelModule],
    providers: [],
    bootstrap: [AppComponent]
})
export class AppModule { }
```

The `import` statement provides access to the `ProductDetailComponent` class, which is added to the `NgModule` decorator's `declarations` property. Now that the component can be used, edit the root component's template to add the element that will apply the new component, as shown in Listing 7-12.

Listing 7-12. Adding an Element in the app.component.html File in the ClientApp Folder

```
<div class="container">
    <div class="row">
        <div class="col">
            <category-filter></category-filter>
            <product-table></product-table>
        </div>
        <div class="col">
            <product-detail></product-detail>
        </div>
    </div>
</div>
```

The listing also adds some structure to the HTML document, using Bootstrap CSS classes to position the new component side-by-side with the existing ones.

Selecting a Product

The new component will display the details of a single product when it is selected, which means that the next step is to provide the user with the means to make that selection. First, add the elements shown in Listing 7-13 to the template for the product table.

Listing 7-13. New Elements in the productTable.component.html File in the ClientApp/app/structure Folder

```
<table class="table table-striped">
    <tr><th>Name</th><th>Category</th><th>Price</th><th></th></tr>
    <tr *ngFor="let product of products">
        <td>{{product.name}}</td>
        <td>{{product.category}}</td>
        <td>{{product.price}}</td>
        <td>
            <button class="btn btn-primary btn-sm"
                    (click)="selectProduct(product.productId)">
                Details
            </button>
        </td>
    </tr>
</table>
```

The new elements add a column to the table containing a Details button for each row produced by the `ngFor` directive. The `click` event binding will invoke a method called `selectProduct` when the `button` is clicked, providing the ID value of the corresponding product. To define the method that the event binding invokes, add the code shown in Listing 7-14 to the product table component.

145

Listing 7-14. Adding a Method in the productTable.component.ts File in the ClientApp/app/structure Folder

```
import { Component } from '@angular/core';
import { Repository } from "../models/repository";
import { Product } from "../models/product.model";

@Component({
    selector: "product-table",
    templateUrl: "productTable.component.html"
})
export class ProductTableComponent {

    constructor(private repo: Repository) { }

    get products(): Product[] {
        return this.repo.products;
    }

    selectProduct(id: number) {
        this.repo.getProduct(id);
    }
}
```

The selectProduct method calls a repository object's getProduct method, which will cause it to send a request to the web service. When you save the changes, you will see the new content, and clicking one of the Details buttons will lead to the detailed view being populated with data, as shown in Figure 7-4.

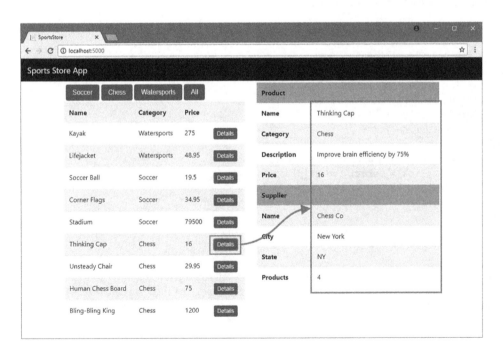

Figure 7-4. *Displaying detailed data*

Understanding the Revised Application Structure

The three new components rely on the data model, either as the target for the operations they perform for the user or as the source of the data they display. None of the components depends directly on any of the others, and any of them can be changed without requiring corresponding changes in the other components. And, as the addition of the third component has shown, components can be both consumers of the data in the model and the source of changes to that data, as illustrated by Figure 7-5.

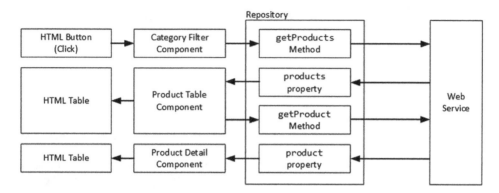

Figure 7-5. *The revised structure of the Angular application*

Understanding Angular Routing

Using the data model as the heart of an Angular application makes it easy to add and integrate components that add new features. For all but the simplest applications, however, you will soon reach the point where you want to display different components to the user at different times. For the SportsStore application, for example, it doesn't make sense to display the product table and the product detail components at the same time. Instead, the application should display the table until the user clicks a Details button, at which time the detailed view should be shown.

In an Angular application, this is done using URL routing, which provides another way for components to cooperate. As an ASP.NET Core MVC developer, you may already be familiar with the idea of URL routing, in which the segments of a URL are used to select a controller and action method to handle an HTTP request. In Angular applications, the segments in the URL are used to decide which components should be displayed to the user. This feature relies on the fact that browsers will allow small changes to the URL without sending a new request to the server, a process that becomes clearer with an example. In the sections that follow, I will add support for URL routing to the SportsStore application and use it to display either the product table or the detailed view.

Creating the Routing Configuration

The first step in setting up the configuration for URL routing is to add a base element to the head section Razor layout, as shown in Listing 7-15.

Listing 7-15. Adding an Element in the _Layout.cshtml File in the Views/Shared Folder

```
<!DOCTYPE html>
<html>
<head>
    <base href="/">
    <meta charset="utf-8" />
    <meta name="viewport" content="width=device-width, initial-scale=1.0" />
    <title>SportsStore @ViewData["Title"]</title>
    <link rel="stylesheet" href="~/lib/bootstrap/dist/css/bootstrap.css" />
</head>
<body>
    @RenderBody()
    @RenderSection("Scripts", required: false)
</body>
</html>
```

The value of the `href` attribute sets the base URL against which the URL routing configuration is applied and is set to / for most applications.

The next step is to define a list of the URL routes that the application will support and the components that they will display. Add a TypeScript file called `app.routing.ts` to the `ClientApp/app` folder, with the code shown in Listing 7-16. This is the conventional name of the routing configuration for an Angular application.

Listing 7-16. The Contents of the app.routing.ts File in the ClientApp/app Folder

```
import { Routes, RouterModule } from "@angular/router";
import { ProductTableComponent } from "./structure/productTable.component"
import { ProductDetailComponent } from "./structure/productDetail.component";

const routes: Routes = [
    { path: "table", component: ProductTableComponent },
    { path: "detail", component: ProductDetailComponent },
    { path: "", component: ProductTableComponent }]

export const RoutingConfig = RouterModule.forRoot(routes);
```

As with ASP.NET Core MVC, there are a lot of options available for URL routing in Angular, and this is a simple configuration. The first step is to define the set of URL segments and the components that they will display, which are combined with the value of the `href` attribute of the `base` element from Listing 7-16.

Just as with ASP.NET Core MVC, Angular routes are evaluated in the order in which they are defined, which means that the most specific routes must be defined first. The segments that the route will match are defined using the `path` property, and the component that will be displayed is specified by the `component` property. There are three routes in the listing, and they produce the mappings described in Table 7-2.

▪ **Tip** You won't be able to navigate to the URLs shown in the table by entering them into the browser manually. I explain why and how this is resolved later in the chapter.

Table 7-2. *The URL Routes and Components*

URL	Description
http://localhost:5000	This URL is matched by the last route in the listing and displays the product table component.
http://localhost:5000/table	This URL is matched by the route whose path is table and displays the product table component.
http://localhost:5000/detail	This URL is matched by the route whose path is detail and displays the product detail component.

The second step to setting up the routing configuration is to call the RouterModule.forRoot method and export the result as a constant (using the const keyword) so that it can be accessed in other TypeScript files.

```
...
export const RoutingConfig = RouterModule.forRoot(routes);
...
```

The forRoot method takes the array of routes as its argument and creates an Angular module that contains the routing configuration, which is then exported as a constant value called RoutingConfig.

Applying the Routing Configuration

Once you have created a routing configuration, it must be enabled in the application's root module, as shown in Listing 7-17.

Listing 7-17. Enabling the Routing Configuration in the app.module.ts File in the ClientApp/app Folder

```
import { BrowserModule } from '@angular/platform-browser';
import { NgModule } from '@angular/core';
import { FormsModule } from '@angular/forms';
import { HttpModule } from '@angular/http';
import { AppComponent } from './app.component';
import { ModelModule } from "./models/model.module";
import { ProductTableComponent } from "./structure/productTable.component"
import { CategoryFilterComponent } from "./structure/categoryFilter.component"
import { ProductDetailComponent } from "./structure/productDetail.component";
import { RoutingConfig } from "./app.routing";

@NgModule({
    declarations: [AppComponent, ProductTableComponent,
        CategoryFilterComponent, ProductDetailComponent],
    imports: [BrowserModule, FormsModule, HttpModule, ModelModule, RoutingConfig],
    providers: [],
    bootstrap: [AppComponent]
})
export class AppModule { }
```

The const value to which the routing module has been assigned is imported with an import statement and added to the NgModule decorator's imports property. When the Angular application starts, the routing configuration will be processed and integrated into the application.

Angular uses a special HTML element, router-outlet, to display the components selected by the routing configuration. This element is used in the root component's template, replacing the existing content, as shown in Listing 7-18.

Listing 7-18. Adding a Router Outlet in the app.component.html File in the ClientApp/app Folder

```
<router-outlet></router-outlet>
```

When all the changes to the Angular files are saved, you will see just the product table when the application has been reloaded, as shown in Figure 7-6. This is because the route from Listing 7-16 whose path is the empty string ("") has matched the URL displayed by the browser and the routing system has selected the product table component to show in the router-outlet element.

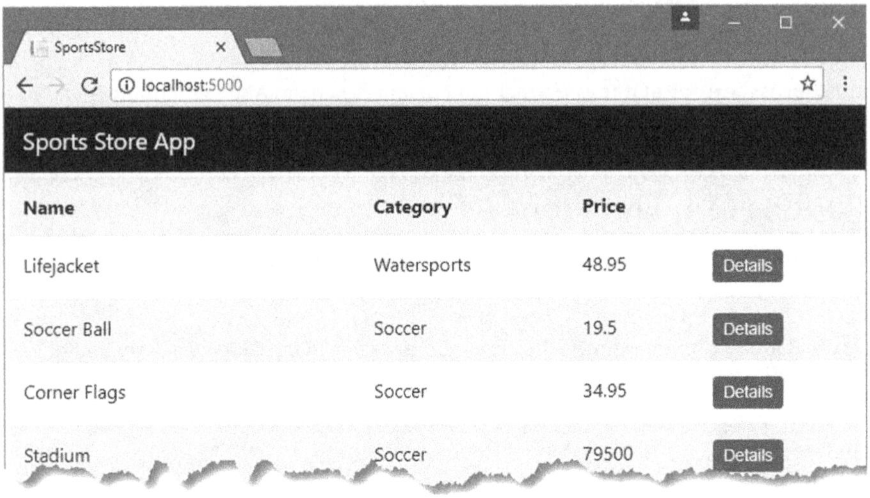

Figure 7-6. *A component selected by the routing system*

Navigating Using Routes

Clicking the Details buttons has no visible effect at the moment because the event binding applied to the button elements just triggers an HTTP request to the web service. To navigate to the URL that will display the product details component, add the code shown in Listing 7-19 to the ProductTableComponent class.

Listing 7-19. Navigating in the productTable.component.ts File in the ClientApp/app/structure Folder

```
import { Component } from '@angular/core';
import { Repository } from "../models/repository";
import { Product } from "../models/product.model";
import { Router } from "@angular/router";
```

```
@Component({
    selector: "product-table",
    templateUrl: "productTable.component.html"
})
export class ProductTableComponent {

    constructor(private repo: Repository,
                private router: Router) { }

    get products(): Product[] {
        return this.repo.products;
    }

    selectProduct(id: number) {
        this.repo.getProduct(id);
        this.router.navigateByUrl("/detail");
    }
}
```

The Router class, which is defined in the @angular/router module, provides support for navigating to a URL through its navigateByUrl method. The constructor for the ProductTableComponent accepts a Router object, which will be provided by dependency injection, and uses it in the selectProduct method to move to the /detail URL, which will display the product detail component.

Save the change, reload the browser, and click one of the Details buttons once the application has reloaded. The product detail component will replace the table, showing the details of the selected product. Notice that the URL displayed by the browser changes, as shown in Figure 7-7.

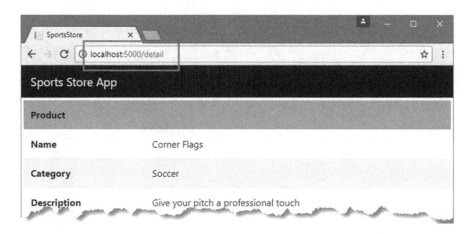

Figure 7-7. *Using the URL routing feature*

Navigating Using a Directive

The Router.navigateByUrl method isn't the only way to navigate using the routing system. Angular also provides a directive that can be applied to an element, which allows a URL to be specified in a template without needing a corresponding method in the component. To allow the user to navigate back from the detailed component to the table, add the elements shown in Listing 7-20.

Listing 7-20. Navigating in the productDetail.component.html File in the ClientApp/app/structure Folder

```
<table class="table table-striped">
    <tr><th colspan="2" class="bg-info">Product</th></tr>
    <tr><th>Name</th><td>{{product?.name || 'No Data'}}</td></tr>
    <tr><th>Category</th><td>{{product?.category || 'No Data'}}</td></tr>
    <tr>
        <th>Description</th>
        <td>{{product?.description || 'No Data'}}</td>
    </tr>
    <tr><th>Price</th><td>{{product?.price  || 'No Data'}}</td></tr>
    <tr><th colspan="2" class="bg-info">Supplier</th></tr>
    <tr><th>Name</th><td>{{product?.supplier?.name}}</td></tr>
    <tr><th>City</th><td>{{product?.supplier?.city}}</td></tr>
    <tr><th>State</th><td>{{product?.supplier?.state}}</td></tr>

<tr><th>Products</th><td>{{product?.supplier?.products?.length}}</td></tr>
</table>
<div class="text-center">
    <button class="btn btn-primary" routerLink="/table">Back</button>
</div>
```

The routerLink attribute applies a directive that tells Angular to navigate to the /table URL when the button is clicked, which corresponds to the route from Listing 7-16 that will show the product table. Save the changes, use the browser to navigate to http://localhost:5000, and use the Details and Back buttons to move navigate between the components, as shown in Figure 7-8.

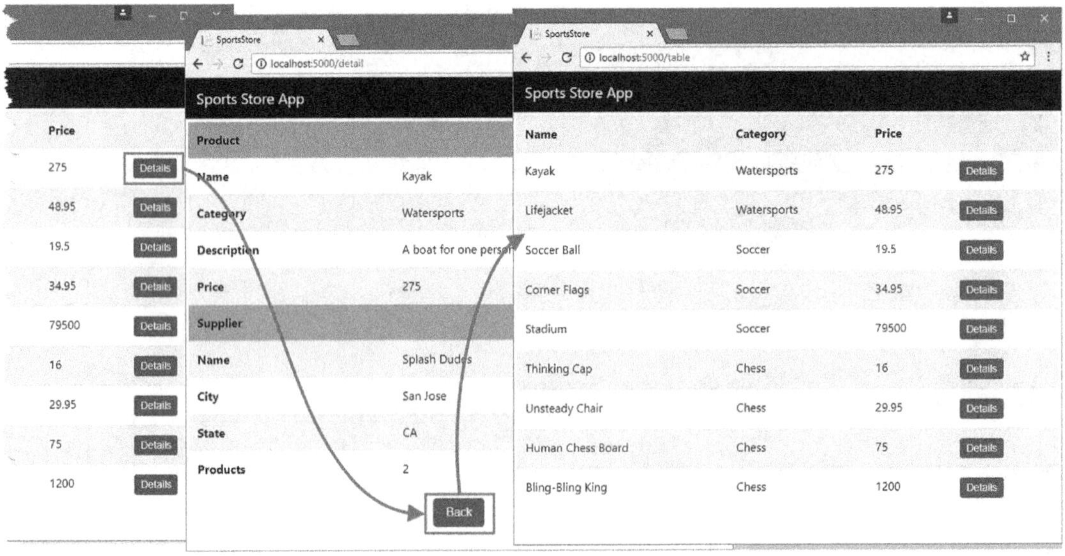

Figure 7-8. *Navigating using a directive*

Improving Navigation

The routing system is being used to handle navigation in the SportsStore application, but it has some rough edges that will just confuse users. In the sections that follow, I describe the problems and explain how to solve them.

Allowing Direct Navigation

If you try to manually navigate to one of the URLs in the routing configuration, such as `http://localhost:5000/table`, by entering it into the browser's URL bar, you will receive a 404 Not Found response. (Some browsers, such as Google Chrome, will just display an empty window, and you will need to look at the browser's JavaScript console to see the HTTP status code.)

When Angular navigates to a new URL, it does so using a JavaScript API that allows the URL to be changed without triggering an HTTP request. But when you enter a URL manually, that API isn't used, and the browser sends an HTTP request to the ASP.NET Core server, requesting the URL that you specified. There is no controller set up to handle requests for the /table URL, so the 404 response is sent.

Solving this problem requires adding additional URL routes to the MVC part of the project so that requests to the /table URL are directed to an action method that will produce a useful response. You could set up new routing entries in the MVC application for all of the URLs supported by the Angular application, but that's an error-prone process, and it is easy to get out of sync. A more robust approach is to take advantage of a feature provided by Microsoft that is included in one of the packages I used in Chapter 3 to set up the project. Add the statements shown in Listing 7-21 to the Startup class to prevent the MVC application from returning a 404 error when the user enters a URL directly.

Listing 7-21. Adding a Fallback Route in the Startup.cs File in the SportsStore Folder

```
...
public void Configure(IApplicationBuilder app,
        IHostingEnvironment env, ILoggerFactory loggerFactory) {
    loggerFactory.AddConsole(Configuration.GetSection("Logging"));
    loggerFactory.AddDebug();

    app.UseDeveloperExceptionPage();
    app.UseWebpackDevMiddleware(new WebpackDevMiddlewareOptions {
        HotModuleReplacement = true
    });

    app.UseStaticFiles();

    app.UseMvc(routes => {
        routes.MapRoute(
            name: "default",
            template: "{controller=Home}/{action=Index}/{id?}");

        routes.MapSpaFallbackRoute("angular-fallback",
            new { controller = "Home", action = "Index" });
    });

    SeedData.SeedDatabase(app.ApplicationServices
        .GetRequiredService<DataContext>());
}
...
```

The MapSpaFallbackRoute extension method is part of the Microsoft.AspNetCore.SpaServices package, which handles integrating Angular with ASP.NET Core MVC. This method sets up a fallback route that specifies a controller and action that will be used for HTTP requests that would otherwise produce a 404 response. The listing specifies that these requests should be handled by the Index action on the Home controller, which will ensure that the client receives the HTML document for the Angular application.

■ **Tip**   The MapSpaFallbackRoute extension method doesn't handle requests that contain a period (the . character) in the last segment of the URL. This is to ensure that requests for static content, such as images, are handled normally, but it also means you should avoid using periods in the URLs used by the Angular application. It also means that all requests that would otherwise generate a 404 response, including those you intended for a web service, will receive the fallback HTML content.

To see the effect of the fallback route, restart the ASP.NET Core MVC application and use a browser to navigate directly to http://localhost:5000/table. The MVC fallback route will direct the request so that it is handled by the Index action on the Home controller, which will render the Index.cshtml view and provide the browser with the HTML that contains the Angular application. When Angular starts, it uses the application's routing configuration to determine how the browser's current URL should be handled and displays the product table, as shown in Figure 7-9.

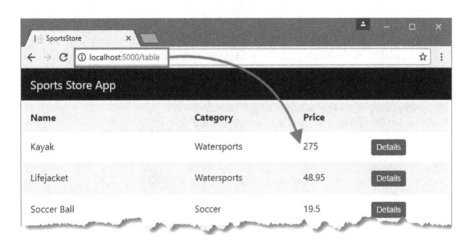

Figure 7-9. *Navigating directly to an Angular URL*

Using a Segment Variable

Allowing the user to navigate directly to one of the Angular application's URLs is a step forward but not perfect. You can see the problem by requesting http://localhost:5000/detail. The Angular application will display the detailed view component, but the placeholder data will never be replaced with real data, as shown in Figure 7-10.

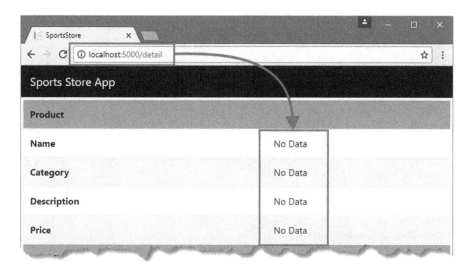

Figure 7-10. *Navigating directly to the detailed view URL*

When the user clicks a Details button, the template's component asks the repository to get the product data and then navigates to the URL that displays the detailed view. When the user navigates directly to a URL, the repository is never asked to get the product data, so the component has nothing to display. Solving this problem means extending the product detail component so it can request its own data and to include details of the product to be displayed to be included in the URL.

The first step is to change the routing configuration to add a segment variable, which will allow the route to match a range of URLs. Angular routing segments are similar to those in ASP.NET Core MVC, although the syntax is different. To add a segment to the Angular route for the product details component, add the route shown in Listing 7-22.

Listing 7-22. Adding a Route in the app.routing.ts File in the ClientApp/app Folder

```
import { Routes, RouterModule } from "@angular/router";
import { ProductTableComponent } from "./structure/productTable.component"
import { ProductDetailComponent } from "./structure/productDetail.component";

const routes: Routes = [
    { path: "table", component: ProductTableComponent },
    { path: "detail/:id", component: ProductDetailComponent },
    { path: "detail", component: ProductDetailComponent },
    { path: "", component: ProductTableComponent }]

export const RoutingConfig = RouterModule.forRoot(routes);
```

The segment variable is denoted using a colon (the : character), so the new route in the listing will match a URL like /table/1, and the value of the last segment will be assigned to a routing variable called id.

To access the value of the segment variable and use it to request data from the repository, make the changes shown in Listing 7-23.

Listing 7-23. Routing in the productDetail.component.ts File in the ClientApp/app/structure Folder

```
import { Component } from '@angular/core';
import { Repository } from "../models/repository";
import { Product } from "../models/product.model";
import { Router, ActivatedRoute } from "@angular/router";

@Component({
    selector: "product-detail",
    templateUrl: "productDetail.component.html"
})
export class ProductDetailComponent {

    constructor(private repo: Repository,
                router: Router,
                activeRoute: ActivatedRoute) {

        let id = Number.parseInt(activeRoute.snapshot.params["id"]);
        if (id) {
            this.repo.getProduct(id);
        } else {
            router.navigateByUrl("/");
        }
    }

    get product(): Product {
        return this.repo.product;
    }
}
```

The current route is available through the `ActivatedRoute` class, which is defined in the `@angular/router` module. In the listing, the component receives an `ActivatedRoute` object, which will be provided by dependency injection, and uses its `snapshot.params` property to get the value of the `id` segment variable. If the variable has a value and it can be parsed into an integer, then details of the product are requested through the repository. If there is no value for the `id` segment or it cannot be parsed, then the `Router` object is used to navigate to the / URL, which will display the product table.

The final adjustment is to change the way that the user navigates from the table to the detailed view for a product. At the moment, clicking a Details button invokes a method that triggers the HTTP request and then navigates to the detailed view, but that is no longer needed. To take advantage of the self-contained nature of the product details component, change the Details button elements in the product table component's template, as shown in Listing 7-24.

Listing 7-24. Navigating in the productTable.component.html File in the ClientApp/app/structure Folder

```
<table class="table table-striped">
    <tr><th>Name</th><th>Category</th><th>Price</th><th></th></tr>
    <tr *ngFor="let product of products">
        <td>{{product.name}}</td>
        <td>{{product.category}}</td>
        <td>{{product.price}}</td>
```

```
    <td>
        <button class="btn btn-primary btn-sm"
                [routerLink]="['/detail', product.productId]">
            Details
        </button>
    </td>
  </tr>
</table>
```

The routerLink directive is applied differently when you need to include a variable in the navigation URL. The name of the attribute is enclosed in square brackets (the [and] characters), and the value is an array of values that will be combined to create the navigation URL. The individual values can be string literal values, such as '/detail', or variables, such as product.productId. When the user clicks the element, Angular will evaluate each element in the array, combine the results, and navigate to the URL. In the listing, this means that clicking a button element will navigate to a URL such as /detail/2.

Save the changes and reload the application. When you click a Details button in the product table, the routing system is used to navigate to a URL with a segment variable that provides the product detail component with the information it needs to request the data from the repository, shown in Figure 7-11.

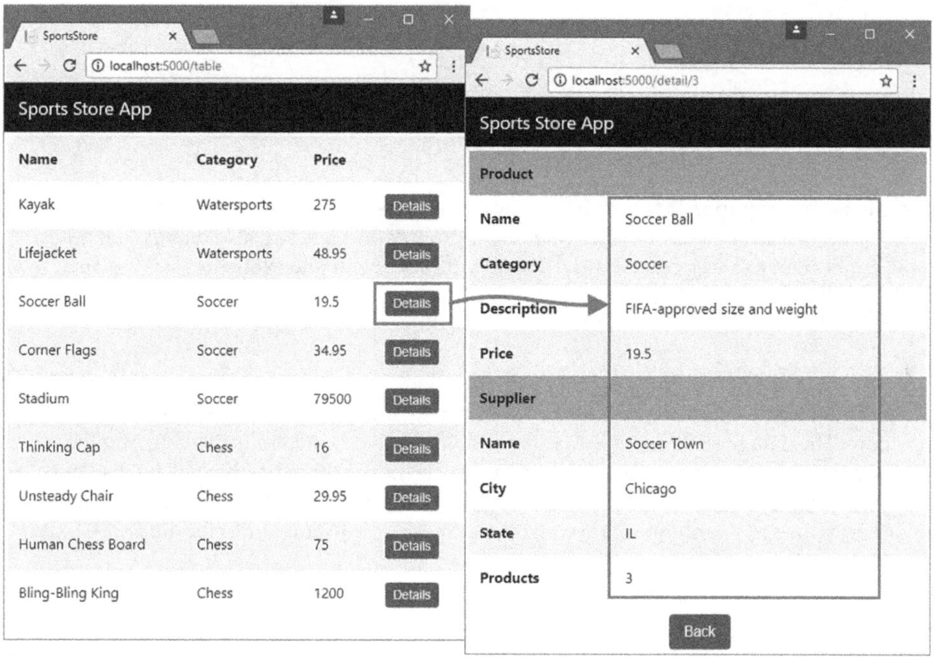

Figure 7-11. Navigating using a segment variable

Understanding the Application Structure

The URL routing feature provides an alternative way for Angular components to cooperate without being tightly coupled together. Clicking a Details button in the SportsStore application lets the table component tell the detail component which product should be displayed, but neither component has knowledge of the other or depends on the code they define. Introducing URL routing has changed the structure of the application, as illustrated in Figure 7-12.

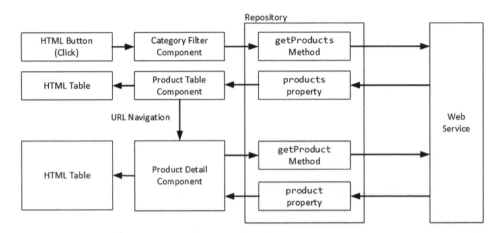

Figure 7-12. The effect of URL routing on the application structure

Being able to choose how components coordinate allows for more flexibility during development. In this case, using URL routing allows the user to navigate directly to a detail view and also means that other components in the application can trigger a detailed display without needing to explicitly load the data.

Summary

In this chapter, I explained how Angular applications are structured around the data model and the URL navigation feature. The data model provides the shared state for the application, allowing Angular components to work consistently together. The URL feature selects the components that will be displayed to the user, allowing features to be used without overwhelming the user with content. In the next chapter, I use the techniques described in this chapter to start working on the end-user features for the SportsStore application.

CHAPTER 8

Creating the Store

The publicly accessible part of the SportsStore application will allow customers to view the products that are on sale, add items to a cart, go through a checkout process, and provide ratings for the products they have purchased. All these features are standard for most online stores, but as you might expect by now, there are some tricks and techniques required to get Angular and ASP.NET Core MVC to work together to create a good experience. In this chapter, I create the structure of the Angular application's store feature and start adding features. Table 8-1 puts the store features in context.

Table 8-1. *Putting End-User Features in Context*

Question	Answer
What are they?	The end-user functionality provides the publicly accessible features of the application.
Why are they useful?	For most applications, the end-user functionality is the most important part of the project and is the reason that development was started. Other features, such as those required to administer the application, tend to receive less attention and effort.
How are they used?	The end user will use their browser to navigate to a URL that presents them with the Angular application, which displays the publicly accessible features. The HTML document that tells the browser to load the Angular application is produced by ASP.NET Core MVC, which is also responsible for delivering the data to the Angular application through the web service controllers.
Are there any pitfalls or limitations?	It is important to start with the structure of the application so that you have a sense of the Angular components that are required, how they will collaborate, and what data is required from the web service. Without this foundation, the Angular part of the project can become complex and difficult to manage.
Are there any alternatives?	No. If you are using Angular and ASP.NET Core MVC in the same project, there will be some type of end user.

Preparing for This Chapter

This chapter uses the SportsStore project I created in Chapter 3 and modified in the chapters since. To ensure that the contents of the database are reset, open a command prompt, navigate to the SportsStore folder, and run the commands shown in Listing 8-1.

■ **Tip** You can download the complete project for this chapter from https://github.com/apress/esntl-angular-for-asp.net-core-mvc. This is where you will also find updates and corrections for this book.

Listing 8-1. Resetting the Database

```
docker-compose down
docker-compose up
```

The first command removes the Docker database container from the previous chapter. The second command creates and starts a fresh container. Start the application to apply the database schema and add the seed data. If you are using Visual Studio, you can do this by selecting Debug ➤ Start Without Debugging. If you are using Visual Studio Code or just prefer working with the command line, then open a command prompt, navigate to the SportsStore folder, and run the command shown in Listing 8-2.

Listing 8-2. Starting the Application

```
dotnet run
```

Use a browser to navigate to http://localhost:5000 and you will see the content shown in Figure 8-1.

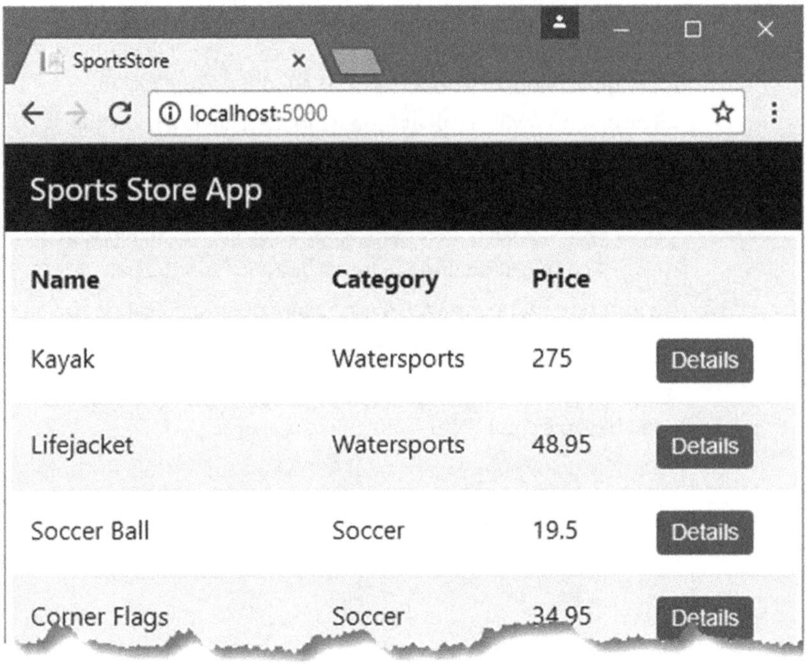

Figure 8-1. *Running the example application*

Starting the Product Selection Feature

The starting point for the store feature is presenting the user with details of the products that are for sale. The earlier chapters included some of the functionality required for this feature, but there are some important additions that will allow the user to filter the content, page through the data, and perform other common tasks.

To provide some context, Figure 8-2 shows the structure that I will be working toward. The layout for product selection will present the user with a list of products, which can be selected to add them to a shopping cart. The user will be able to navigate through the products by selecting a category filter and by moving between pages of products. This is a conventional layout for presenting products and will be familiar if you have followed the SportsStore example in my other books.

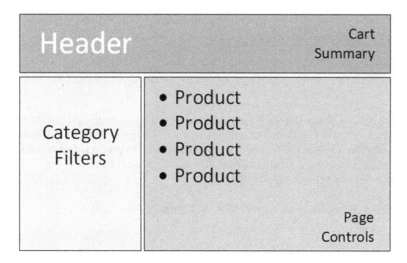

Figure 8-2. *The intended product selection structure*

In the sections that follow, I show you how to create this layout using Angular and how to enhance the ASP.NET Core MVC part of the application.

Blocking Out the Feature Components

When working on a new feature, I find it useful to start by creating components that display placeholder content so that I can define the basic structure shown in Figure 8-2. Once the placeholders are done, I can return to each component and implement the functionality that will be presented to the user.

Creating the Product List Component

Create the ClientApp/app/store folder. This is where the Angular classes and HTML templates for the product selection feature will live. Create a TypeScript file called productList.component.ts in the store folder and add the code shown in Listing 8-3.

Listing 8-3. The Contents of the productList.component.ts File in the ClientApp/app/store Folder

```
import { Component } from "@angular/core";
import { Repository } from "../models/repository";
import { Product } from "../models/product.model";

@Component({
    selector: "store-product-list",
    templateUrl: "productList.component.html"
})
export class ProductListComponent {

    constructor(private repo: Repository) { }

    get products(): Product[] {
        return this.repo.products;
    }
}
```

This component will be responsible for displaying the list of products to the user. Even though I am just blocking out the content at the moment, I know that the set of products in the repository is needed, so I have declared a Repository dependency in the constructor and defined a get-only products property that returns the data. To provide the component with a template, create an HTML file called productList.component. html in the store folder and add the element shown in Listing 8-4.

Listing 8-4. The Contents of the productList.component.html File in the ClientApp/app/store Folder

```
<h3>Placeholder: Product List</h3>
```

I will replace this HTML content with more useful elements once the structure of the application has been completed, but this is enough with which to get started.

Creating the Pagination Component

The pagination component will make long lists of products more manageable by allowing the user to navigate through smaller pages. Add a TypeScript file called pagination.component.ts in the store folder and add the code shown in Listing 8-5.

Listing 8-5. The Contents of the pagination.component.ts File in the ClientApp/app/store Folder

```
import { Component } from "@angular/core";
import { Repository } from "../models/repository";

@Component({
    selector: "store-pagination",
    templateUrl: "pagination.component.html"
})
export class PaginationComponent {

    constructor(private repo: Repository) { }

}
```

This component has a constructor that declares a dependency on the Repository class, which will be used to manage the page navigation. To provide the component with its template, create an HTML file called pagination.component.html in the store folder and add the element shown in Listing 8-6.

Listing 8-6. The Contents of the pagination.component.html File in the ClientApp/app/store Folder

```
<h3>Placeholder: Page Controls</h3>
```

Creating the Category Filter Component

The category filter component will allow the user to select a single category to display. Add a TypeScript file called categoryFilter.component.ts to the store folder with the code shown in Listing 8-7.

Listing 8-7. The Contents of the categoryFilter.component.ts File in the ClientApp/app/store Folder

```
import { Component } from "@angular/core";
import { Repository } from "../models/repository";

@Component({
    selector: "store-categoryfilter",
    templateUrl: "categoryFilter.component.html"
})
export class CategoryFilterComponent {

    constructor(private repo: Repository) { }

}
```

This component follows the pattern of defining a constructor that declares a Repository dependency, which will be resolved using the dependency injection feature and provide access to the filter feature defined in Chapter 5. To provide the component with its template, create an HTML file called categoryFilter.component.html in the store folder and add the element shown in Listing 8-8.

Listing 8-8. The Contents of the categoryFilter.component.html File in the ClientApp/app/store Folder

```
<h3>Placeholder: Category Filter</h3>
```

Creating the Cart Summary Component

The cart summary component will display an overview of the user's shopping cart. Create a TypeScript file called cartSummary.component.ts in the store folder and add the code shown in Listing 8-9.

Listing 8-9. The Contents of the cartSummary.component.ts File in the ClientApp/app/store Folder

```
import { Component } from "@angular/core";

@Component({
    selector: "store-cartsummary",
    templateUrl: "cartSummary.component.html"
})
export class CartSummaryComponent {

}
```

163

Unlike most of the other components created in this chapter, the cart summary component won't need access to the data repository. To provide the component with the template specified by the templateUrl property in the @Component decorator, create an HTML file called cartSummary.component.html in the store folder and add the element shown in Listing 8-10.

Listing 8-10. The Contents of the cartSummary.component.html File in the ClientApp/app/store Folder

```
<h5>Placeholder: Cart Summary</h5>
```

Creating the Ratings Component

The ratings component will display the ratings for a product. Create a TypeScript file called ratings.component.ts in the store folder and add the code shown in Listing 8-11.

Listing 8-11. The Contents of the ratings.component.ts File in the ClientApp/app/store Folder

```
import { Component } from "@angular/core";
import { Product } from "../models/product.model";

@Component({
    selector: "store-ratings",
    templateUrl: "ratings.component.html"
})
export class RatingsComponent {

}
```

This component doesn't need the repository to do its job, so it doesn't define a constructor. To provide the component with the template specified by the templateUrl property in the @Component decorator, create an HTML file called ratings.component.html in the store folder and add the elements shown in Listing 8-12.

Listing 8-12. The Contents of the ratings.component.html File in the ClientApp/app/store Folder

```
<h5>Placeholder: Ratings</h5>
```

Creating the Structural Component

The final component required for this chapter will provide the layout for the others. Angular doesn't have support for creating stand-alone HTML templates, which means that a component is required even when only the HTML structure is required. Add a TypeScript file called productSelection.component.ts to the store folder with the code shown in Listing 8-13.

Listing 8-13. The Contents of the productSelection.component.ts File in the ClientApp/app/store Folder

```
import { Component } from "@angular/core";

@Component({
    selector: "store-products",
    templateUrl: "productSelection.component.html"
})
export class ProductSelectionComponent {

}
```

To provide the component with its template, which is what will provide the layout structure, create an HTML file called productSelection.component.html in the store folder and add the elements shown in Listing 8-14.

Listing 8-14. The Contents of the productSelection.component.html File in the ClientApp/app/store Folder

```
<div class="navbar bg-inverse ">
    <div class="row">
        <div class="col">
            <a class="navbar-brand text-white">
                SPORTS STORE
            </a>
        </div>
        <div class="col text-white mr-1">
            <store-cartsummary></store-cartsummary>
        </div>
    </div>
</div>
<div class="row no-gutters">
    <div class="col-3">
        <store-categoryfilter></store-categoryfilter>
    </div>
    <div class="col">
        <store-product-list></store-product-list>
        <store-pagination></store-pagination>
    </div>
</div>
```

This template uses the Bootstrap classes to create a grid layout, which makes it easy to position content without getting bogged down in the complexities of CSS. The ratings component isn't included in the layout, but I'll integrate it into the application later in the chapter.

Creating and Registering the Store Feature Module

To create a feature module for the product selection feature, create a TypeScript file called store.module.ts in the store folder and add the code shown in Listing 8-15.

Listing 8-15. The Contents of the store.module.ts File in the ClientApp/app/store Folder

```
import { NgModule } from "@angular/core";
import { BrowserModule } from '@angular/platform-browser';
import { CartSummaryComponent } from "./cartSummary.component";
import { CategoryFilterComponent } from "./categoryFilter.component";
import { PaginationComponent } from "./pagination.component";
import { ProductListComponent } from "./productList.component";
import { RatingsComponent } from "./ratings.component";
import { ProductSelectionComponent } from "./productSelection.component";
```

```
@NgModule({
    declarations: [CartSummaryComponent, CategoryFilterComponent,
        PaginationComponent, ProductListComponent, RatingsComponent,
        ProductSelectionComponent],
    imports: [BrowserModule],
    exports: [ProductSelectionComponent]
})
export class StoreModule { }
```

The declarations property of the StoreModule feature module is used to register the components created in this section so they can be used by the Angular application. The exports property tells Angular which components can be used outside the feature module and has been used to specify the ProductSelectionComponent, which will be responsible for managing the others. (By default, the classes specified by the declarations property can only be referred to in templates defined in the same feature module.)

The imports property tells Angular which other modules this module depends on. In this case, this is the BrowserModule, which provides the standard directives and data bindings required for an Angular application running in a browser.

To tell Angular about the store feature module, register it with the root module, as shown in Listing 8-16.

Listing 8-16. Registering a Feature Module in the app.module.ts File in the ClientApp/app Folder

```
import { BrowserModule } from '@angular/platform-browser';
import { NgModule } from '@angular/core';
import { FormsModule } from '@angular/forms';
import { HttpModule } from '@angular/http';
import { AppComponent } from './app.component';
import { ModelModule } from "./models/model.module";
//import { ProductTableComponent } from "./structure/productTable.component"
//import { CategoryFilterComponent } from "./structure/categoryFilter.component"
//import { ProductDetailComponent } from "./structure/productDetail.component";
import { RoutingConfig } from "./app.routing";
import { StoreModule } from "./store/store.module";
import { ProductSelectionComponent } from "./store/productSelection.component";

@NgModule({
    declarations: [AppComponent],
    imports: [BrowserModule, FormsModule, HttpModule, ModelModule,
                RoutingConfig, StoreModule],
    providers: [],
    bootstrap: [AppComponent]
})
export class AppModule { }
```

Unlike ASP.NET Core MVC, Angular doesn't discover its building blocks automatically, so every module or component that you rely on must be registered either directly with the root module or in a feature module (which must then be registered with the root module).

Configuring the Angular URL Routes

The routing configuration for the Angular application is still set up for the components from Chapter 7. To update the configuration for the components in this chapter, replace the routes with the ones shown in Listing 8-17.

Listing 8-17. Configuring the Routes in the app.routing.ts File in the ClientApp/app Folder

```
import { Routes, RouterModule } from "@angular/router";
//import { ProductTableComponent } from "./structure/productTable.component"
//import { ProductDetailComponent } from "./structure/productDetail.component";
import { ProductSelectionComponent } from "./store/productSelection.component";

const routes: Routes = [
    { path: "store", component: ProductSelectionComponent },
    { path: "", component: ProductSelectionComponent }]

export const RoutingConfig = RouterModule.forRoot(routes);
```

There are two routes in this configuration, which will show the ProductSelectionComponent for the default URL and the /store URL.

Removing the Layout Header

The Index.cshtml Razor view duplicates the SportsStore header contained in the template for the product selection component. I need to use the component's header because it contains the cart summary component, so comment out the duplicate, as shown in Listing 8-18.

Listing 8-18. Commenting Out a Header in the Index.cshtml File in the Views/Home Folder

```
@section scripts {
    <script src="~/dist/inline.bundle.js" asp-append-version="true"></script>
    <script src="~/dist/polyfills.bundle.js" asp-append-version="true"></script>
    <script src="~/dist/vendor.bundle.js" asp-append-version="true"></script>
    <script src="~/dist/main.bundle.js" asp-append-version="true"></script>
}

@*<div class="navbar bg-inverse">*@
@*    <a class="navbar-brand text-white">@(ViewBag.Message ?? "SPORTS STORE")</a>*@
@*</div>*@

<div class="p-1">
    <app-root></app-root>
</div>
```

The Razor view now contains only the script elements for the Angular JavaScript files and the app-root element in which the Angular application will be displayed. Once you have saved all the changes, reload the browser, and you will see the content shown in Figure 8-3. It doesn't look like much, but it provides the basic structure of the product selection feature.

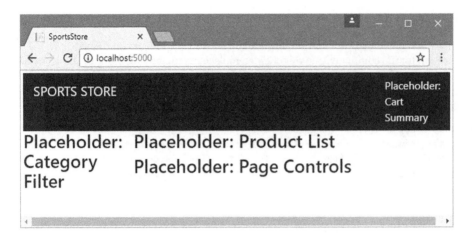

Figure 8-3. *Creating the structure for the product selection feature*

Displaying the Product List

Showing a list of available products is relatively easy because this is one of the features that I used in Chapter 5 to create the web service. The product list component, created in Listing 8-3, already has a products property that provides access to the Product objects in the repository. Edit the component's template as shown in Listing 8-19 to display the Product objects provided by the Repository and the component.

Listing 8-19. Displaying Data in the productList.component.html File in the ClientApp/app/store Folder

```
<div *ngIf="products?.length > 0; else nodata">
    <div *ngFor="let product of products" class="card card-outline-primary m-1">
        <div class="card-header">
            <span class="h4">{{product.name}}</span>
            <span class="float-right badge badge-pill badge-primary">
                {{product.price | currency:"USD":true }}
            </span>
        </div>
        <div class="card-block">
            <span class="card-text p-a-1">{{product.description}}</span>
            <button class="float-right btn btn-sm btn-success"
                    (click)="addToCart(product)">
                Add to Cart
            </button>
        </div>
    </div>
</div>

<ng-template #nodata>
    <h4 class="m-1">Waiting for data...</h4>
</ng-template>
```

Save the change to the template and reload the Angular application to see the list of products illustrated in Figure 8-4.

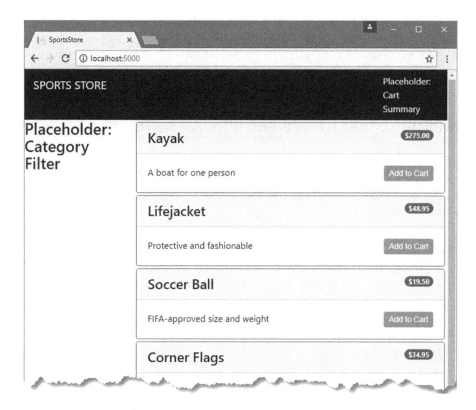

Figure 8-4. *Displaying a list of products*

Understanding the Product List Template Features

This template uses some of the Angular features shown in previous chapters but introduces some new ones, too. In the sections that follow, I describe each of the template features used in Listing 8-19.

Understanding the ngIf Directive

The first Angular feature used in the template is the ngIf directive, which comes in two parts, like this:

```
<div *ngIf="products?.length > 0; else nodata">
  <!-- content to be displayed if expression evaluates as true -->
</div>

<ng-template #nodata>
  <!-- content to be displayed if expression evaluates as false -->
</ng-template>
```

If the ngIf directive's expression evaluates to true, then the element it has been applied to and its content are inserted into the HTML shown to the user. If the expression is false, then the element is removed. Like other Angular directives, ngIf reevaluates its expression when there is a data change, which means it allows elements to be created or deleted dynamically. In this case, the expression checks to see that there are Product objects to display, and if there are, the div element to which the ngIf directive has been applied will be added to the HTML document.

This listing uses an optional feature of the ngIf directive. The directive's expression is followed by a semicolon (the ; character) and the else keyword, followed by a name. The name corresponds to the ng-template element, which will be added to the HTML document when the ngIf directive's expression is false. In this case, the effect is that a "Waiting for Data" message will be displayed when there is no Product data to display.

STRUCTURAL DIRECTIVES REQUIRE AN ASTERISK

Some Angular directives are applied with an asterisk before their names, such as *ngIf and *ngFor, and you will receive an error if you omit it. Directives that add or remove content contained in the element they are applied to are known as structural directives, and they can be used in two ways: the full syntax and the concise syntax.

The asterisk tells Angular that you want to use the concise syntax, which is much easier to work with and is what I use throughout this book. The full syntax is required only when you can't apply the directive directly to an element, which I demonstrate in Chapter 10. It can be difficult to remember which directives require an asterisk when you first start working with Angular, but it quickly becomes second nature.

Understanding the ngFor Directive

The ngFor directive generates the same content for each object in a sequence, such as an array. The directive assigns each object to a temporary variable, whose name is defined in the expression, and which can be used for data bindings (and other directives) inside the directive's element. In this case, the ngFor directive is applied to the set of objects returned by the component's products property and assigns each object in turn to a variable called product, like this:

```
...
<div *ngFor="let product of products" class="card card-outline-primary m-1">
...
```

Directives and data bindings applied to elements contained within the div element that the ngFor directive has been applied to can access the current object by using the product variable, like this:

```
...
<span class="h4">{{product.name}}</span>
...
```

In Listing 8-19, the ngFor directive generates content for each Product object, and the content and data bindings that are produced provide the user with the name, price, and description of each product that is available.

Understanding the Currency Pipe

Angular pipes are responsible for formatting data values so they can be presented to the user. Angular includes a set of pipes that perform common formatting tasks, as described in Table 8-2.

Table 8-2. *The Built-in Angular Piples*

Name	Description
number	This pipe is used for specify the number of integer and fraction digits shown for a number value.
currency	This pipe is used to format a number value as a currency amount.
percent	This pipe is used to format a number value as a percentage.
uppercase	This pipe is used to convert a string value to uppercase characters.
lowercase	This pipe is used to convert a string value to lowercase characters.
json	This pipe is used to serialize an object to JSON data.
slice	This pipe is used to select elements from an array.

I used the currency pipe in Listing 8-19 to format the price of a product as a currency value, like this:

```
...
{{product.price  | currency:"USD":true }}
...
```

Pipes are applied to a data value using the vertical bar (the | character), followed by the name of the pipe and its configuration settings. Each built-in pipe has its own options, and the ones used in this case specify the U.S. dollar as the currency and select the currency symbol rather than the currency code so that $ is displayed rather than USD.

Understanding the Click Handler

The final template feature used in Listing 8-19 is the event binding, which is used to handle the click event on the button element and allows the user to add a product to the shopping cart.

```
...
<button class="float-right btn btn-sm btn-success" (click)="addToCart(product)">
    Add to Cart
</button>
...
```

The binding tells Angular to invoke a method called addToCart, using the value of the product variable created by the ngFor directive as an argument. The addToCart method doesn't exist yet, but I will create it in Chapter 9 when I create the shopping cart functionality. Until then, clicking the button element will produce an error in the browser's JavaScript console.

Creating the Category Filter

The key challenge in implementing the category filter is getting the complete set of categories. The requests made by the Repository class to the web service to get Product objects may return only a subset of the available data, which means deriving the categories from that data may return an incomplete list.

As a consequence, I need additional information that describes the complete set of data that is available, even if not all of the data is being sent to the client. In the sections that follow, I enhance the ASP. NET Core MVC web service to provide a description of the data available and demonstrate how to consume that data in the Angular application.

171

Enhancing the ASP.NET Core MVC Application

To provide the client with category information, add a new method to the `ProductValues` controller and update the `GetProducts` method, as shown in Listing 8-20.

Listing 8-20. Providing Category Data in the ProductValuesController.cs File in the Controllers Folder

```
using Microsoft.AspNetCore.Mvc;
using SportsStore.Models;
using Microsoft.EntityFrameworkCore;
using System.Linq;
using System.Collections.Generic;
using SportsStore.Models.BindingTargets;
using Microsoft.AspNetCore.JsonPatch;

namespace SportsStore.Controllers {

    [Route("api/products")]
    public class ProductValuesController : Controller {
        private DataContext context;

        public ProductValuesController(DataContext ctx) {
            context = ctx;
        }

        // ...other methods omitted for brevity...

        [HttpGet]
        public IActionResult GetProducts(string category, string search,
                bool related = false, bool metadata = false) {
            IQueryable<Product> query = context.Products;

            if (!string.IsNullOrWhiteSpace(category)) {
                string catLower = category.ToLower();
                query = query.Where(p => p.Category.ToLower().Contains(catLower));
            }
            if (!string.IsNullOrWhiteSpace(search)) {
                string searchLower = search.ToLower();
                query = query.Where(p => p.Name.ToLower().Contains(searchLower)
                    || p.Description.ToLower().Contains(searchLower));
            }

            if (related) {
                query = query.Include(p => p.Supplier).Include(p => p.Ratings);
                List<Product> data = query.ToList();
                data.ForEach(p => {
                    if (p.Supplier != null) {
                        p.Supplier.Products = null;
                    }
                    if (p.Ratings != null) {
                        p.Ratings.ForEach(r => r.Product = null);
                    }
                });
```

```
            return metadata ? CreateMetadata(data) : Ok(data);
        } else {
            return metadata ? CreateMetadata(query) : Ok(query);
        }
    }

    private IActionResult CreateMetadata(IEnumerable<Product> products) {
        return Ok(new {
            data = products,
            categories = context.Products.Select(p => p.Category)
                .Distinct().OrderBy(c => c)
        });
    }
}
}
```

This listing adds an optional parameter called metadata to the GetProducts method. When this parameter is true, then the CreateMetadata method is used to generate a result with data and categories properties, which allows the product data and the category data to be combined in a single response. The data property is set to the sequence of Product objects that the client has requested, and the categories property is set using a LINQ query that produces an ordered set of distinct category names.

Receiving Category Data in the Angular Data Repository

To allow the Angular application to receive the category data, make the changes shown in Listing 8-21 to the Repository class.

Listing 8-21. Receiving Category Data in the repository.ts File in the ClientApp/app/models Folder

```
...
@Injectable()
export class Repository {
    private filterObject = new Filter();

    constructor(private http: Http) {
        this.filter.related = true;
        this.getProducts();
    }

    getProduct(id: number) {
        this.sendRequest(RequestMethod.Get, productsUrl + "/" + id)
            .subscribe(response => this.product = response);
    }

    getProducts() {
        let url = productsUrl + "?related=" + this.filter.related;

        if (this.filter.category) {
            url += "&category=" + this.filter.category;
        }
```

```
        if (this.filter.search) {
            url += "&search=" + this.filter.search;
        }

        url += "&metadata=true";
        this.sendRequest(RequestMethod.Get, url)
            .subscribe(response => {
                this.products = response.data;
                this.categories = response.categories;
            });
    }

    // ...other methods omitted for brevity...

    product: Product;
    products: Product[];
    suppliers: Supplier[] = [];
    categories: string[] = [];

    get filter(): Filter {
        return this.filterObject;
    }
}
...
```

Although it would be possible to be selective about getting the category data, I have chosen to receive a new set of categories every time the application refreshes its product data by calling the getProducts method, ensuring that any changes to the data stored in the database will be reflected in the client. The set of category names returned by the web service is made available through the Repository class's categories property, which is initialized to an empty array until the data from the web service is assigned to it.

Updating the Filter Component and Template

All that remains is to present the user with a list of categories and use their selection to filter the list of products. The first step is to update the component class so that it defines properties that expose the list of categories and the currently selected category and a method that will change the category selection, as shown in Listing 8-22.

Listing 8-22. Exposing Data in the categoryFilter.component.ts File in the ClientApp/app/store Folder

```
import { Component } from "@angular/core";
import { Repository } from "../models/repository";

@Component({
    selector: "store-categoryfilter",
    templateUrl: "categoryFilter.component.html"
})
export class CategoryFilterComponent {

    constructor(private repo: Repository) { }
```

```
    get categories(): string[] {
        return this.repo.categories;
    }

    get currentCategory(): string {
        return this.repo.filter.category;
    }

    setCurrentCategory(newCategory: string) {
        this.repo.filter.category = newCategory;
        this.repo.getProducts();
    }
}
```

The categories and currentCategory properties provide read-only access to the data provided by the Repository object. The current category is determined by reading the repository's Filter object, which is used to control the URL used to query the web service for data. The setCurrentCategory method updates the repository's filter.category property and then calls the getProducts method to refresh the data, which will be filtered using the specified category.

To use the method and properties defined by the component, replace the content in its template with the elements shown in Listing 8-23.

Listing 8-23. Categories in the categoryFilter.component.html File in the ClientApp/app/store Folder

```html
<div class="m-1">
    <button class="btn btn-outline-primary btn-block"
            (click)="setCurrentCategory(null)">
        All Categories
    </button>
    <button *ngFor="let category of categories"
            class="btn btn-outline-primary btn-block"
            [class.active]="currentCategory == category"
            (click)="setCurrentCategory(category)">
        {{category}}
    </button>
</div>
```

The template has two button elements. The first button element allows the user to select all the categories and has a click event binding that calls the setCurrentCategory method with null as the argument.

The ngFor directive has been applied to the other element, with an expression that operates on the category names and produces a button for each of them. There is a click event binding that calls the setCurrentCategory method to select a category. There is also a new kind of binding, known as the *class binding*.

```html
...
<button *ngFor="let category of categories"
    class="btn btn-outline-primary btn-block"
    [class.active]="currentCategory == category"
    (click)="setCurrentCategory(category)">
...
```

The class binding is applied using square brackets (the [and] characters) containing the `class` keyword, followed by a period, followed by the name of a class, such as the Bootstrap `active` class, which applies a style to the element that shows it is selected. The element is added to the class when the expression evaluates as `true` and is removed when it is `false`. The expression is reevaluated when the data model is changed, which means that the button elements will be added and removed from the `active` class automatically as the selected category changes.

Restart the application and use a browser to navigate to `http://localhost:5000` to see the category filter. Clicking the buttons filters the products so that only those in the selected category are displayed, as shown in Figure 8-5.

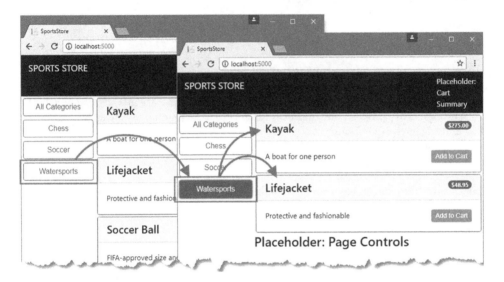

Figure 8-5. *Filtering categories*

Creating the Pagination Controls

Most applications have too much data to display in one go or even to send to the client in one go. The most common solution is to break the data into pages and allow the user to navigate between pages on demand.

Creating and Registering a Pagination Service

I am going to create multiple building blocks to implement the pagination controls. To help them cooperate, I am going to create a class that represents the current pagination state and provide access to it through the Repository class. Add the class shown in Listing 8-24 to the `configClasses.repository.ts` file.

Listing 8-24. Adding a Class in the configClasses.repository.ts File in the ClientApp/app/model Folder

```
export class Filter {
    category?: string;
    search?: string;

    related: boolean = false;
```

```
    reset() {
        this.category = this.search = null;
        this.related = false;
    }
}

export class Pagination {

    productsPerPage: number = 4;
    currentPage = 1;
}
```

The Pagination class defines properties that specify how many products will be displayed by each page and which page is currently selected. These are simple data values, but making them available through the Repository class will make it easy to write the building blocks that will provide the pagination feature and get them to work together. Make the changes shown in Listing 8-25 to the Repository class to create a shared pagination state and to reset the selected page when the product data is refreshed by the getProducts method.

Listing 8-25. Exposing Page Data in the repository.ts File in the ClientApp/app/models Folder

```
import { Product } from "./product.model";
import { Injectable } from "@angular/core";
import { Http, RequestMethod, Request, Response } from "@angular/http";
import { Observable } from "rxjs/Observable";
import "rxjs/add/operator/map";
import { Filter, Pagination } from "./configClasses.repository";
import { Supplier } from "./supplier.model";

const productsUrl = "/api/products";
const suppliersUrl = "/api/suppliers";

@Injectable()
export class Repository {
    private filterObject = new Filter();
    private paginationObject = new Pagination();

    constructor(private http: Http) {
        this.filter.related = true;
        this.getProducts();
    }

    getProduct(id: number) {
        this.sendRequest(RequestMethod.Get, productsUrl + "/" + id)
            .subscribe(response => this.product = response);
    }

    getProducts() {
        let url = productsUrl + "?related=" + this.filter.related;

        if (this.filter.category) {
            url += "&category=" + this.filter.category;
        }
```

```
        if (this.filter.search) {
            url += "&search=" + this.filter.search;
        }
        url += "&metadata=true";
        this.sendRequest(RequestMethod.Get, url)
            .subscribe(response => {
                this.products = response.data;
                this.categories = response.categories;
                this.pagination.currentPage = 1;
            });
    }

    // ...other methods and properties omitted for brevity...

    get filter(): Filter {
        return this.filterObject;
    }

    get pagination(): Pagination {
        return this.paginationObject;
    }
}
```

Updating the Pagination Button Component

Now that the repository provides access to pagination data, I can update the component so that it can provide the support required for the page navigation buttons, as shown in Listing 8-26.

Listing 8-26. Adding Page Support in the pagination.component.ts File in the ClientApp/app/store Folder

```
import { Component } from "@angular/core";
import { Repository } from "../models/repository";

@Component({
    selector: "store-pagination",
    templateUrl: "pagination.component.html"
})
export class PaginationComponent {

    constructor(private repo: Repository) { }

    get current(): number {
        return this.repo.pagination.currentPage;
    }

    get pages(): number[] {
        if (this.repo.products != null) {
            return Array(Math.ceil(this.repo.products.length
                    / this.repo.pagination.productsPerPage))
                .fill(0).map((x, i) => i + 1);
        } else {
```

```
        return [];
    }
}

changePage(newPage: number) {
    this.repo.pagination.currentPage = newPage;
}
}
```

The current property and the changePage method get and set the Pagination.currentPage property. The pages method generates a sequence of page numbers, which will provide the ngFor directive with the objects it needs to create and configure the buttons that will change the page. (The ngFor directive cannot be used to create a for loop and must always be provided with a sequence of objects to work with.)

Edit the component's template to generate the elements that will allow the user to change pages, as shown in Listing 8-27.

Listing 8-27. Adding Page Support in the pagination.component.html File in the ClientApp/app/store Folder

```
<div *ngIf="pages.length > 1" class="text-right my-2">
    <button *ngFor="let page of pages"
            class="btn btn-outline-primary mx-1"
            [class.active]="current == page"
            (click)="changePage(page)">
        {{page}}
    </button>
</div>
```

All the features used in this template have been described in earlier examples. The ngIf directive is used to ensure that page buttons are displayed only if there are multiple pages of products available. The ngFor directive is used to generate button elements for each page, with the class binding showing the active page and the click event binding allowing the user to change pages. Save the changes and reload the browser and you will see the page buttons displayed at the end of the product list, as shown in Figure 8-6. The buttons are displayed only when there are more than four products to display, which means they are not shown when a category filter is applied because there are not enough products to require pagination in any of the categories.

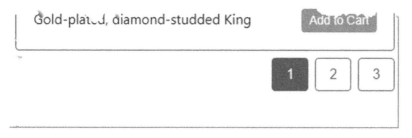

Figure 8-6. *The page navigation buttons*

Paging the Product Data

The page navigation buttons are in place, but clicking them has no effect on the list of products displayed to the user. To address this, update the product list component so that its `products` property takes into account the pagination data, as shown in Listing 8-28.

Listing 8-28. Paging Data in the productList.component.ts File in the ClientApp/app/store Folder

```
import { Component } from "@angular/core";
import { Repository } from "../models/repository";
import { Product } from "../models/product.model";

@Component({
    selector: "store-product-list",
    templateUrl: "productList.component.html"
})
export class ProductListComponent {

    constructor(private repo: Repository) { }

    get products(): Product[] {
        if (this.repo.products != null && this.repo.products.length > 0) {
            let pageIndex = (this.repo.pagination.currentPage - 1)
                * this.repo.pagination.productsPerPage;
            return this.repo.products.slice(pageIndex,
                pageIndex + this.repo.pagination.productsPerPage);
        }
    }
}
```

The implementation of the `products` getter uses the JavaScript array `slice` method to select a subset of the `Product` objects available in the repository. Save the change, and you will see that the list of products is paginated and changes when a new page is selected, as shown in Figure 8-7.

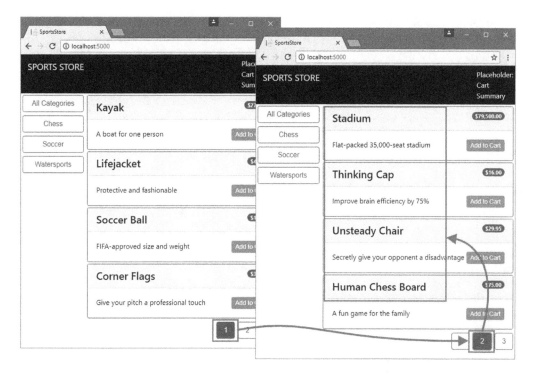

Figure 8-7. *Paginating products*

Displaying Ratings

Displaying ratings requires some different techniques, since multiple instances of the ratings component will be created, each of which will be responsible for displaying the rating of a single product. In the sections that follow, I add a package to the project that will provide the graphics required for the rating and show you how to create a component that handles a single data object.

Adding the Font Awesome Package

The Font Awesome package provides access to a large collection of icons that can be easily integrated into web applications. To add Font Awesome to the SportsStore project, add details of the package to the bower. json file, as shown in Listing 8-29.

Listing 8-29. Adding a Package in the bower.json File in the SportsStore Folder

```
{
  "name": "asp.net",
  "private": true,
  "dependencies": {
    "bootstrap": "4.0.0-alpha.6",
    "jquery": "2.2.0",
    "jquery-validation": "1.14.0",
    "jquery-validation-unobtrusive": "3.2.6",
    "font-awesome": "4.7.0"
  }
}
```

If you are using Visual Studio Code, run the command shown in Listing 8-30 in the SportsStore folder to update the client-side packages. (Visual Studio will perform the update automatically).

Listing 8-30. Updating the Client-Side Packages

```
bower install
```

To ensure that the browser receives the Font Awesome files, add the elements shown in Listing 8-31 to the _Layout.cshtml file in the Views/Shared folder.

Listing 8-31. Adding an Element in the _Layout.cshtml File in the Views/Shared Folder

```
<!DOCTYPE html>
<html>
<head>
    <base href="/">
    <meta charset="utf-8" />
    <meta name="viewport" content="width=device-width, initial-scale=1.0" />
    <title>SportsStore @ViewData["Title"]</title>
    <link rel="stylesheet" href="~/lib/bootstrap/dist/css/bootstrap.css" />
    <link href="~/lib/font-awesome/css/font-awesome.min.css" rel="stylesheet" />
</head>
<body>
    @RenderBody()
    @RenderSection("Scripts", required: false)
</body>
</html>
```

Updating the Rating Component and Template

To display the ratings for a product, I am going to average the number of stars that have been awarded. The component will display five star icons, which will be shown in solid color or outline to indicate the overall rating. The component needs to provide its template with a sequence of five values that indicate whether a star should be solid or outline, as shown in Listing 8-32.

Listing 8-32. Generating Rating Data in the ratings.component.ts File in the ClientApp/app/store Folder

```
import { Component, Input } from "@angular/core";
import { Product } from "../models/product.model";

@Component({
    selector: "store-ratings",
    templateUrl: "ratings.component.html"
})
export class RatingsComponent {

    @Input()
    product: Product;
```

```
    get stars(): boolean[] {
        if (this.product != null && this.product.ratings != null) {
            let total = this.product.ratings.map(r => r.stars)
                .reduce((prev, curr) => prev + curr, 0);
            let count = Math.round(total / this.product.ratings.length);
            return Array(5).fill(false).map((value, index) => {
                return index < count;
            });
        } else {
            return [];
        }
    }
}
```

The component needs to know which Product object it is responsible for, and for this I have used an Angular *input property*. Input properties are decorated with the @Input decorator, which is defined in the @angular/core module, like this:

```
...
@Input()
product: Product;
...
```

Input properties allow components to receive data from the template in which they are applied. You'll see how is used in the next section, but when Angular creates this component, it will set the value of the product property to the Product object for which rating information should be displayed.

The stars function uses the Product object to generate an array of boolean values that can be used with the ngFor directive. If a Product has an average of three stars, for example, then the stars property will return an array containing the values true, true, true, false, false. To display the star rating, add the elements shown in Listing 8-33 to the component's template.

Listing 8-33. Displaying Ratings in the ratings.component.html File in the ClientApp/app/store Folder

```
<span class="h6 ml-1">
    <i *ngFor="let s of stars"
        [class]="s ? 'fa fa-star' : 'fa fa-star-o'"
        [style.color]="s ? 'goldenrod' : 'gray'">
    </i>
</span>
```

The i element is how Font Awesome icons are applied, with the classes to which the element is assigned determining which icon is shown.

The ngFor directive creates an i element for each of the five entries in the array returned by the stars property. To configure the i element, the listing uses two data bindings, which are the attributes whose names are in square brackets.

The class data binding evaluates an expression and uses the result to set the classes to which an element is a member. In the listing, this binding is used to choose between two different sets of classes that select Font Awesome icons.

```
...
[class]="s ? 'fa fa-star' : 'fa fa-star-o'"
...
```

This is another example of the class data binding, except that it sets all the classes that the element is assigned to using the result of its expression. In this case, the expression uses the JavaScript ternary operator to examine the value of the s variable and selects the fa and fa-star classes if it is true (which creates a solid star icon) and the fa and fa-star-o classes if it is false (which creates an outline star icon). Notice that the classes in the expression are specified as string literals and that the fa class is required for both outcomes, since this binding replaces all existing classes.

■ **Tip**   If you don't like including string literals for classes in templates, you can define a method in the component that returns the classes that are required and invoke it in the class binding expression.

The color CSS property is used to set the color of the Font Awesome icons. The style data binding is used to set style properties and has been used in this listing to set the color property.

```
...
[style.color]="s ? 'goldenrod' : 'gray'">
...
```

The expression for this data binding uses the ternary operator to inspect the s variable and chooses goldenrod if it is true and gray if it is false.

Applying the Rating Component

The last step required to display the product ratings is to add the store-ratings element, which tells Angular to apply the ratings component. Add the element shown in Listing 8-34 to the product list component's template.

Listing 8-34. Adding an Element in the productList.component.html File in the ClientApp/app/model Folder

```html
<div *ngIf="products?.length > 0; else nodata">
    <div *ngFor="let product of products" class="card card-outline-primary m-1">
        <div class="card-header">
            <span class="h4">
                {{product.name}}
                <store-ratings [product]="product"></store-ratings>
            </span>
            <span class="float-right badge badge-pill badge-primary">
                {{product.price | currency:"USD":true }}
            </span>
        </div>
        <div class="card-block">
            <span class="card-text p-a-1">{{product.description}}</span>
            <button class="float-right btn btn-sm btn-success"
                    (click)="addToCart(product)">
                Add to Cart
            </button>
        </div>
    </div>
</div>
```

```
<ng-template #nodata>
    <h4 class="m-1">Waiting for data...</h4>
</ng-template>
```

The store-ratings element has been applied inside the content generated by the ngFor directive, which means that Angular will create an instance of the controller class for each product that is displayed to the user. To provide the ratings component with the Product object whose ratings will be displayed, a data binding is applied to the store-ratings element, like this:

```
...
<store-ratings [product]="product"></store-ratings>
...
```

The square brackets are used to denote the binding, enclosing the name of the input property defined in Listing 8-32. The value for the input property is set using the binding expression, which is the value of the product variable created by the ngFor directive.

Save the changes, and you will see that the product list has been updated so that each product includes its rating data, as shown in Figure 8-8.

Figure 8-8. *Displaying ratings*

Summary

In this chapter, I started work on using the Angular application to present the product selection feature to the user. I created the components that will cooperate to provide features to the user and organized them with placeholder content to create the overall structure. I then added support for listing the products available, filtering the products by category, paging through products when there are too many to display, and showing the ratings awarded to each product. In the next chapter, I complete the SportsStore store.

CHAPTER 9

Completing the Angular Store

In this chapter, I complete the customer-facing features for the SportsStore application, allowing the user to add products to a shopping cart and complete an order.

Preparing for This Chapter

This chapter uses the SportsStore project created in Chapter 3 and modified in the chapters since. To ensure that the contents of the database are reset, open a command prompt, navigate to the SportsStore folder, and run the commands shown in Listing 9-1.

■ **Tip**   You can download the complete project for this chapter from https://github.com/apress/esntl-angular-for-asp.net-core-mvc. This is also where you will find updates and corrections for this book.

Listing 9-1. Resetting the Database

```
docker-compose down
docker-compose up
```

The first command removes the Docker database container from the previous chapter. The second command creates and starts a fresh container. Start the application to apply the database schema and add the seed data. If you are using Visual Studio, you can do this by selecting Debug ➤ Start Without Debugging. If you are using Visual Studio Code or just prefer working with the command line, then open a command prompt, navigate to the SportsStore folder, and run the command shown in Listing 9-2.

Listing 9-2. Starting the Application

```
dotnet run
```

Use a browser to navigate to http://localhost:5000 and you will see the content shown in Figure 9-1.

© Adam Freeman 2017
A. Freeman, *Essential Angular for ASP.NET Core MVC*, DOI 10.1007/978-1-4842-2916-3_9

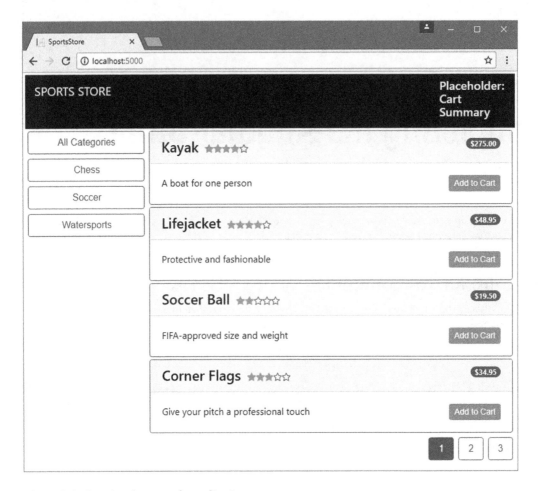

Figure 9-1. *Running the example application*

Creating the Shopping Cart

Most online stores allow users to gather the products they require into a shopping cart, which is then used to complete a purchase. In the sections that follow, I demonstrate how to create a shopping cart in the Angular application and how to store the contents of carts using ASP.NET Core MVC and Entity Framework Core.

Extending the Angular Data Model

The starting point is to define a new class that will represent the cart in the Angular application. Add a new TypeScript file called cart.model.ts in the models folder and use it to define the class shown in Listing 9-3.

Listing 9-3. The Contents of the cart.model.ts File in the ClientApp/app/models Folder

```
import { Injectable } from "@angular/core";
import { Product } from "./product.model";

@Injectable()
export class Cart {
    selections: ProductSelection[] = [];
    itemCount: number = 0;
    totalPrice: number = 0;

    addProduct(product: Product) {
        let selection = this.selections
            .find(ps => ps.productId == product.productId);
        if (selection) {
            selection.quantity++;
        } else {
            this.selections.push(new ProductSelection(this,
                product.productId, product.name,
                product.price, 1));
        }
        this.update();
    }

    updateQuantity(productId: number, quantity: number) {
        if (quantity > 0) {
            let selection = this.selections.find(ps => ps.productId == productId);
            if (selection) {
                selection.quantity = quantity;
            }
        } else {
            let index = this.selections.findIndex(ps => ps.productId == productId);
            if (index != -1) {
                this.selections.splice(index, 1);
            }
            this.update();
        }
    }

    clear() {
        this.selections = [];
        this.update();
    }

    update() {
        this.itemCount = this.selections.map(ps => ps.quantity)
            .reduce((prev, curr) => prev + curr, 0);
        this.totalPrice = this.selections.map(ps => ps.price * ps.quantity)
            .reduce((prev, curr) => prev + curr, 0);
    }
}
```

```
export class ProductSelection {

    constructor(public cart: Cart,
        public productId?: number,
        public name?: string,
        public price?: number,
        private quantityValue?: number) { }

    get quantity() {
        return this.quantityValue;
    }

    set quantity(newQuantity: number) {
        this.quantityValue = newQuantity;
        this.cart.update();
    }
}
```

The Cart class represents the user's shopping cart, using the ProductSelection class to represent individual product choices. The Cart class provides methods that allow the product selections to be managed and provides properties whose values report on the number of items in the cart and their total cost.

The update method must be called each time the product selection changes to recalculate the total cost and number of items in the cart. Remember that Angular evaluates data binding expressions repeatedly when there is an update, and it is a good idea to perform this kind of calculation only when required to avoid repeatedly inspecting the products in the cart.

Registering the Cart as a Service

I am going to register the Cart class as a service, which will allow other classes, including components, to declare a constructor dependency that will be resolved using dependency injection and will ensure that a single Cart object is shared throughout the application. To register the service, add the Cart class to the providers property of the model feature module, as shown in Listing 9-4.

Listing 9-4. Registering a Service in the model.module.ts File in the ClientApp/app/models Folder

```
import { NgModule } from "@angular/core";
import { Repository } from "./repository";
import { Cart } from "./cart.model";

@NgModule({
    providers: [Repository, Cart]
})
export class ModelModule { }
```

Angular will create a Cart object and use it to satisfy constructor dependencies for the components that will provide the user-facing cart functionality.

Wiring Up the Buttons

The Add to Cart buttons that are displayed for each product in the list invoke a method in the template's component. This method doesn't yet exist but is required so that the user can select the products they want to buy. To allow the user to add products to the cart, make the changes shown in Listing 9-5 to the product list component.

Listing 9-5. Adding Cart Items in the productList.component.ts File in the ClientApp/app/store Folder

```
import { Component } from "@angular/core";
import { Repository } from "../models/repository";
import { Product } from "../models/product.model";
import { Cart } from "../models/cart.model";

@Component({
    selector: "store-product-list",
    templateUrl: "productList.component.html"
})
export class ProductListComponent {

    constructor(private repo: Repository, private cart: Cart) { }

    get products(): Product[] {
        if (this.repo.products != null && this.repo.products.length > 0) {
            let pageIndex = (this.repo.pagination.currentPage - 1)
                * this.repo.pagination.productsPerPage;
            return this.repo.products.slice(pageIndex,
                pageIndex + this.repo.pagination.productsPerPage);
        }
    }

    addToCart(product: Product) {
        this.cart.addProduct(product);
    }
}
```

The constructor receives a Cart object, whose addProduct method is called by the component's addToCart method.

Creating the Cart Summary Component

The first cart-related component will appear at the top of the product list and show the number of products that the user has in the cart and their total cost. Make the changes to the cartSummary.component.ts file in the store folder, as shown in Listing 9-6.

Listing 9-6. Adding Code in the cartSummary.component.ts File in the ClientApp/app/store Folder

```
import { Component } from "@angular/core";
import { Cart } from "../models/cart.model";

@Component({
    selector: "store-cartsummary",
    templateUrl: "cartSummary.component.html"
})
export class CartSummaryComponent {

    constructor(private cart: Cart) { }

    get itemCount(): number {
        return this.cart.itemCount;
    }

    get totalPrice(): number {
        return this.cart.totalPrice;
    }
}
```

The new constructor declares a dependency on the Cart class, which will be resolved using the service defined in Listing 9-5 and which is used to provide the values for the read-only itemCount and totalPrice properties. To display a summary of the cart to the user, replace the placeholder content in the component's template with the elements shown in Listing 9-7.

Listing 9-7. The cartSummary.component.html File in the ClientApp/app/store Folder

```
<div class="text-right p-1">
    <small *ngIf="itemCount > 0; else empty">
        ({{ itemCount }} item(s) {{ totalPrice | currency:"USD":true }})
    </small>
    <button class="btn btn-sm ml-1"
            [disabled]="itemCount == 0"
            routerLink="/cart">
        <i class="fa fa-shopping-cart"></i>
    </button>
</div>

<ng-template #empty>
    <small class="text-muted">
        (cart is empty)
    </small>
</ng-template>
```

This template uses features shown in earlier examples to present a summary of the cart to the user. The ngIf directive is used to change the content displayed to the user based on the number of items in the shopping cart. If there are no items, the empty template is displayed. If the cart contains items, then the number and total cost are shown instead.

There is a `button` element that uses a Font Awesome icon for a shopping cart and that is configured with a data binding on the `disable` attribute like this:

```
...
<button class="btn btn-sm ml-1" [disabled]="itemCount == 0" routerLink="/cart">
...
```

This data binding disables the button when there are no items in the cart. The button element has also been configured with the `routerLink` attribute so that the application will navigate to the `/cart` URL when the button is clicked. This URL is not yet defined, but it will display a details list of the cart contents and allow the user to start the checkout process.

Save the changes and reload the application in the browser to see the cart summary. The summary will indicate that the cart is empty until you click the Add to Cart button for one or more products, after which the number of items in the cart and their cost will be displayed, as shown in Figure 9-2.

Figure 9-2. *Displaying the cart summary*

Displaying the Cart Detail

The next step is to create the component that will display a detailed view of the cart, allowing the user to make changes to the quantities of each product, to remove products from the cart, and to commence the checkout process. Create a TypeScript file called `cartDetail.component.ts` in the `store` folder and add the code shown in Listing 9-8.

Listing 9-8. The Contents of the cartDetail.component.ts File in the ClientApp/app/store Folder

```
import { Component } from "@angular/core";
import { Cart } from "../models/cart.model";

@Component({
    templateUrl: "cartDetail.component.html"
})
export class CartDetailComponent {

    constructor(public cart: Cart) { }
}
```

This component defines a constructor Cart parameter that is used to create a cart property that can be accessed by the template. To create the template, create an HTML file called cartDetail.component.html in the store folder with the content shown in Listing 9-9.

■ **Tip**   Notice that the decorator for this component doesn't define a selector property. A selector is required only when you want Angular to apply the component to a specific HTML element in an HTML template and can be omitted if the component is going to be displayed only in a router-outlet element by the URL routing system.

Listing 9-9. The Contents of the cartDetail.component.html File in the ClientApp/app/store Folder

```
<div class="navbar bg-inverse ">
    <a class="navbar-brand text-white">SPORTS STORE</a>
</div>

<div class="m-1">
    <h2 class="text-center">Your Cart</h2>
    <table class="table table-bordered table-striped p-1">
        <thead>
            <tr>
                <th>Quantity</th><th>Product</th>
                <th class="text-right">Price</th>
                <th class="text-right">Subtotal</th>
            </tr>
        </thead>
        <tbody>
            <tr *ngIf="cart.selections.length == 0">
                <td colspan="4" class="text-xs-center">
                    Your cart is empty
                </td>
            </tr>
            <tr *ngFor="let sel of cart.selections">
                <td>
                    <input type="number" class="form-control-sm"
                            style="width:5em" [(ngModel)]="sel.quantity" />
                </td>
```

```
            <td>{{sel.name}}</td>
            <td class="text-right">
                {{sel.price | currency:"USD":true:"2.2-2"}}
            </td>
            <td class="text-right">
                {{(sel.quantity * sel.price) | currency:"USD":true:"2.2-2" }}
            </td>
            <td class="text-center">
                <button class="btn btn-sm btn-danger"
                        (click)="cart.updateQuantity(sel.productId, 0)">
                    Remove
                </button>
            </td>
        </tr>
    </tbody>
    <tfoot>
        <tr>
            <td colspan="3" class="text-right">Total:</td>
            <td class="text-right">
                {{cart.totalPrice | currency:"USD":true:"2.2-2"}}
            </td>
        </tr>
    </tfoot>
</table>
</div>
<div class="text-center">
    <button class="btn btn-primary" routerLink="/store">Continue Shopping</button>
    <button class="btn btn-secondary" routerLink="/checkout"
            [disabled]="cart.selections.length == 0">
        Checkout
    </button>
</div>
```

The HTML elements in the template list the contents of the cart, along with the subtotal for each item and the overall total. This is done using standard data bindings (denoted by the {{ and }} characters), built-in directives (ngFor and ngIf), and pipes (for formatting currency amounts). There is one new feature in this template, which allows the user to change the quantity of a product in the cart by changing the value in an input element, like this:

```
...
<input type="number" class="form-control-sm"
    style="width:5em" [(ngModel)]="sel.quantity" />
...
```

This is a two-way data binding, which means that a single binding can read a data value and modify it. Two-way data bindings are used with form elements and are denoted by square brackets and parentheses ([(and)]), which is known as the "banana in a box," where the parentheses are the banana and the square brackets are the box. Two-way data bindings are most frequently used with the ngModel directive, which knows how to set the value displayed by form elements and which events to listen to in order to detect a change. The expression used with the ngModel binding specifies the property whose value will be displayed by the form element and which will be updated when the user makes a change. In this case, the quantity property of the product selection is specified.

195

To make the component available for use in the application, register it in the store feature module, as shown in Listing 9-10.

Listing 9-10. Registering a Component in the store.module.ts File in the ClientApp/app/store Folder

```
import { NgModule } from "@angular/core";
import { BrowserModule } from '@angular/platform-browser';
import { CartSummaryComponent } from "./cartSummary.component";
import { CategoryFilterComponent } from "./categoryFilter.component";
import { PaginationComponent } from "./pagination.component";
import { ProductListComponent } from "./productList.component";
import { RatingsComponent } from "./ratings.component";
import { ProductSelectionComponent } from "./productSelection.component";
import { CartDetailComponent } from "./cartDetail.component";
import { RouterModule } from "@angular/router";
import { FormsModule } from "@angular/forms";

@NgModule({
    declarations: [CartSummaryComponent, CategoryFilterComponent,
        PaginationComponent, ProductListComponent, RatingsComponent,
        ProductSelectionComponent, CartDetailComponent],
    imports: [BrowserModule, RouterModule, FormsModule],
    exports: [ProductSelectionComponent]
})
export class StoreModule { }
```

In addition to adding the CartDetailComponent class to the NgModule decorator's declarations property, this listing also adds two of the Angular modules to the imports property. The RouterModule is required because there are button elements in the template in Listing 9-9 to which the routerLink directive has been applied, but this won't work if the RouterModule isn't imported into the component's feature module. The FormsModule is required to enable the ngModel directive, which is used in the two-way data binding that allows the user to change product quantities.

To create the URL route that will display the cart detail, add the configuration entry to the routing configuration, as shown in Listing 9-11.

Listing 9-11. Adding a Route in the app.routing.ts File in the ClientApp/app Folder

```
import { Routes, RouterModule } from "@angular/router";
import { ProductSelectionComponent } from "./store/productSelection.component";
import { CartDetailComponent } from "./store/cartDetail.component";

const routes: Routes = [
    { path: "cart", component: CartDetailComponent },
    { path: "store", component: ProductSelectionComponent },
    { path: "", component: ProductSelectionComponent }]

export const RoutingConfig = RouterModule.forRoot(routes);
```

Reload the application and click one of the Add to Cart buttons to add something to the cart. Click the cart icon at the top of the page to navigate to the /cart URL, which shows the detailed view of the cart, as shown in Figure 9-3.

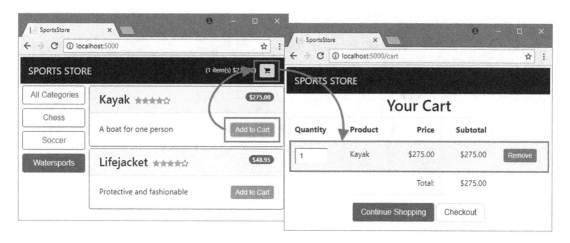

Figure 9-3. *Displaying the cart detail*

The two-way data binding allows the user to change the quantity for a product using the input element. If you change the value 1 in the input element to 5, for example, the subtotal and total will be updated to reflect the change, as shown in Figure 9-4.

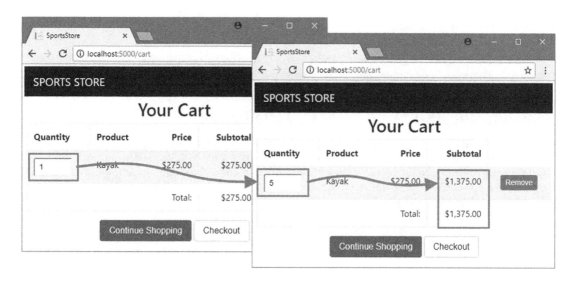

Figure 9-4. *Changing a product quantity*

Storing Carts

There is a hidden problem with the way that the cart works at the moment. To see the issue, add some products to the cart and then reload the browser window. The Angular application is reloaded, which means that the contents of the cart are lost, as shown in Figure 9-5.

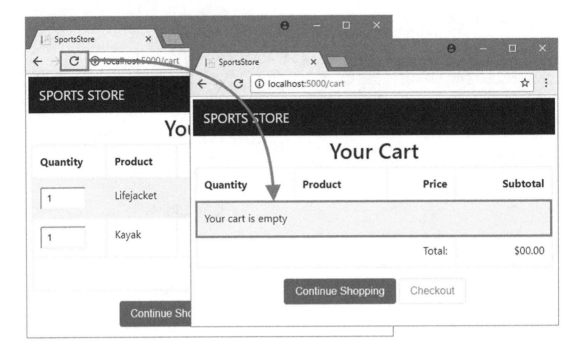

Figure 9-5. *The effect of reloading the browser window*

In the sections that follow, I demonstrate how to store the cart data using the ASP.NET Core MVC session data feature and explain how this can be used to prevent the problem shown in Figure 9-5.

Extending the ASP.NET Core MVC Data Model

The first step is to define a C# model class that will represent a cart. The mechanism that I will use to store the data can be used to store any string data but using a C# class and the MVC model binding feature will ensure only cart data can be stored, preventing this feature from being abused to store any arbitrary data that a client sends. Add a new C# class file called CartProductSelection.cs to the Models folder and use it to define the class shown in Listing 9-12.

Listing 9-12. The Contents of the CartProductSelection.cs File in the Models Folder

```
namespace SportsStore.Models {

    public class ProductSelection {
        public long productId { get; set; }
        public string name { get; set; }
        public decimal price { get; set; }
        public int quantity { get; set; }
    }
}
```

This class will allow the MVC model binder to process the data sent by the client and represent each product that the user has added to the cart.

> ■ **Tip** Notice that the property names start with lowercase letters in Listing 9-12. This is to ensure that the Angular application can parse the JSON session data correctly and is required when working directly with JSON strings rather than .NET objects.

Creating the Cart Storage Web Service

The next step is to create an HTTP web service that will allow the client to send cart data to ASP.NET Core MVC to be stored. The web service will store the data using the ASP.NET Core MVC session data feature, which will automatically manage the life of the data. Not all cart data will result in completed purchases, and using session data will ensure that abandoned cart data will automatically expire and, as you will see, make it simple to provide the client with its client data when the user reloads the browser.

Installing the NuGet Packages

Add the NuGet packages shown in Listing 9-13 to install the ASP.NET Core MVC support for session data. (If you are using Visual Studio, right-click the SportsStore project item in the Solution Explorer and select Edit SportsStore.csproj from the pop-up menu).

Listing 9-13. Adding Packages in the SportsStore.csproj File in the SportsStore Folder

```
<Project Sdk="Microsoft.NET.Sdk.Web">
  <PropertyGroup>
    <TargetFramework>netcoreapp1.1</TargetFramework>
  </PropertyGroup>
  <ItemGroup>
    <PackageReference Include="Microsoft.AspNetCore" Version="1.1.1" />
    <PackageReference Include="Microsoft.AspNetCore.Mvc" Version="1.1.2" />
    <PackageReference Include="Microsoft.AspNetCore.SpaServices" Version="1.1.0" />
    <PackageReference Include="Microsoft.AspNetCore.StaticFiles" Version="1.1.1" />
    <PackageReference Include="Microsoft.EntityFrameworkCore" Version="1.1.1" />
    <PackageReference Include="Microsoft.EntityFrameworkCore.Design"
        Version="1.1.1" />
    <PackageReference Include="Microsoft.EntityFrameworkCore.SqlServer"
        Version="1.1.1" />
    <PackageReference Include="Microsoft.Extensions.Logging.Debug" Version="1.1.1" />
    <PackageReference Include="Microsoft.VisualStudio.Web.BrowserLink"
        Version="1.1.0" />
    <DotNetCliToolReference Include="Microsoft.EntityFrameworkCore.Tools"
        Version="1.0.0" />
    <DotNetCliToolReference Include="Microsoft.EntityFrameworkCore.Tools.DotNet"
        Version="1.0.0" />
    <PackageReference Include="Microsoft.AspNetCore.Session" Version="1.1.1" />
    <PackageReference Include="Microsoft.Extensions.Caching.SqlServer"
        Version="1.1.1" />
    <DotNetCliToolReference Include="Microsoft.Extensions.Caching.SqlConfig.Tools"
        Version="1.0.1" />
  </ItemGroup>
</Project>
```

Save the changes to the file. If you are using Visual Studio, then the new packages will be downloaded automatically. If you are using Visual Studio Code, run the command shown in Listing 9-14 in the SportsStore project to download the new packages.

Listing 9-14. Installing New Packages

```
dotnet restore
```

Preparing the Database

The next step is to prepare the database so that it can be used to store session data. Run the command shown in Listing 9-15 in the SportsStore folder.

■ **Note**   ASP.NET Core MVC can store its session data in a number of ways, including using an in-memory store. I have chosen SQL Server for this example because it simplifies the infrastructure required to deploy the application. The in-memory option means that each ASP.NET Core MVC server has its own session data and requires that HTTP requests from a single client are always handled by the same server. Using a database allows ASP.NET Core MVC to share session data and means that any server can handle any request.

Listing 9-15. Creating the Session Database Schema

```
dotnet sql-cache create "Server=localhost,5100;Database=SportsStore;User Id=sa;
Password=mySecret123;MultipleActiveResultSets=true" "dbo" "SessionData"
```

The dotnet sql-cache command sets up the schema and required arguments for the connection string, the schema (a SQL Server feature that groups related database together), and the name of the table that will be used to store session data. The connection string is the same one specified in the appsettings. json file and must be copied exactly and entered on a single line. The schema argument is dbo (which is the default value used by SQL Server), and the final argument is SessionData.

Configuring the ASP.NET Core MVC Application

To set up the ASP.NET Core MVC to use the session database, add the statements shown in Listing 9-16 to the Startup class.

■ **Note**   You may find that Visual Studio and Visual Studio Code highlight the additions in Listing 9-16 as errors. This problem will be resolved if you restart the IDE and open the SportsStore project again.

Listing 9-16. Configuring Session Data in the Startup.cs File in the SportsStore Folder

```
using Microsoft.AspNetCore.Builder;
using Microsoft.AspNetCore.Hosting;
using Microsoft.Extensions.Configuration;
using Microsoft.Extensions.DependencyInjection;
using Microsoft.Extensions.Logging;
```

```csharp
using Microsoft.AspNetCore.SpaServices.Webpack;
using SportsStore.Models;
using Microsoft.EntityFrameworkCore;
using Newtonsoft.Json;

namespace SportsStore {
    public class Startup {
        public Startup(IHostingEnvironment env) {
            var builder = new ConfigurationBuilder()
              .SetBasePath(env.ContentRootPath)
              .AddJsonFile("appsettings.json", optional: false, reloadOnChange: true)
              .AddJsonFile($"appsettings.{env.EnvironmentName}.json", optional: true)
              .AddEnvironmentVariables();
            Configuration = builder.Build();
        }

        public IConfigurationRoot Configuration { get; }

        public void ConfigureServices(IServiceCollection services) {
            services.AddDbContext<DataContext>(options =>
                options.UseSqlServer(Configuration
                    ["Data:Products:ConnectionString"]));
            services.AddMvc().AddJsonOptions(opts => {
                opts.SerializerSettings.ReferenceLoopHandling
                    = ReferenceLoopHandling.Serialize;
                opts.SerializerSettings.NullValueHandling = NullValueHandling.Ignore;
            });

            services.AddDistributedSqlServerCache(options => {
                options.ConnectionString =
                    Configuration["Data:Products:ConnectionString"];
                options.SchemaName = "dbo";
                options.TableName = "SessionData";
            });

            services.AddSession(options => {
                options.CookieName = "SportsStore.Session";
                options.IdleTimeout = System.TimeSpan.FromHours(48);
                options.CookieHttpOnly = false;
            });
        }

        public void Configure(IApplicationBuilder app,
                IHostingEnvironment env, ILoggerFactory loggerFactory) {
            loggerFactory.AddConsole(Configuration.GetSection("Logging"));
            loggerFactory.AddDebug();

            app.UseDeveloperExceptionPage();
            app.UseWebpackDevMiddleware(new WebpackDevMiddlewareOptions {
                HotModuleReplacement = true
            });
```

```
        app.UseStaticFiles();
        app.UseSession();
        app.UseMvc(routes => {
            routes.MapRoute(
                name: "default",
                template: "{controller=Home}/{action=Index}/{id?}");

            routes.MapSpaFallbackRoute("angular-fallback",
                new { controller = "Home", action = "Index" });
        });

        SeedData.SeedDatabase(app.ApplicationServices
            .GetRequiredService<DataContext>());
    }
  }
}
```

The AddDistributedSqlServerCache extension method tells ASP.NET Core MVC to use SQL Server as a data cache, with configuration options that correspond to the arguments used on the command line in Listing 9-15.

The AddSession extension method sets up session state and configures the cookie that will be used to identify sessions. The configuration options set the name of the cookie to SportsStore.Session, with an expiry period of 48 hours. The CookieHttpOnly property must be set to false so that it will be accessible to the Angular application.

Creating the Web Service Controller

Now that ASP.NET Core MVC has been configured to use session data, it is time to create the web service that will allow the Angular application to store its cart data. Add a C# class file called SessionValuesController.cs in the Controllers folder and use it to define the class shown in Listing 9-17.

Listing 9-17. The Contents of the SessionValuesController.cs File in the Controllers Folder

```
using Microsoft.AspNetCore.Http;
using Microsoft.AspNetCore.Mvc;
using Newtonsoft.Json;
using SportsStore.Models;

namespace SportsStore.Controllers {

    [Route("/api/session")]
    public class SessionValuesController : Controller {

        [HttpGet("cart")]
        public IActionResult GetCart() {
            return Ok(HttpContext.Session.GetString("cart"));
        }
```

```
[HttpPost("cart")]
public void StoreCart([FromBody] ProductSelection[] products) {
    var jsonData = JsonConvert.SerializeObject(products);
    HttpContext.Session.SetString("cart", jsonData);
    }
  }
}
```

This controller defines actions that can be targeted with HTTP GET and POST requests, allowing cart data to be retrieved and stored. Within the action methods, session data is accessed through the HttpContext.Session property, with the GetString and SetString extension methods being used to read and write string data.

The StoreCart action method defines a ProductSelection array parameter that has been decorated with the FromBody attribute so that the MVC model binder will read the data from the body of the HTTP request. The data is then converted back into JSON and then stored as session data, which will be written to the SQL database. The process of parsing JSON data into a .NET object and then serializing back into JSON ensures that clients can't store arbitrary data.

Storing and Retrieving Cart Data

Now that the ASP.NET Core MVC part of the project can store cart data, I can modify the Angular application so that it sends an HTTP POST request to the server whenever the user makes a change to the cart. Add new methods to the Repository class so that it can get and create session data, as shown in Listing 9-18.

Listing 9-18. Handling Session Data in the repository.ts File in the ClientApp/app/models Folder

```
import { Product } from "./product.model";
import { Injectable } from "@angular/core";
import { Http, RequestMethod, Request, Response } from "@angular/http";
import { Observable } from "rxjs/Observable";
import "rxjs/add/operator/map";
import { Supplier } from "./supplier.model";
import { Filter, Pagination } from "./configClasses.repository";

const productsUrl = "/api/products";
const suppliersUrl = "/api/suppliers";

@Injectable()
export class Repository {
    private filterObject = new Filter();
    private paginationObject = new Pagination();

    constructor(private http: Http) {
        this.filter.related = true;
        this.getProducts();
    }
```

```
// ...other methods and properties omitted for brevity...

storeSessionData(dataType: string, data: any) {
    return this.sendRequest(RequestMethod.Post, "/api/session/" + dataType, data)
        .subscribe(response => { });
}

getSessionData(dataType: string): Observable<any> {
    return this.sendRequest(RequestMethod.Get, "/api/session/" + dataType);
}
}
```

The storeSessionData and getSessionData methods send requests that target the web service URLs defined in Listing 9-17 to store and retrieve session data. These methods are not specific to dealing with carts because I am going to use the same features to store other kinds of data later in this chapter.

▪ **Tip**   The Http class won't send a request until the subscribe method is called. This is why the subscribe method is called in the storeSessionData method in Listing 9-18, even though the result is discarded.

To deal specifically with cart data, make the changes to the Cart class shown in Listing 9-19.

Listing 9-19. Persisting Cart Data in the cart.model.ts File in the ClientApp/app/models Folder

```
import { Injectable } from "@angular/core";
import { Product } from "./product.model";
import { Repository } from "./repository";

@Injectable()
export class Cart {
    selections: ProductSelection[] = [];
    itemCount: number = 0;
    totalPrice: number = 0;

    constructor(private repo: Repository) {
        repo.getSessionData("cart").subscribe(cartData => {
            if (cartData != null) {
                cartData.map(item => new ProductSelection(this, item.productId,
                    item.name, item.price, item.quantity))
                    .forEach(item => this.selections.push(item));
                this.update(false);
            }
        });
    }

    // ...other methods omitted for brevity...

    update(storeData: boolean = true) {
        this.itemCount = this.selections.map(ps => ps.quantity)
            .reduce((prev, curr) => prev + curr, 0);
        this.totalPrice = this.selections.map(ps => ps.price * ps.quantity)
            .reduce((prev, curr) => prev + curr, 0);
```

```
    if (storeData) {
        this.repo.storeSessionData("cart", this.selections.map(s => {
            return {
                productId: s.productId, name: s.name,
                price: s.price, quantity: s.quantity
            }
        }));
    }
}
}
```

The constructor receives a Repository object through dependency injection, which is used to get any stored cart data for the user's session. If there is data available, it is used to populate the cart, and the update method is called in order to update the properties that are used in data bindings and, in doing so, trigger Angular to reevaluate those bindings to present the modified cart to the user.

The update method uses the Repository to store the cart as session data whenever there is a change. The structure of the Cart class makes it easy to use with the ngModel directive but will create a loop reference loop when serialized, so I use the JavaScript array map method to select the properties that should be sent to the server and stored. The Angular application doesn't check the result returned by the web service when session data is stored, producing a fire-and-forget effect.

To see the effect, restart the ASP.NET Core MVC application and use a browser to request the URL http://localhost:5000. Use the Add to Cart buttons to select some products, click the cart icon at the top of the window, and then reload the browser window. Now that the cart data is stored using the ASP.NET Core MVC session feature, reloading the browser doesn't clear the cart, as shown in Figure 9-6. ASP.NET Core MVC adds a cookie to responses, which the browser includes in subsequent HTTP requests, allowing the Angular application to store and retrieve its cart data.

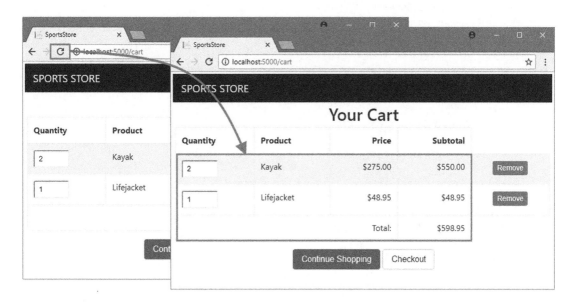

Figure 9-6. *The effect of storing cart data*

Creating the Checkout Process

In the sections that follow, I extend both the ASP.NET Core MVC and Angular parts of the project to support the checkout process and allow the user to complete an order. In a real project, this would include integration with a payment system, but for simplicity, I am going to leave a placeholder for payment in the SportsStore application. Payment systems are country specific and typically require bank account details and anti-money-laundering checks to be performed, all of which is beyond the scope of this book.

■ **Caution**   I store payment detail in the SportsStore database in the sections that follow. This won't always be allowed by your payment provider or local laws. If you do store payment data, then you should pay particular attention to security to avoid leaking sensitive data.

Extending the ASP.NET Core MVC Data Model

Most of the work for the checkout process will be done by the Angular application, but the ASP.NET Core MVC part of the project will be responsible for validating the payment details provided by the user and storing orders at the end of the checkout process.

Create a C# file called Order.cs in the Models folder and add the code shown in Listing 9-20 to create a model class that will represent a user's order.

Listing 9-20. The Contents of the Order.cs File in the Models Folder

```
using Microsoft.AspNetCore.Mvc.ModelBinding;
using System.Collections.Generic;
using System.ComponentModel.DataAnnotations;

namespace SportsStore.Models {

    public class Order {

        [BindNever]
        public long OrderId { get; set; }
        [Required]
        public string Name { get; set; }

        public IEnumerable<CartLine> Products { get; set; }

        [Required]
        public string Address{ get; set; }
        [Required]
        public Payment Payment { get; set; }
        [BindNever]
        public bool Shipped { get; set; } = false;
    }
```

```
public class Payment {
    [BindNever]
    public long PaymentId { get; set; }
    [Required]
    public string CardNumber { get; set; }
    [Required]
    public string CardExpiry { get; set; }
    [Required]
    public int CardSecurityCode { get; set; }
    [BindNever]
    public decimal Total { get; set; }
    [BindNever]
    public string AuthCode { get; set; }
}

public class CartLine {
    [BindNever]
    public long CartLineId { get; set; }
    [Required]
    public long ProductId { get; set; }
    [Required]
    public int Quantity { get; set; }
}
}
```

This is a simplified representation of an order that will let me demonstrate the process for capturing the data without getting bogged down in the details.

■ **Tip**   Notice that the CartLine class doesn't use Product objects to represent a user's selection. This is because Entity Framework Core would try to add a column to the Products table to relate Product objects to CartLine objects, which is not the relationship that the application requires since a single Product can be used in multiple CartLine objects. To avoid this problem, I store just the ProductId value, which can then be used as a key in a query for the Product data.

Creating a New Entity Framework Core Migration

Orders will be stored in the database, which means that Entity Framework Core must be configured so that it knows about Order objects. Edit the database context class to add the property shown in Listing 9-21.

Listing 9-21. Adding a Property in the DataContext.cs File in the Models Folder

```
using Microsoft.EntityFrameworkCore;
using Microsoft.EntityFrameworkCore.Metadata;

namespace SportsStore.Models {
```

```
    public class DataContext : DbContext {

        public DataContext(DbContextOptions<DataContext> opts)
            : base(opts) { }

        public DbSet<Product> Products { get; set; }
        public DbSet<Supplier> Suppliers { get; set; }
        public DbSet<Rating> Ratings { get; set; }
        public DbSet<Order> Orders { get; set; }

        protected override void OnModelCreating(ModelBuilder modelBuilder) {
            modelBuilder.Entity<Product>().HasMany<Rating>(p => p.Ratings)
                .WithOne(r => r.Product).OnDelete(DeleteBehavior.Cascade);
            modelBuilder.Entity<Product>().HasOne<Supplier>(p => p.Supplier)
                .WithMany(s => s.Products).OnDelete(DeleteBehavior.SetNull);
        }
    }
}
```

Open a new command prompt and run the command shown in Listing 9-22 in the SportsStore folder to generate the database that will allow Entity Framework Core to store Order objects in the database.

Listing 9-22. Creating a Database Migration

```
dotnet ef migrations add Orders
```

The migration that this command creates will update the database schema when the ASP.NET Core MVC application is restarted and allow Order data to be stored.

Creating the ASP.NET Core MVC Web Service

To allow Order objects to be accessed by the Angular application, add a new C# class file called OrderValuesController.cs in the Controllers folder and use it to define the web service controller shown in Listing 9-23.

Listing 9-23. The Contents of the OrderValuesController.cs File in the Controllers Folder

```
using Microsoft.AspNetCore.Mvc;
using Microsoft.EntityFrameworkCore;
using SportsStore.Models;
using System.Collections.Generic;
using System.Linq;

namespace SportsStore.Controllers {

    [Route("/api/orders")]
    public class OrderValuesController : Controller {
        private DataContext context;

        public OrderValuesController(DataContext ctx) {
            context = ctx;
        }
```

```csharp
    [HttpGet]
    public IEnumerable<Order> GetOrders() {
        return context.Orders
            .Include(o => o.Products).Include(o => o.Payment);
    }

    [HttpPost("{id}")]
    public void MarkShipped(long id) {
        Order order = context.Orders.Find(id);
        if (order != null) {
            order.Shipped = true;
            context.SaveChanges();
        }
    }

    [HttpPost]
    public IActionResult CreateOrder([FromBody] Order order) {
        if (ModelState.IsValid) {

            order.OrderId = 0;
            order.Shipped = false;
            order.Payment.Total = GetPrice(order.Products);

            ProcessPayment(order.Payment);
            if (order.Payment.AuthCode != null) {
                context.Add(order);
                context.SaveChanges();
                return Ok(new {
                    orderId = order.OrderId,
                    authCode = order.Payment.AuthCode,
                    amount = order.Payment.Total
                });
            } else {
                return BadRequest("Payment rejected");
            }
        }
        return BadRequest(ModelState);
    }

    private decimal GetPrice(IEnumerable<CartLine> lines) {
        IEnumerable<long> ids = lines.Select(l => l.ProductId);
        return context.Products
            .Where(p => ids.Contains(p.ProductId))
            .Select(p => lines
                .First(l => l.ProductId == p.ProductId).Quantity * p.Price)
            .Sum();
    }

    private void ProcessPayment(Payment payment) {
        // integrate your payment system here
        payment.AuthCode = "12345";
    }
    }
}
```

This controller supports HTTP POST requests to create new orders in the CreateOrder method, relying on the MVC model binding feature to create a .NET Order object, which is checked using the model validation process.

Notice that the CreateOrder method calls the GetPrice method, which queries the database to get the prices for the products selected by the user to determine the total cost of the order. It is important not to trust the client to provide critical information because it is easy for a malicious user to craft an HTTP request that contains arbitrary data, such as specifying the cost of all products as $1.

The CreateOrder method calls the ProcessPayment method to process payment for the order. This is where you would integrate a payment system into the project, but this method simply returns a placeholder authorization code that is returned to the client, along with the transaction amount and the ID value used to store the order in the database.

Creating the Angular Checkout Process

Now that the back-end services are in place, the next step is to extend the Angular application so that it can get the data required to create an order that is submitted to the ASP.NET Core MVC part of the project. In the sections that follow, I create a model class that will represent the order. I will also create a component that uses HTML form elements to get the required data from the user and sends it using an HTTP POST request.

Extending the Angular Data Model

To describe the order that will be sent to the server, add a TypeScript file called order.model.ts in the models folder and add the code shown in Listing 9-24.

Listing 9-24. The Contents of the order.model.ts File in the ClientApp/app/models Folder

```
import { Injectable } from "@angular/core";
import { Cart } from "./cart.model";
import { Repository } from "./repository";

@Injectable()
export class Order {

    constructor(private repo: Repository, public cart: Cart) { }

    orderId: number;
    name: string;
    address: string;
    payment: Payment = new Payment();

    submitted: boolean = false;
    shipped: boolean = false;
    orderConfirmation: OrderConfirmation;

    get products(): CartLine[] {
        return this.cart.selections
            .map(p => new CartLine(p.productId, p.quantity));
    }
}
```

```
    clear() {
        this.name = null;
        this.address = null;
        this.payment = new Payment();
        this.cart.clear();
        this.submitted = false;
    }

    submit() {
        this.submitted = true;
        this.repo.createOrder(this);
    }
}

export class Payment {
    cardNumber: string;
    cardExpiry: string;
    cardSecurityCode: string;
}

export class CartLine {

    constructor(private productId: number,
        private quantity: number) { }
}

export class OrderConfirmation {

    constructor(public orderId: number,
        public authCode: string,
        public amount: number) { }
}
```

Checkout processes can be complex, and I am going make it easier for the user by presenting them with a series of individual steps that solicit the different pieces of information required to create the order. To make this easier to code, the Order and Payment classes defines properties outside of its constructor, which means that I will be able to use data bindings to build up the data gradually.

The Order class defines a submit method that will send the data to the server using a method called createOrder defined by the Repository class, which is shown in Listing 9-25.

Listing 9-25. Creating Orders in the repository.ts File in the ClientApp/app/models Folder

```
import { Product } from "./product.model";
import { Injectable } from "@angular/core";
import { Http, RequestMethod, Request, Response } from "@angular/http";
import { Observable } from "rxjs/Observable";
import "rxjs/add/operator/map";
import { Supplier } from "./supplier.model";
import { Filter, Pagination } from "./configClasses.repository";
import { Order } from "./order.model";
```

```
const productsUrl = "/api/products";
const suppliersUrl = "/api/suppliers";
const ordersUrl = "/api/orders";

@Injectable()
export class Repository {
    private filterObject = new Filter();
    private paginationObject = new Pagination();

    constructor(private http: Http) {
        this.filter.related = true;
        this.getProducts();
    }

    // ...other methods and properties omitted for brevity...

    getOrders() {
        this.sendRequest(RequestMethod.Get, ordersUrl)
            .subscribe(data => this.orders = data);
    }

    createOrder(order: Order) {
        this.sendRequest(RequestMethod.Post, ordersUrl, {
            name: order.name,
            address: order.address,
            payment: order.payment,
            products: order.products
        }).subscribe(data => {
            order.orderConfirmation = data
            order.cart.clear();
            order.clear();
        });
    }

    shipOrder(order: Order) {
        this.sendRequest(RequestMethod.Post, ordersUrl + "/" + order.orderId)
            .subscribe(r => this.getOrders())
    }

    product: Product;
    products: Product[];
    suppliers: Supplier[] = [];
    categories: string[] = [];
    orders: Order[] = [];

    get filter(): Filter {
        return this.filterObject;
    }

    get pagination(): Pagination {
        return this.paginationObject;
    }
}
```

The new method sends a POST request to the /api/orders URL with a data payload that the MVC model binder will be easily able to process. The response from the web service is assigned to the orderConfirmation property of the Order object, which I will present to the user when the checkout process is complete.

To ensure that a single Order object is used through the checkout process, register a new service, as shown in Listing 9-26.

Listing 9-26. Registering a Service in the model.module.ts File in the ClientApp/app/models Folder

```
import { NgModule } from "@angular/core";
import { Repository } from "./repository";
import { Cart } from "./cart.model";
import { Order } from "./order.model";

@NgModule({
    providers: [Repository, Cart, Order]
})
export class ModelModule { }
```

The addition of the Order class to the model feature module's providers property will allow other parts of the application to declare Order constructor parameters that will be resolved using dependency injection.

Creating the Checkout Components

To provide the user with the HTML forms that will be required to complete the checkout process, I am going to create a series of Angular components, each of which will present a single set of form elements, and navigate between them using the URL routing system. In the sections that follow, I create the components and use them to build up the data required to send an order to the ASP.NET Core MVC part of the project.

Creating the Checkout Details Component

The first component will ask the user to provide their name and address. Create a store/checkout folder for the Angular application and add to it a TypeScript file called checkoutDetails.component.ts, with the code shown in Listing 9-27.

Listing 9-27. The checkoutDetails.component.ts File in the ClientApp/app/store/checkout Folder

```
import { Component } from "@angular/core";
import { Router } from "@angular/router";
import { Order } from "../../models/order.model";

@Component({
    templateUrl: "checkoutDetails.component.html"
})
export class CheckoutDetailsComponent {

    constructor(private router: Router,
                public order: Order) {
        if (order.products.length == 0) {
            this.router.navigateByUrl("/cart");
        }
    }
}
```

The component defines a constructor that receives an Order object through dependency injection so that it can be accessed in the template. It also receives a Router object, which is used to navigate to the shopping cart if the user navigates directly to the component without having selected any products.

To create the template, add a file called checkoutDetails.component.html in the store/checkout folder, with the content shown in Listing 9-28.

Listing 9-28. The checkoutDetails.component.html File in the ClientApp/app/store/checkout Folder

```html
<div class="navbar bg-inverse ">
    <a class="navbar-brand text-white">SPORTS STORE</a>
</div>

<h2 class="text-center mt-1">Step 1: Your Details</h2>

<form novalidate #detailsForm="ngForm">
    <div class="form-group">
        <label>Name</label>
        <input #name="ngModel" name="name" class="form-control"
                [(ngModel)]="order.name" required />
        <div *ngIf="name.invalid" class="text-danger">
            Please enter your name
        </div>
    </div>
    <div class="form-group">
        <label>Address</label>
        <input #address="ngModel" name="street" class="form-control"
                [(ngModel)]="order.address" required />
        <div *ngIf="address.invalid" class="text-danger">
            Please enter your address
        </div>
    </div>
    <div class="text-center pt-2">
        <button class="btn btn-outline-primary" routerLink="/cart">Back</button>
        <button class="btn btn-danger" [disabled]="detailsForm.invalid"
                routerLink="/checkout/step2">
            Next
        </button>
    </div>
</form>
```

This template takes advantage of the features that Angular provides for managing HTML forms and validating the data that users enter. Two-way data bindings, defined using the ngModel directive and the banana-in-a-box brackets, tell Angular which data value should be associated with the input element, like this:

```html
...
<input #name="ngModel" name="name" class="form-control"
    [(ngModel)]="order.name" required />
...
```

This data binding creates a two-way binding on the component's order.name property, which will be used to set the value of the input element and updated when the user enters a value.

To support data validation, Angular uses the standard HTML validation attributes, which are applied to input elements like this:

```
...
<input #name="ngModel" name="name" class="form-control"
    [(ngModel)]="order.name" required />
...
```

The required attribute specifies that a value is required for this input element. To allow the validation status of the input element to be inspected, the #name attribute is used to create a variable, called name and assigned the value ngModel, which can be used elsewhere in the template. In this case, a validation message is displayed alongside the element, like this:

```
...
<div *ngIf="name.invalid" class="text-danger">Please enter your name</div>
...
```

The name variable is assigned an object that defines invalid and valid properties that indicate whether the contents of the element meet the validation constraints that have been applied to it. In this case, the invalid property is used with an ngIf directive to display a message.

▓ **Caution**   Do not apply the ASP.NET Core MVC client-side validation attributes to HTML elements in an Angular application. Doing so will apply two different validation systems to the same content and cause errors and confusion for users.

The same approach can be used to check the validation status of the entire form. A template variable is declared on the form element like this:

```
...
<form novalidate #detailsForm="ngForm">
...
```

This attribute creates a variable called detailsForm, which is assigned ngForm to provide access to the overall validation status of the form. The same valid and invalid properties are provided, but they reflect the combined status of the individual elements in the form so that, for example, the invalid property will return true if any of the input elements in the form contains an invalid value. These properties can be accessed through the detailsForm to prevent the user from proceeding with the checkout process, like this:

```
...
<button class="btn btn-danger" [disabled]="detailsForm.invalid"
        routerLink="/checkout/step2">Next</button>
...
```

This binding sets the disabled property on the button element such that it will be disabled unless all the input elements in the form meet the validation constraints that have been applied to them.

Creating the Checkout Payment Component

The second step in the checkout process will be to provide payment details. Add a TypeScript file called checkoutPayment.component.ts to the store/checkout folder, with the code shown in Listing 9-29.

Listing 9-29. The checkoutPayment.component.ts File in the ClientApp/app/store/checkout Folder

```
import { Component } from "@angular/core";
import { Router } from "@angular/router";
import { Order } from "../../models/order.model";

@Component({
    templateUrl: "checkoutPayment.component.html"
})
export class CheckoutPaymentComponent {

    constructor(private router: Router,
                public order: Order) {
        if (order.name == null || order.address == null) {
            router.navigateByUrl("/checkout/step1");
        }
    }
}
```

This component follows the same pattern as the one for the previous step in the process and defines a constructor that will provide the template with access to the Order and that uses the Router to return to the previous step if the user has navigated directly without providing a name and address.

COMPONENTS ARE THE BASIC ANGULAR UNIT

To an MVC developer, the process of creating nearly identical classes to provide support for templates can feel awkward since it conflicts with the ASP.NET Core MVC model of a single controller class that can select multiple templates.

The architecture of Angular makes components the basic unit of application functionality, and there is no way to create interchangeable templates that correspond to the way that Razor views work. Although it can feel odd, you should embrace the Angular design philosophy and accept that each template has its own component, even if that component only exists to provide access to a shared service and is largely similar to other components in the same application.

To define the template, create an HTML file called checkoutPayment.component.html in the store/ checkout folder and add the elements shown in Listing 9-30.

Listing 9-30. The checkoutPayment.component.html File in the ClientApp/app/store/checkout Folder

```
<div class="navbar bg-inverse ">
    <a class="navbar-brand text-white">SPORTS STORE</a>
</div>

<h2 class="text-center mt-1">Step 2: Payment</h2>

<form novalidate #paymentForm="ngForm">
    <div class="form-group">
        <label>Card Number</label>
        <input #cardNumber="ngModel" name="cardNumber" class="form-control"
            [(ngModel)]="order.payment.cardNumber" required />
        <div *ngIf="cardNumber.invalid" class="text-danger">
            Please enter your card number
        </div>
    </div>
    <div class="form-group">
        <label>Card Expiry</label>
        <input #cardExpiry="ngModel" name="cardExpiry" class="form-control"
            [(ngModel)]="order.payment.cardExpiry" required />
        <div *ngIf="cardExpiry.invalid" class="text-danger">
            Please enter your card expiry
        </div>
    </div>
    <div class="form-group">
        <label>Security Code</label>
        <input #cardCode="ngModel" name="cardCode" class="form-control"
            [(ngModel)]="order.payment.cardSecurityCode" required />
        <div *ngIf="cardCode.invalid" class="text-danger">
            Please enter your security code
        </div>
    </div>
    <div class="text-center pt-2">
        <button class="btn btn-outline-primary" routerLink="/checkout/step1">
            Back
        </button>
        <button class="btn btn-danger" [disabled]="paymentForm.invalid"
                routerLink="/checkout/step3">Next</button>
    </div>
</form>
```

This template works in the same way as the one in Listing 9-28, except that it is the Payment object whose properties are selected by the two-way data bindings. The button elements that appear at the end of the template allow the user to navigate to the previous stage in the checkout process or progress to the next stage.

Creating the Checkout Summary Component

The third step in the checkout process presents the user with a summary of the order that is about to be placed. Create a TypeScript file called checkoutSummary.component.ts in the store/checkout folder and add the code shown in Listing 9-31.

Listing 9-31. The checkoutSummary.component.ts File in the ClientApp/app/store/checkout Folder

```
import { Component } from "@angular/core";
import { Router } from "@angular/router";
import { Order } from "../../models/order.model";

@Component({
    templateUrl: "checkoutSummary.component.html"
})
export class CheckoutSummaryComponent {

    constructor(private router: Router,
                public order: Order) {
        if (order.payment.cardNumber == null
            || order.payment.cardExpiry == null
            || order.payment.cardSecurityCode == null) {
            router.navigateByUrl("/checkout/step2");
        }
    }

    submitOrder() {
        this.order.submit();
        this.router.navigateByUrl("/checkout/confirmation");
    }
}
```

This component uses its constructor to receive an Order object that will be provided by dependency injection and is accessible to its template, as well as using the Route to navigate away from the summary if the values required by the previous step have not been provided. It also defines a submitOrder method, which sends the order to the web service and navigates to the final step in the process.

To create the template, add an HTML file called checkoutSummary.component.html to the store/checkout folder, with the elements shown in Listing 9-32.

Listing 9-32. The checkoutSummary.component.html File in the ClientApp/app/store/checkout Folder

```
<h2 class="text-center">Summary</h2>

<div class="container">
    <table class="table m-2">
        <tr><th>Name</th><td>{{order.name}}</td></tr>
        <tr><th>Address</th><td>{{order.address}}</td></tr>
        <tr><th>Products</th><td>{{order.cart.itemCount}}</td></tr>
        <tr>
            <th>Total Price</th>
            <td>{{order.cart.totalPrice | currency:USD:true }}</td>
        </tr>
    </table>
```

```
<div class="text-center pt-2">
    <button class="btn btn-outline-primary" routerLink="/checkout/step2">
        Back
    </button>
    <button class="btn btn-danger" (click)="submitOrder()">
        Place Order
    </button>
</div>
</div>
```

The Place Order button uses a click event binding to invoke the component's `submitOrder` method to complete the checkout process.

Creating the Confirmation Component

The final component required for the checkout sequence displays a summary of the order, displaying its ID, the payment authorization code, and the price. Create a TypeScript file called `orderConfirmation.component.ts` in the store/checkout folder and add the code shown in Listing 9-33.

Listing 9-33. The orderConfirmation.component.ts File in the ClientApp/app/store/checkout Folder

```
import { Component } from "@angular/core";
import { Router } from "@angular/router";
import { Order } from "../../models/order.model";

@Component({
    templateUrl: "orderConfirmation.component.html"
})
export class OrderConfirmationComponent {

    constructor(private router: Router,
                public order: Order) {
        if (!order.submitted) {
            router.navigateByUrl("/checkout/step3");
        }
    }
}
```

This component prevents direct navigation by checking to see whether the order has been submitted and navigating to the previous step if it is not. To provide the component with its template, add an HTML file called `orderConfirmation.component.html` to the store/checkout folder with the elements shown in Listing 9-34.

Listing 9-34. The orderConfirmation.component.html File in the ClientApp/app/store/checkout Folder

```
<h2 class="text-center">Order Confirmation</h2>

<div class="container">
    <table *ngIf="order.orderConfirmation; else nodata" class="table m-2">
        <tr><th>Order</th><td>{{order.orderConfirmation.orderId}}</td></tr>
        <tr><th>Price</th><td>{{order.orderConfirmation.amount}}</td></tr>
        <tr><th>Payment Code</th><td>{{order.orderConfirmation.authCode}}</td></tr>
    </table>
```

```
<div class="text-center">
    <button class="btn btn-primary" routerLink="/">Done</button>
</div>

<ng-template #nodata>
    <h3 class="text-center">Submitting Order...</h3>
</ng-template>
</div>
```

The template displays the confirmation data in a table, along with a Done button that navigates back to the store.

Registering the Components and Creating the Routes

To set up the checkout process, the four new components have to be registered with the store feature module, and the Angular application's URL routing configuration must be updated to include the routes that are used to navigate between them.

First, register the components so they are included in the application, as shown in Listing 9-35.

Listing 9-35. Registering Components in the store.module.ts File in the ClientApp/app/store Folder

```
import { NgModule } from "@angular/core";
import { BrowserModule } from '@angular/platform-browser';
import { CartSummaryComponent } from "./cartSummary.component";
import { CategoryFilterComponent } from "./categoryFilter.component";
import { PaginationComponent } from "./pagination.component";
import { ProductListComponent } from "./productList.component";
import { RatingsComponent } from "./ratings.component";
import { ProductSelectionComponent } from "./productSelection.component";
import { CartDetailComponent } from "./cartDetail.component";
import { RouterModule } from "@angular/router";
import { FormsModule } from "@angular/forms";
import { CheckoutDetailsComponent } from "./checkout/checkoutDetails.component";
import { CheckoutPaymentComponent } from "./checkout/checkoutPayment.component";
import { CheckoutSummaryComponent } from "./checkout/checkoutSummary.component";
import { OrderConfirmationComponent } from "./checkout/orderConfirmation.component";

@NgModule({
    declarations: [CartSummaryComponent, CategoryFilterComponent,
        PaginationComponent, ProductListComponent, RatingsComponent,
        ProductSelectionComponent, CartDetailComponent,
        CheckoutDetailsComponent, CheckoutPaymentComponent,
        CheckoutSummaryComponent, OrderConfirmationComponent],
    imports: [BrowserModule, RouterModule, FormsModule],
    exports: [ProductSelectionComponent]
})
export class StoreModule { }
```

Finally, add the routes shown in Listing 9-36, which will allow the user to work through the checkout process.

Listing 9-36. Creating Routes in the app.routing.ts File in the ClientApp/app Folder

```
import { Routes, RouterModule } from "@angular/router";
import { ProductSelectionComponent } from "./store/productSelection.component";
import { CartDetailComponent } from "./store/cartDetail.component";
import { CheckoutDetailsComponent }
    from "./store/checkout/checkoutDetails.component";
import { CheckoutPaymentComponent }
    from "./store/checkout/checkoutPayment.component";
import { CheckoutSummaryComponent }
    from "./store/checkout/checkoutSummary.component";
import { OrderConfirmationComponent }
    from "./store/checkout/orderConfirmation.component";

const routes: Routes = [

    { path: "checkout/step1", component: CheckoutDetailsComponent },
    { path: "checkout/step2", component: CheckoutPaymentComponent },
    { path: "checkout/step3", component: CheckoutSummaryComponent },
    { path: "checkout/confirmation", component: OrderConfirmationComponent },
    { path: "checkout", component: CheckoutDetailsComponent },
    { path: "cart", component: CartDetailComponent },
    { path: "store", component: ProductSelectionComponent },
    { path: "", component: ProductSelectionComponent }]

export const RoutingConfig = RouterModule.forRoot(routes);
```

Restart the ASP.NET Core MVC application, use a browser to navigate to `http://localhost:5000`, and add some items to the cart. Click the cart icon and then click the Checkout button to start the process. For each step in the process, validation messages will be displayed alongside the form elements until you enter values, at which point they will disappear. When all of the form elements have valid values, the button that allows you to proceed to the next step will be activated, as illustrated by Figure 9-7.

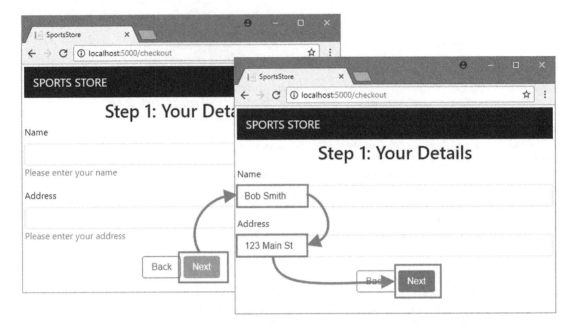

Figure 9-7. *Using Angular data validation*

Continue through the checkout process and provide the data required to create the order. When you get to the summary stage, click the Place Order button and the Angular application will send the data to the ASP. NET Core MVC web service and present a confirmation, as shown in Figure 9-8.

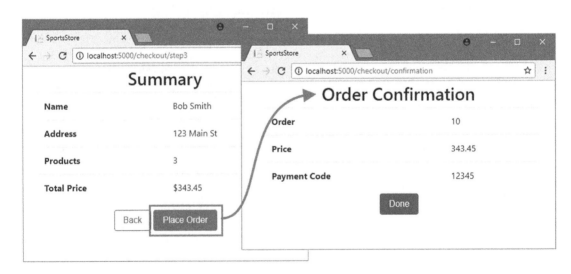

Figure 9-8. *Sending an order to the web service*

Storing Checkout Details as Session Data

The data entered by the user will be lost if they reload the browser window during the checkout process, which can be especially confusing when a task is presented as a series of distinct steps. The problem can be solved by storing progress through the checkout process as session data, similar to the way that the shopping cart is stored.

Extending the Session Data Web Service

To provide the MVC model binder with a class that it can use to parse checkout data values from HTTP requests, create a C# class file called CheckoutState.cs in the Models/BindingTargets folder and add the code shown in Listing 9-37.

Listing 9-37. The Contents of the CheckoutState.cs File in the Models/BindingTargets Folder

```
namespace SportsStore.Models.BindingTargets {

    public class CheckoutState  {

        public string name { get; set; }
        public string address { get; set; }
        public string cardNumber { get; set; }
        public string cardExpiry { get; set; }
        public string cardSecurityCode { get; set; }
    }
}
```

The names of the properties defined by the CheckoutState class follow the JavaScript capitalization convention, which will make the data easier to handle in the Angular part of the project. To add support for storing checkout state data, add the methods shown in Listing 9-38 to the SessionValues controller.

Listing 9-38. Adding Methods in the SessionValuesController.cs File in the Controllers Folder

```
using Microsoft.AspNetCore.Http;
using Microsoft.AspNetCore.Mvc;
using Newtonsoft.Json;
using SportsStore.Models;
using SportsStore.Models.BindingTargets;

namespace SportsStore.Controllers {

    [Route("/api/session")]
    public class SessionValuesController : Controller {

        [HttpGet("cart")]
        public IActionResult GetCart() {
            return Ok(HttpContext.Session.GetString("cart"));
        }
```

```
    [HttpPost("cart")]
    public void StoreCart([FromBody] ProductSelection[] products) {
        var jsonData = JsonConvert.SerializeObject(products);
        HttpContext.Session.SetString("cart", jsonData);
    }

    [HttpGet("checkout")]
    public IActionResult GetCheckout() {
        return Ok(HttpContext.Session.GetString("checkout"));
    }

    [HttpPost("checkout")]
    public void StoreCheckout([FromBody] CheckoutState data) {
        HttpContext.Session.SetString("checkout",
            JsonConvert.SerializeObject(data));
    }
  }
}
```

The StoreCheckout method receives data from the client through the MVC model binder, serializes it as JSON, and stores it as session data. As with the cart data, this means that the data is received as JSON from the client, parsed to create a .NET object, and then serialized into JSON again, which is a redundant process but helps ensure that clients can't use this web service to store arbitrary data. The GetCheckout method retrieves the serialized data and returns it, as is, to the client.

Storing Checkout Data

The final change is to store the values that the user enters in the checkout process as session data. The two-way data bindings used by the Angular checkout components are updated every time that the user makes a change, which would generate too many HTTP requests if used as the trigger for HTTP requests. Instead, I am going to store data when the application navigates to a new URL that begins with checkout, which will indicate that a transition between checkout stages has occurred. The Router class, which I used in Chapter 7 to navigate within a component, generates events that can be observed to learn about routing changes. Add the code shown in Listing 9-39 to the Angular Order class to register for these events and use them to send session data to the service.

Listing 9-39. Using Session Data in the order.model.ts File in the ClientApp/app/models Folder

```
import { Injectable } from "@angular/core";
import { Cart } from "./cart.model";
import { Repository } from "./repository";
import { Router, NavigationStart } from "@angular/router";
import "rxjs/add/operator/filter";

@Injectable()
export class Order {

    constructor(private repo: Repository,
                public cart: Cart,
                router: Router) {
```

```
router.events
    .filter(event => event instanceof NavigationStart)
    .subscribe(event => {
        if (router.url.startsWith("/checkout")
                && this.name != null && this.address != null) {
            repo.storeSessionData("checkout", {
                name: this.name,
                address: this.address,
                cardNumber: this.payment.cardNumber,
                cardExpiry: this.payment.cardExpiry,
                cardSecurityCode: this.payment.cardSecurityCode
            });
        }
    });

    repo.getSessionData("checkout").subscribe(data => {
        if (data != null) {
            this.name = data.name;
            this.address = data.address;
            this.payment.cardNumber = data.cardNumber;
            this.payment.cardExpiry = data.cardExpiry;
            this.payment.cardSecurityCode = data.cardSecurityCode;
        }
    })
}

// ...other methods and properties omitted for brevity...
}
```

The Router.events property returns an observable for the routing events. I use the Reactive Extensions filter operator to select only the NavigationStart event so that I don't send multiple requests to the server for the same navigation change (there are corresponding event types for the end of a navigation, for example).

I use the subscribe method to handle events by sending session data to the server but only if there are values assigned to the name and address properties, which ensures that I don't try to store the data before the user has entered something into the form elements and started the checkout process.

To retrieve previously stored session data, the constructor uses the Repository.getSessionData method and uses the data that is received to populate the properties. Notice that I don't have to worry about handling the product selections, which are already stored as cart session data.

The result is that reloading the browser during the checkout process will return the user to the cart detail component but ensure that the form elements are correctly populated when they resume the checkout process. Restart the ASP.NET Core MVC, navigate to http://localhost:5000, and reload the browser during the checkout process to ensure that the values you enter have been persisted, as shown in Figure 9-9.

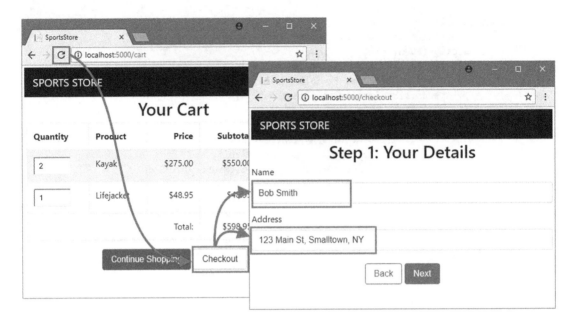

Figure 9-9. *Resuming the checkout process*

Summary

In this chapter, I showed you how to use ASP.NET Core MVC session state to store cart data, which bridges the gap between the way that Angular URL routing works and the way that the user can reload the browser or navigate directly to a URL. I also showed you how to create a multistage checkout process, which validates the data provided by the user and sends it to an ASP.NET Core MVC web service. In the next chapter, I add the administration features for the SportsStore application.

CHAPTER 10

■ ■ ■

Creating Administration Features

In this chapter, I build on the Angular and ASP.NET Core MVC features from earlier chapters to create the basic administration features required by the application. To keep the example application manageable, I don't use all of the features that allowed me to demonstrate different aspects of Angular or ASP.NET Core MVC programming in earlier chapters, but I create enough new functionality to show that new additions can be assembled quickly and easily once the right foundation is in place. Table 10-1 puts this chapter in context.

Table 10-1. *Putting Administration Features in Context*

Question	Answer
What are they?	The administration features allow the management of the application and its data.
Why are they useful?	Most applications require some kind of administration, either to manage the publicly accessible data or to manage user accounts.
How are they used?	Administration features can be built with the same techniques used for the end-user features.
Are there any pitfalls or limitations?	Depending on the complexity of the administration features, it may make sense to create a completely separate administration application. In this chapter, I have included the administration code as part of the Angular application so that it can be accessed using the /admin URL.
Are there any alternatives?	Not all applications require administration features.

Preparing for This Chapter

This chapter uses the SportsStore project created in Chapter 3 and modified in the chapters since. To ensure that the contents of the database are reset, open a command prompt, navigate to the SportsStore folder, and run the commands shown in Listing 10-1.

■ **Tip**   You can download the complete project for this chapter from https://github.com/apress/esntl-angular-for-asp.net-core-mvc. This is also where you will find updates and corrections for this book.

© Adam Freeman 2017
A. Freeman, *Essential Angular for ASP.NET Core MVC*, DOI 10.1007/978-1-4842-2916-3_10

Listing 10-1. Resetting the Database

```
docker-compose down
docker-compose up
```

The first command removes the Docker database container from the previous chapter. The second command creates and starts a fresh container. Wait until SQL Server is up and running, open a second command prompt, and run the commands shown in Listing 10-2 in the SportsStore folder.

Listing 10-2. Preparing the Database

```
dotnet ef database update
dotnet sql-cache create "Server=localhost,5100;Database=SportsStore;User Id=sa;
Password=mySecret123;MultipleActiveResultSets=true" "dbo" "SessionData"
```

These commands are required now that the application uses the ASP.NET Core MVC session state feature. The first command applies the migrations in the project to the database, which creates the SportsStore database. The second command creates the additional table required to store session data.

Start the application to add the seed data and begin handling HTTP requests. If you are using Visual Studio, you can do this by selecting Debug ➤ Start Without Debugging. If you are using Visual Studio Code or just prefer working with the command line, then run the command shown in Listing 10-3 in the SportsStore folder.

Listing 10-3. Starting the Application

```
dotnet run
```

Use a browser to navigate to http://localhost:5000 and you will see the content shown in Figure 10-1.

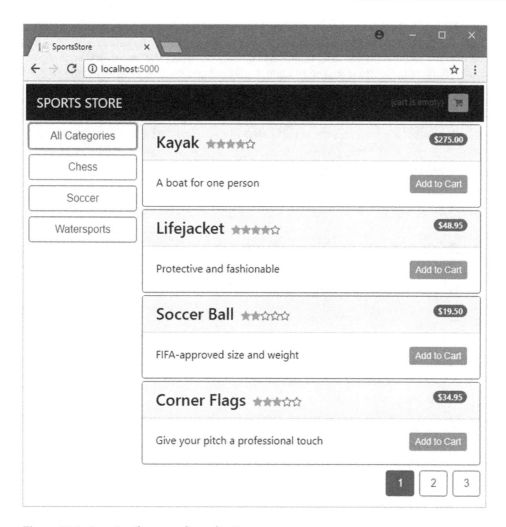

Figure 10-1. *Running the example application*

Adding Administration Features

Angular provides a number of different ways to define features that will not be used by all users, although they all have different advantages and drawbacks. If you want to avoid sending the administration code and content to regular users, you can create a feature module that is loaded only when the Angular application navigates to a specific URL. This is an elegant approach, but it requires third-party packages to load the module and depends on some complex configuration changes.

Alternatively, you can create an entirely separate application, which contains just the administration features. You can still use the components and content defined for the main SportsStore Angular application, but you create an entirely separate infrastructure, including root modules, routing configurations, and root components, which complicates the development process and is prone to errors.

I take a simpler approach, which is to include the administration features in the application, even for users who won't use them. This has the drawback of sending code to clients that is unlikely to be used but has the advantage of being easier to develop and simple to maintain. And, since the administration features build on the existing SportsStore functionality, the additional code and content don't add an enormous amount of overhead to the files that the client has to download.

■ **Tip**   The choice that works for the SportsStore example application may not be the one that makes sense for your project. You should give some consideration to all of the available options, trading off the development and configuration complexity against the additional bandwidth required to deliver code and content that is unlikely to be used by most clients.

Creating the Administration Components

Create the ClientApp/app/admin folder and add to it a TypeScript file called admin.component.ts with the code shown in Listing 10-4. This will be the top-level component for the administration features.

Listing 10-4. The Contents of the admin.component.ts File in the ClientApp/app/admin Folder

```
import { Component } from "@angular/core";
import { Repository } from "../models/repository";

@Component({
    templateUrl: "admin.component.html"
})
export class AdminComponent {

    constructor(private repo: Repository) {
        repo.filter.reset();
        repo.filter.related = true;
        this.repo.getProducts();
        this.repo.getSuppliers();
        this.repo.getOrders();
    }
}
```

The constructor clears the filter used to query for product data and calls the repository's getProducts, getSuppliers, and getOrders methods to request the application data, ensuring that the administration features will have all the data they require.

To create the template, add an HTML file called admin.component.html to the admin folder with the content shown in Listing 10-5.

Listing 10-5. The Contents of the admin.component.html File in the ClientApp/app/admin Folder

```
<div class="navbar bg-info mb-1">
    <a class="navbar-brand text-white">SPORTS STORE Admin</a>
</div>
<div class="row no-gutters">
    <div class="col-3">
        <button class="btn btn-block btn-outline-info" routerLink="/admin"
                routerLinkActive="active" [routerLinkActiveOptions]="{exact: true}">
            Overview
        </button>
        <button class="btn btn-block btn-outline-info" routerLink="/admin/products"
                routerLinkActive="active">Products</button>
        <button class="btn btn-block btn-outline-info" routerLink="/admin/orders"
                routerLinkActive="active">Orders</button>
    </div>
    <div class="col p-2">
        <router-outlet></router-outlet>
    </div>
</div>
</div>
```

The template provides a banner to make it obvious to the user that this is the administration part of the application. There are button elements that use the routerLink directive to navigate to URLs that will be managed by the routing system, combined with the routerLinkActive directive, which assigns an element to a class when the route it navigates to has been selected. In this listing, the button elements are assigned to the active class, which applies the Bootstrap CSS styles for an activated button.

The template also includes a router-outlet element, which will display components based on the current URL, selected by clicking the button elements and managed through the URL routing system. Angular applications can have more than one router-outlet element, which allows for complex navigation schemes.

Creating the Administration Feature Components

With the top-level administration component defined, it is time to create the individual components that will be used to manage products and orders. I am going to display placeholder content so that I can focus on the structure of the application and routing configuration, before implementing the administration features later in the chapter.

The component that the administrator will see when navigating to the /admin URL will provide an overview of the data and operations available. For this component, create a TypeScript file called overview.component.ts in the admin folder, with the code shown in Listing 10-6.

Listing 10-6. The Contents of the overview.component.ts File in the ClientApp/app/admin Folder

```
import { Component } from "@angular/core";
import { Repository } from "../models/repository";
import { Product } from "../models/product.model";
import { Order } from "../models/order.model";
```

```
@Component({
    templateUrl: "overview.component.html"
})
export class OverviewComponent {

    constructor(private repo: Repository) { }

    get products(): Product[] {
        return this.repo.products;
    }

    get orders(): Order[] {
        return this.repo.orders;
    }
}
```

To provide the overview component with its template, create an HTML file called overview.component.html in the admin folder and add the elements shown in Listing 10-7.

Listing 10-7. The Contents of the overview.component.html File in the ClientApp/app/admin Folder

```
<table class="table m-1">
    <tr>
        <td>There are {{products?.length || 0}} products for sale</td>
        <td><button class="btn btn-sm btn-info btn-block"
                    routerLink="/admin/products">Manage Products</button></td>
    </tr>
    <tr>
        <td>There are {{orders?.length || 0}} orders</td>
        <td><button class="btn btn-sm btn-info btn-block"
                    routerLink="/admin/orders">Manage Orders</button></td>
    </tr>
</table>
```

The template contains a table that displays the number of products and orders and the buttons that navigate to the URLs for managing each of them.

For the component that will be used to manage products, create a TypeScript file called productAdmin.component.ts in the admin folder, with the code shown in Listing 10-8.

Listing 10-8. The Contents of the productAdmin.component.ts File in the ClientApp/app/admin Folder

```
import { Component } from "@angular/core";

@Component({
    templateUrl: "productAdmin.component.html"
})
export class ProductAdminComponent {
}
```

Add an HTML file called productAdmin.component.html to the admin folder with the markup shown in Listing 10-9. This is placeholder content that I will replace with more useful features once the structure of the administration part of the application has been set up.

Listing 10-9. The Contents of the productAdmin.component.html File in the ClientApp/app/admin Folder

```
<h4 class="text-center m-2">Product Admin Placeholder</h4>
```

To create the component for managing orders, add a TypeScript file called orderAdmin.component.ts in the admin folder with the code shown in Listing 10-10.

Listing 10-10. The Contents of the orderAdmin.component.ts File in the ClientApp/add/admin Folder

```
import { Component } from "@angular/core";

@Component({
    templateUrl: "orderAdmin.component.html"
})
export class OrderAdminComponent {
}
```

To provide the component with a template, create an HTML file called orderAdmin.component.html in the admin folder and add the placeholder elements shown in Listing 10-11, which I will replace later in the chapter.

Listing 10-11. The Contents of the orderAdmin.component.html File in the ClientApp/app/admin Folder

```
<h4 class="text-center m-2">Order Admin Placeholder</h4>
```

Creating the Feature Module and Routing Configuration

To create a feature module that will incorporate the new components into the application, add a TypeScript file called admin.module.ts in the admin folder with the code shown in Listing 10-12.

Listing 10-12. The Contents of the admin.module.ts File in the ClientApp/app/admin Folder

```
import { NgModule } from "@angular/core";
import { BrowserModule } from "@angular/platform-browser";
import { RouterModule } from "@angular/router";
import { FormsModule } from "@angular/forms";
import { AdminComponent } from "./admin.component";
import { OverviewComponent } from "./overview.component";
import { ProductAdminComponent } from "./productAdmin.component";
import { OrderAdminComponent } from "./orderAdmin.component";

@NgModule({
    imports: [BrowserModule, RouterModule, FormsModule],
    declarations: [AdminComponent, OverviewComponent,
        ProductAdminComponent, OrderAdminComponent]
})
export class AdminModule { }
```

The feature module follows the pattern established in earlier chapters and uses the @NgModule decorator to register the AdminComponent class in the declarations property, making it available for use in the rest of the application. The RouterModule is required for the imports property to support the URL navigation between components.

To integrate the new feature module into the rest of the application, make the change shown in Listing 10-13 to the Angular application's root module.

Listing 10-13. Adding a Feature Module in the app.module.ts File in the ClientApp/app Folder

```
import { BrowserModule } from '@angular/platform-browser';
import { NgModule } from '@angular/core';
import { FormsModule } from '@angular/forms';
import { HttpModule } from '@angular/http';
import { AppComponent } from './app.component';
import { ModelModule } from "./models/model.module";
import { RoutingConfig } from "./app.routing";
import { StoreModule } from "./store/store.module";
import { ProductSelectionComponent } from "./store/productSelection.component";
import { AdminModule } from "./admin/admin.module";

@NgModule({
    declarations: [AppComponent],
    imports: [BrowserModule, FormsModule, HttpModule, ModelModule,
        RoutingConfig, StoreModule, AdminModule],
    providers: [],
    bootstrap: [AppComponent]
})
export class AppModule { }
```

The final step is to add a route to the routing configuration that will display the administration features, as shown in Listing 10-14.

Listing 10-14. Defining a Route in the app.routing.ts File in the ClientApp/app Folder

```
import { Routes, RouterModule } from "@angular/router";
import { ProductSelectionComponent } from "./store/productSelection.component";
import { CartDetailComponent } from "./store/cartDetail.component";
import { CheckoutDetailsComponent }
    from "./store/checkout/checkoutDetails.component";
import { CheckoutPaymentComponent }
    from "./store/checkout/checkoutPayment.component";
import { CheckoutSummaryComponent }
    from "./store/checkout/checkoutSummary.component";
import { OrderConfirmationComponent }
    from "./store/checkout/orderConfirmation.component";
import { AdminComponent } from "./admin/admin.component";
import { OverviewComponent } from "./admin/overview.component";
import { ProductAdminComponent } from "./admin/productAdmin.component";
import { OrderAdminComponent } from "./admin/orderAdmin.component";

const routes: Routes = [
    {
        path: "admin", component: AdminComponent,
        children: [
            { path: "products", component: ProductAdminComponent },
            { path: "orders", component: OrderAdminComponent },
```

```
            { path: "overview", component: OverviewComponent },
            { path: "", component: OverviewComponent }
        ]
    },
    { path: "checkout/step1", component: CheckoutDetailsComponent },
    { path: "checkout/step2", component: CheckoutPaymentComponent },
    { path: "checkout/step3", component: CheckoutSummaryComponent },
    { path: "checkout/confirmation", component: OrderConfirmationComponent },
    { path: "checkout", component: CheckoutDetailsComponent },
    { path: "cart", component: CartDetailComponent },
    { path: "store", component: ProductSelectionComponent },
    { path: "", component: ProductSelectionComponent }]

export const RoutingConfig = RouterModule.forRoot(routes);
```

The new router uses the `children` property to specify the set of routes that will target the `router-outlet` element defined in Listing 10-5. This lets the user navigate between the overview, product, and order components using the `/admin/overview`, `/admin/products`, and `/admin/orders` URLs. There is also a route for the `/admin` URL, which ensures that there isn't a URL for which there isn't a route defined.

Save the changes and use the browser to navigate to `http://localhost:5000/admin`. The SPA fallback route added to the ASP.NET Core configuration will intercept this request and direct it to the `Index` action on the `Home` controller, which will send the client the HTML document required to load the Angular application. When the Angular application starts, it will examine the URL, which matches the last of the `children` routes from Listing 10-14 and displays the overview component. The `button` elements can be used to navigate between administration components, as shown in Figure 10-2.

Figure 10-2. *The structure of administration components*

Administering Products

Now that the basic structure is in place, I can start to define the features that an administrator will require, starting with the ability to manage the product available for sale. As you will see in the sections that follow, most of the heavy-lifting has been done in earlier chapters, and the administration features can take advantage of the data model and the repository that mediates access to the ASP.NET Core MVC web service.

Creating the Editor Component

First, create a new TypeScript file called productEditor.component.ts in the admin folder and add the code shown in Listing 10-15. This component will be used to present a set of fields to users so they can create or edit products.

Listing 10-15. The Contents of the productEditor.component.ts File in the ClientApp/app/admin Folder

```
import { Component } from "@angular/core";
import { Repository } from "../models/repository";
import { Product } from "../models/product.model";
import { Supplier } from "../models/supplier.model";

@Component({
    selector: "admin-product-editor",
    templateUrl: "productEditor.component.html"
})
export class ProductEditorComponent {

    constructor(private repo: Repository) { }

    get product(): Product {
        return this.repo.product;
    }

    get suppliers(): Supplier[] {
        return this.repo.suppliers;
    }

    compareSuppliers(s1: Supplier, s2: Supplier) {
        return s1 && s2 && s1.name == s2.name;
    }
}
```

This component provides access to the currently edited Product object through its product property. The selection of the Product object and the actions that are performed on it are left to other components. The job of this component is only to provide access to the data so that the same set of HTML form fields can be presented without duplication to support both editing and creating data. The suppliers property and the compareSuppliers method support editing the relationship between a product and its supplier, which I describe shortly.

To provide the component with its template, add an HTML file called productEditor.component.html in the admin folder with the elements shown in Listing 10-16.

Listing 10-16. The Contents of the productEditor.component.html File in the ClientApp/app/admin Folder

```
<div class="form-group">
    <label>Name</label>
    <input class="form-control" [(ngModel)]="product.name" />
</div>
```

```
<div class="form-group">
    <label>Category</label>
    <input class="form-control" [(ngModel)]="product.category" />
</div>
<div class="form-group">
    <label>Supplier</label>
    <select class="form-control" [(ngModel)]="product.supplier"
            [compareWith]="compareSuppliers">
        <option *ngFor="let s of suppliers" [ngValue]="s">{{s.name}}</option>
    </select>
</div>
<div class="form-group">
    <label>Description</label>
    <textarea class="form-control" [(ngModel)]="product.description"></textarea>
</div>
<div class="form-group">
    <label>Price</label>
    <input class="form-control" [(ngModel)]="product.price" />
</div>
```

The template uses two-way data bindings and the ngModel directive to allow the user to edit the properties of the Product object. Most of the properties are simple input or textarea elements, but some extra work is required to get the select element working correctly.

The ngModel directive on the select element works with the ngValue directive on the option elements to ensure that the appropriate option is selected by default, which is done by comparing the model value and the option value. If the two values are the same, then the option is selected in order to display the current value to the user.

A common problem when working with complex data obtained from an ASP.NET Core MVC web service is that the objects that are being compared are obtained using separate HTTP requests. In this case, the Supplier objects returned by the Product.supplier properties were created by parsing the response to a GET request sent to the /api/products URL. However, the Supplier objects that are used to create the option elements were created by parsing the response to a GET request sent to the /api/suppliers URL. This means that the ngModel directive has to compare objects from two different sources, which prevents the select element from correctly displaying the current value. To work around this problem, the compareWith directive is used to provide Angular with a method defined by the component that can be used to determine whether two objects are equal. In this case, the compareSuppliers method is specific, which compares Supplier objects using the value of the name property.

Make the changes shown in Listing 10-17 to register the new component in the administration feature module.

Listing 10-17. Registering a Component in the admin.module.ts File in the ClientApp/app/admin Folder

```
import { NgModule } from "@angular/core";
import { BrowserModule } from "@angular/platform-browser"
import { RouterModule } from "@angular/router";
import { FormsModule } from "@angular/forms";
import { AdminComponent } from "./admin.component";
import { OverviewComponent } from "./overview.component";
import { ProductAdminComponent } from "./productAdmin.component";
import { OrderAdminComponent } from "./orderAdmin.component";
import { ProductEditorComponent } from "./productEditor.component";
```

```
@NgModule({
    imports: [BrowserModule, RouterModule, FormsModule],
    declarations: [AdminComponent, OverviewComponent,
        ProductAdminComponent, OrderAdminComponent, ProductEditorComponent]
})
export class AdminModule { }
```

Creating the Product Table

The next step is to complete the main product administration component so that it will present the user with a list of products and support creating, editing, and deleting them. Add the code shown in Listing 10-18 to the ProductAdminComponent class.

Listing 10-18. Adding Features to the productAdmin.component.ts File in the ClientApp/app/admin Folder

```
import { Component } from "@angular/core";
import { Repository } from "../models/repository";
import { Product } from "../models/product.model";
import { Supplier } from "../models/supplier.model";


@Component({
    templateUrl: "productAdmin.component.html"
})
export class ProductAdminComponent {

    constructor(private repo: Repository) {}

    tableMode: boolean = true;

    get product(): Product {
        return this.repo.product;
    }

    selectProduct(id: number) {
        this.repo.getProduct(id);
    }

    saveProduct() {
        if (this.repo.product.productId == null) {
            this.repo.createProduct(this.repo.product);
        } else {
            this.repo.replaceProduct(this.repo.product);
        }
        this.clearProduct()
        this.tableMode = true;
    }

    deleteProduct(id: number) {
        this.repo.deleteProduct(id);
    }
```

```
    clearProduct() {
        this.repo.product = new Product();
        this.tableMode = true;
    }

    get products(): Product[] {
        return this.repo.products;
    }
}
```

The properties and methods defined by the component provide access to the product data, allow a
product to be selected for editing, and send changes to the web service. There is also a `tableMode` property
that will be used to display the editor fields when the user creates a new product. To present the content,
replace the elements in the component's template with those shown in Listing 10-19.

Listing 10-19. Displaying Data in the productAdmin.component.html File in the ClientApp/app/admin Folder

```
<table *ngIf="tableMode; else create" class="table table-sm table-striped">
    <tr>
        <th>ID</th><th>Name</th><th>Category</th><th>Supplier</th>
        <th>Price</th><th></th>
    </tr>
    <tr *ngFor="let p of products">
        <ng-template [ngIf]="product?.productId != p.productId" [ngIfElse]="edit">
            <td>{{p.productId}}</td>
            <td>{{p.name}}</td>
            <td>{{p.category}}</td>
            <td>{{p.supplier?.name || '(None)'}}</td>
            <td>{{p.price | currency:USD:true}}</td>
            <td>
                <button class="btn btn-sm btn-primary"
                        (click)="selectProduct(p.productId)">Edit</button>
                <button class="btn btn-sm btn-danger"
                        (click)="deleteProduct(p.productId)">Delete</button>
            </td>
        </ng-template>
    </tr>
    <tfoot>
        <tr>
            <td colspan="6" class="text-center">
                <button class="btn btn-primary"
                    (click)="clearProduct(); tableMode = false">Create</button>
            </td>
        </tr>
    </tfoot>
</table>
```

```
<ng-template #edit>
    <td colspan="6">
        <admin-product-editor></admin-product-editor>
        <div class="text-center">
            <button class="btn btn-sm btn-primary" (click)="saveProduct()">
                Save
            </button>
            <button class="btn btn-sm btn-info" (click)="clearProduct()">
                Cancel
            </button>
        </div>
    </td>
</ng-template>

<ng-template #create>
    <admin-product-editor></admin-product-editor>
    <button class="btn btn-primary" (click)="saveProduct()">
        Save
    </button>
    <button class="btn btn-info" (click)="clearProduct()">
        Cancel
    </button>
</ng-template>
```

The centerpiece of the template is a table that contains a row for each product, which you can see by reloading the application and navigating to http://localhost:5000/admin/products. Each row contains Edit and Delete buttons, as shown in Figure 10-3.

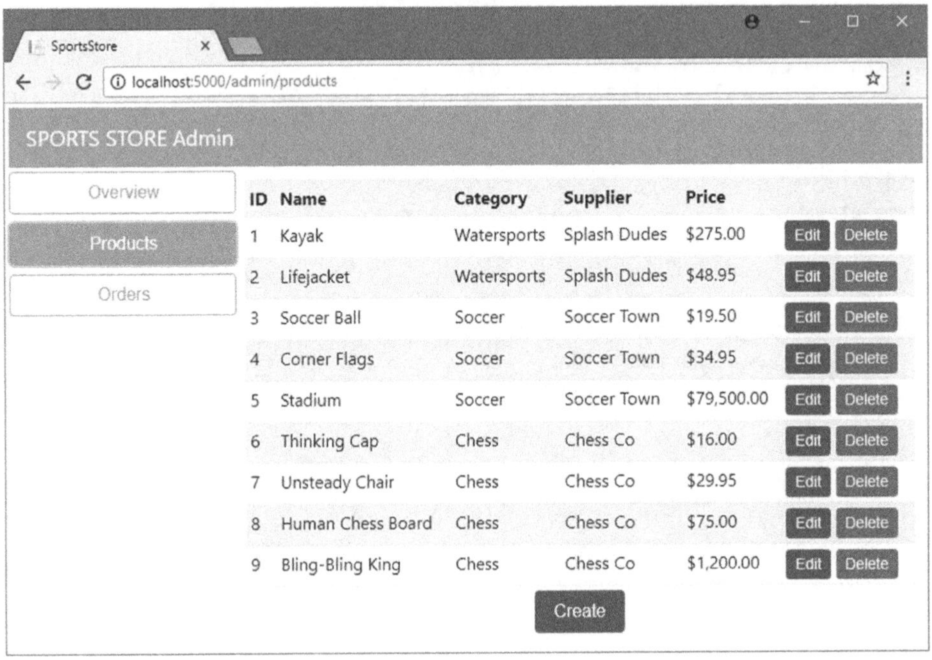

Figure 10-3. The product administration table

240

If you click one of the Edit buttons, the table row is replaced with an inline editor that allows the property values to be changed, as shown in Figure 10-4, which also shows how the same editor is used when the Create button is clicked.

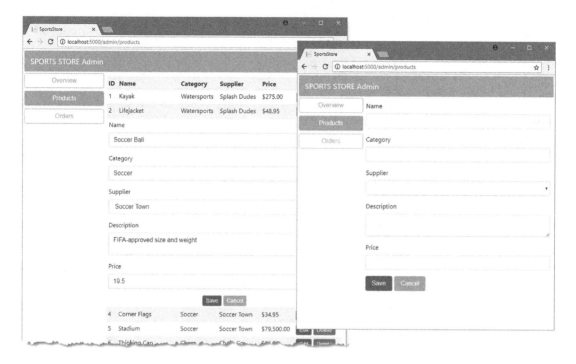

Figure 10-4. *Using the product editor*

In most situations, the concise syntax for structural directives is more convenient because it allows the directive can be applied directly to the element. In Listing 10-19, the concise syntax for the ngIf directive is used to display the table of products or the editor for creating new products, like this:

```
...
<table *ngIf="tableMode; else create" class="table table-sm table-striped">
...
```

The concise syntax can't be used when there isn't a suitable element to apply it to. The template in Listing 10-19 changes the contents of a table row so that different sets of td elements are used in a table row when the user is editing a product. The ngIf directive can't be applied to the tr element because the contents of each row will be different for each product and there is no suitable intermediate element between the tr and td elements that should be displayed. In this situation, the full syntax can be used, like this:

```
...
<ng-template [ngIf]="product?.productId != p.productId" [ngIfElse]="edit">
    <td>{{p.productId}}</td>
    <td>{{p.name}}</td>
    <td>{{p.category}}</td>
    <td>{{p.supplier?.name || '(None)'}}</td>
    <td>{{p.price | currency:USD:true}}</td>
```

```
    <td>
        <button class="btn btn-sm btn-primary"
            (click)="selectProduct(p.productId)">Edit</button>
        <button class="btn btn-sm btn-danger"
            (click)="deleteProduct(p.productId)">Delete</button>
    </td>
</ng-template>
...
```

The ng-template element allows the ngIf directive to be applied without changing the structure of the table. When using the full syntax, the name of the directive is not preceded by an asterisk, and a different set of data bindings is required to control how the directive works. In this case, the ngIf binding specifies the condition that the directive should evaluate, and the ngIfElse binding specifies the template that should be displayed when the expression is false.

Administering Orders

The process for dealing with orders follows the same basic pattern for products and relies on the data model and repository created in earlier chapters. Replace the OrderAdminComponent class with the code shown in Listing 10-20.

Listing 10-20. Adding Features in the orderAdmin.component.ts File in the ClientApp/app/admin Folder

```
import { Component } from "@angular/core";
import { Repository } from "../models/repository";
import { Order } from "../models/order.model";

@Component({
    templateUrl: "orderAdmin.component.html"
})
export class OrderAdminComponent {

    constructor(private repo: Repository) {}

    get orders(): Order[] {
        return this.repo.orders;
    }

    markShipped(order: Order) {
        this.repo.shipOrder(order);
    }
}
```

The component receives a Repository object through dependency injection and uses it to provide its template with the orders data and a method that will mark an order as shipped. To use these members, replace the contents of the component's template with the code shown in Listing 10-21.

Listing 10-21. Managing Orders in the orderAdmin.component.html File in the ClientApp/app/admin Folder

```
<table *ngIf="orders?.length > 0; else nodata" class="table table-striped">
    <tr>
        <th>Customer</th><th>Address</th><th>Products</th>
        <th>Total</th><th></th>
    </tr>
    <tr *ngFor="let o of orders">
        <td>{{o.name}}</td>
        <td>{{o.address}}</td>
        <td>{{o.products.length}}</td>
        <td>{{o.payment.total | currency:USD:true}}</td>
        <td *ngIf="!o.shipped; else shipped">
            <button class="btn btn-sm btn-primary"
                    (click)="markShipped(o)">
                Ship
            </button>
        </td>
    </tr>
</table>

<ng-template #shipped>
    <td>Shipped</td>
</ng-template>

<ng-template #nodata>
    <h3 class="text-center">There are no orders</h3>
</ng-template>
```

There are no new Angular features used in this template. There a table that is displayed only when there are orders available, managed using the ngIf directive. Within the table, rows are generated for each order using the ngFor directive. Each row contains a button element that uses a click event binding to invoke the component's markShipped method, which causes the repository to send an HTTP POST request to the ASP.NET Core MVC to update the order and then send an HTTP GET request to refresh the data.

To see the result, use the store section of the SportsStore application to create one or more orders and then navigate to http://localhost:5000/admin/orders to manage them, as shown in Figure 10-5.

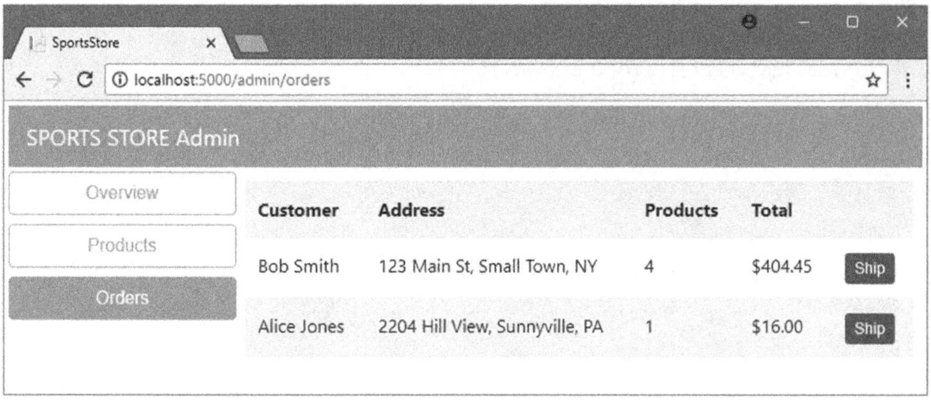

Figure 10-5. Administering orders

Dealing with Request Errors

Not all HTTP requests will produce a successful result, especially when dealing with data entered by a user, which may not pass the ASP.NET Core MVC model validation process.

Ideally, when an application receives an error response, it will deal with it in such a way that the user is able to understand what has gone wrong and is put in a position to correct the problem with the minimum of effort and lost work. But this can be hard to achieve in a real project without adding a lot of complexity to the application, which presents its own risk of errors.

For most projects, the best compromise is to try to avoid errors but simply display them to the user when they occur and then try to return the application to a known good state. Avoiding errors is most effectively done by using the Angular data validation features, which were used in Chapter 9 to ensure that the user provided all of the data values required by the checkout process. The Angular validation features can be awkward to work with, but they are effective and can be customized to handle custom validation requirements.

Angular also makes it easy to determine when an error has occurred and display it to the user, which is the focus of this part of the chapter. In the sections that follow, I create a component that displays errors and integrates it into the application.

Creating the Error Handling and Distribution Service

Angular makes it easy to change the way that errors are handled by defining a new service. Add a TypeScript file called errorHandler.service.ts in the app folder and use it to define the class shown in Listing 10-22.

Listing 10-22. The Contents of the errorHandler.service.ts File in the ClientApp/app Folder

```
import { Injectable } from "@angular/core";
import { Subject } from "rxjs/Subject";
import { Observable } from "rxjs/Observable";

@Injectable()
export class ErrorHandlerService  {
    private subject = new Subject<string[]>();

    handleError(error: any) {
        setTimeout(() => {
            if (error instanceof ValidationError) {
                this.subject.next(error.errors);
            } else if (error instanceof Error) {
                this.subject.next([error.message]);
            } else {
                this.subject.next(["An error has occurred"]);
            }
        });
    }

    get errors(): Observable<string[]> {
        return this.subject;
    }
}
```

```
export class ValidationError implements Error {

    constructor(public errors: string[]) {}

    name: string;
    message: string;
}
```

Angular will call the handleError method when there is an exception raised in the code that isn't handled anywhere else in the application. This allows the try/throw/catch keywords to be used normally while ensuring that there is a fallback for dealing with problems that were not expected or are unhandled.

In Chapter 5, I explained that Angular uses Reactive Extensions behind the scenes and that you only have to work directly with observables when you are working at the edges of the application, typically when introducing data into the application. The custom error handler in Listing 10-22 intercepts errors and reintroduces them into the application so they can be displayed to the user; as a consequence, the error handler relies on an Observable to distribute details of the errors. The Subject class is the easiest way to create an Observable that you can feed your own data values into, using the next method. The result is that errors are received from Angular through the handleError method and then fed back into the application through the Subject.next method.

■ **Note**   Notice that I wrapped the calls to the Subject object's next method using the setTimeout function. This ensures that errors are distributed in a separate update within the Angular application, without which errors won't be displayed until some other change in the application occurs, working around a wrinkle in the way that Angular handles changes.

To register the error handler class as a service, make the changes shown in Listing 10-23 to the application's root module.

Listing 10-23. Registering a Service in the app.module.ts File in the ClientApp/app Folder

```
import { BrowserModule } from '@angular/platform-browser';
import { NgModule } from '@angular/core';
import { FormsModule } from '@angular/forms';
import { HttpModule } from '@angular/http';
import { AppComponent } from './app.component';
import { ModelModule } from "./models/model.module";
import { RoutingConfig } from "./app.routing";
import { StoreModule } from "./store/store.module";
import { ProductSelectionComponent } from "./store/productSelection.component";
import { AdminModule } from "./admin/admin.module";
import { ErrorHandler } from "@angular/core";
import { ErrorHandlerService } from "./errorHandler.service";

const eHandler = new ErrorHandlerService();

export function handler() {
    return eHandler;
}
```

```
@NgModule({
    declarations: [AppComponent],
    imports: [BrowserModule, FormsModule, HttpModule, ModelModule,
        RoutingConfig, StoreModule, AdminModule],
    providers: [
        { provide: ErrorHandlerService, useFactory: handler},
        { provide: ErrorHandler, useFactory: handler}],
    bootstrap: [AppComponent]
})
export class AppModule { }
```

The standard way to configure Angular dependency injection is to specify a class name and let Angular create the object that is used to resolve dependencies in the application.

That doesn't work for the error handler because I want the same object to be used to resolve ErrorHandler and ErrorHandlerService dependencies, which will ensure that Angular handles its errors using the new service as well as providing access to the additional features to the rest of the application. I create the object that I want to use and use it in the configuration entries for the providers property, where the provide property specifies the dependency injection type and the useFactory property specifies a function that will produce the object that will be used to resolve dependencies. The oddity of this approach works around a limitation of the Angular development tools.

Displaying Errors

To provide access to the errors that occur in the application, add the statements shown in Listing 10-24 to the root component. (This class contains methods and properties from an earlier chapter, which I have removed for the sake of brevity).

Listing 10-24. Accessing Errors in the app.component.ts File in the ClientApp/app Folder

```
import { Component } from '@angular/core';
import { ErrorHandlerService } from "./errorHandler.service";

@Component({
    selector: "app-root",
    templateUrl: "./app.component.html"
})
export class AppComponent {
    private lastError: string[];

    constructor(errorHandler: ErrorHandlerService) {
        errorHandler.errors.subscribe(error => {
            this.lastError = error;
        });
    }

    get error(): string[] {
        return this.lastError;
    }

    clearError() {
        this.lastError = null;
    }
}
```

246

To display errors to the user, add the elements shown in Listing 10-25 to the root component's template.

Listing 10-25. Displaying Errors in the app.component.html File in the ClientApp/app Folder

```
<div class="bg-danger text-white text-center p-2 m-2" *ngIf="error != null">
    <h6 *ngFor="let e of error">{{e}}</h6>
    <button class="btn btn-warning" (click)="clearError()">OK</button>
</div>
<router-outlet></router-outlet>
```

There is a div element that is displayed only when there is an error, containing h6 elements that are generated for each string required to describe the error. An error will be displayed until the user clicks the button element, which has a click event binding that calls the error handler's clearError method.

Reporting Validation Errors

All that remains is to update the repository so that it inspects the responses received from the web services and throws errors when there are validation problems, as shown in Listing 10-26.

Listing 10-26. Throwing Errors in the repository.ts File in the ClientApp/app/models Folder

```
import { Product } from "./product.model";
import { Injectable } from "@angular/core";
import { Http, RequestMethod, Request, Response } from "@angular/http";
import { Observable } from "rxjs/Observable";
import "rxjs/add/operator/map";
import { Supplier } from "./supplier.model";
import { Filter, Pagination } from "./configClasses.repository";
import { Order } from "./order.model";
import { ErrorHandlerService, ValidationError } from "../errorHandler.service";
import "rxjs/add/operator/catch";

const productsUrl = "/api/products";
const suppliersUrl = "/api/suppliers";
const ordersUrl = "/api/orders";

@Injectable()
export class Repository {
    private filterObject = new Filter();
    private paginationObject = new Pagination();

    // ...other methods and properties omitted for brevity...

    private sendRequest(verb: RequestMethod, url: string, data?: any)
            : Observable<any> {
```

```
        return this.http.request(new Request({
            method: verb, url: url, body: data
        }))
        .map(response => {
            return response.headers.get("Content-Length") != "0"
                ? response.json() : null;
        })
        .catch((errorResponse: Response) => {
            if (errorResponse.status == 400 ) {
                let jsonData: string;
                try {
                    jsonData = errorResponse.json();
                } catch (e) {
                    throw new Error("Network Error");
                }
                let messages = Object.getOwnPropertyNames(jsonData)
                    .map(p => jsonData[p]);
                throw new ValidationError(messages);
            }
            throw new Error("Network Error");
        });
    }
}
```

The catch operator is used on Observable objects to deal with errors. For HTTP responses, errors include any response that doesn't have a status code in the 200 to 299 range. The new code checks for the 400 Bad Request status code, which is the one that will be returned by the ASP.NET Core MVC web service when there are validation errors. The 400 responses from the web service will contain JSON data in the body that looks like this:

```
{
  "Name":["The Name field is required."],
  "Price":["Price must be at least 1"],
  "Category":["The Category field is required."],
  "Description":["The Description field is required."]
}
```

The new code in Listing 10-26 creates a JavaScript object from the JSON data, extracts the property values, and uses them to create a ValidationError object, which is then used with the throw keyword to create an error that will be passed by Angular to the custom error handler.

To see the result, reload the application in the browser, navigate to the http://localhost:5000/admin URL, and click the Products button to display the list of products. Click the Create button and then click the Save button without entering values into any of the fields. The HTTP request that is sent to the web service fails the MVC model binding process and produces the error messages shown in Figure 10-6.

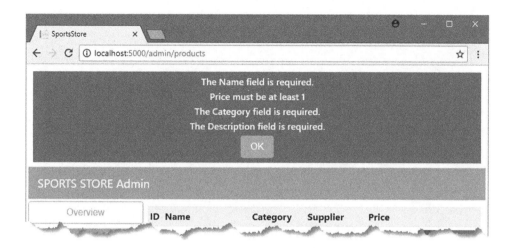

Figure 10-6. *Displaying validation errors*

Bear in mind that the asynchronous nature of the HTTP request means that the response from the ASP.NET Core MVC web service is received after the Angular application has navigated to another URL. It is for this reason that Angular form validation should be used to avoid this kind of error being generated and that handling errors like this should be a last resort.

Summary

In this chapter, I created the administration features for the application, building on the features created in earlier chapters. I also added support for displaying errors to the user, which provides a last-resort technique for problems that cannot be handled in the application code and that could not be avoided using features such as form validation. In the next chapter, I explain how to secure the application so that the administration features can be used only by authorized users.

CHAPTER 11

Securing the Application

In this chapter, I explain how to set up authentication and authorization so that administrative tasks, such as modifying or deleting data, can be done only by approved users. I explain how to restrict access to web services, how to use ASP.NET Core Identity to provide security services, and how to authenticate users using Angular. Table 11-1 puts application security in context.

Table 11-1. *Putting Application Security in Context*

Question	Answer
What is it?	Application security prevents unauthorized users from using sensitive web service actions.
Why is it useful?	Without authorization, any user can administer the application.
How is it used?	ASP.NET Core Identity is used to manage users and roles and is combined with the built-in features of ASP.NET Core MVC to authenticate or authorize users.
Are there any pitfalls or limitations?	You must take care to protect the parts of the API that are required for administration, while ensuring that the parts required for the publicly accessible features are open to anonymous access.
Are there any alternatives?	Not all applications require authorization and authentication, especially if there are no administration features.

Preparing for This Chapter

This chapter uses the SportsStore project created in Chapter 3 and modified since. To ensure that the contents of the database are reset, open a command prompt, navigate to the SportsStore folder, and run the commands shown in Listing 11-1.

■ **Tip**   You can download the complete project for this chapter from https://github.com/apress/esntl-angular-for-asp.net-core-mvc. This is also where you will find updates and corrections for this book.

© Adam Freeman 2017
A. Freeman, *Essential Angular for ASP.NET Core MVC*, DOI 10.1007/978-1-4842-2916-3_11

Listing 11-1. Resetting the Database

```
docker-compose down
docker-compose up
```

The first command removes the Docker database container from the previous chapter. The second command creates and starts a fresh container. Wait until SQL Server is up and running, open a second command prompt, and run the commands shown in Listing 11-2 in the SportsStore folder.

Listing 11-2. Preparing the Database

```
dotnet ef database update
dotnet sql-cache create "Server=localhost,5100;Database=SportsStore;User Id=sa;
Password=mySecret123;MultipleActiveResultSets=true" "dbo" "SessionData"
```

The first command applies the migrations in the project to the database, which creates the SportsStore database. The second command creates the additional table required to store session data.

Start the application to add the seed data and begin handling HTTP requests. If you are using Visual Studio, you can do this by selecting Debug ➤ Start Without Debugging. If you are using Visual Studio Code or just prefer working with the command line, then run the command shown in Listing 11-3 in the SportsStore folder.

Listing 11-3. Starting the Application

```
dotnet run
```

Use a browser to navigate to http://localhost:5000 and you will see the content shown in Figure 11-1.

Figure 11-1. Running the example application

Restricting Access to Action Methods

Restricting access to the sensitive web service features requires applying the Authorize attribute, which specifies the authorization policy for a controller or action method. For the SportsStore application, I am going to restrict access to the administration features to authenticated users who have been assigned a role called Administrator.

Restricting Access to Suppliers

To begin with something simple, apply the Authorize attribute to the SupplierValuesController class, as shown in Listing 11-4, to restrict access to all the action methods used to deal with supplier data.

Listing 11-4. Restricting Access in the SupplierValuesController.cs File in the Controllers Folder

```
using Microsoft.AspNetCore.Mvc;
using SportsStore.Models;
using SportsStore.Models.BindingTargets;
using System.Collections.Generic;
using Microsoft.AspNetCore.Authorization;

namespace SportsStore.Controllers {

    [Route("api/suppliers")]
    [Authorize(Roles = "Administrator")]
    public class SupplierValuesController : Controller {
        private DataContext context;

        // ...methods omitted for brevity...
    }
}
```

Applying the Authorize attribute to the class affects all the action methods defined by the controller. The effect of the attribute in Listing 11-4 is to restrict all actions that operate on Supplier objects from being accessed, except from authenticated users who have been assigned the Administrator role.

Restricting Access to Orders

Access to the action methods defined by the OrderValuesController class is a little more complex; all users should be able to create orders, but the ability to retrieve and modify orders should be restricted. Add the attributes shown in Listing 11-5 to set up the authorization policy on this controller.

Listing 11-5. Restricting Access in the OrderValuesController.cs File in the Controllers Folder

```
using Microsoft.AspNetCore.Mvc;
using Microsoft.EntityFrameworkCore;
using SportsStore.Models;
using System.Collections.Generic;
using System.Linq;
using Microsoft.AspNetCore.Authorization;
```

```
namespace SportsStore.Controllers {

    [Route("/api/orders")]
    [Authorize(Roles = "Administrator")]
    public class OrderValuesController : Controller {
        private DataContext context;

        // ...other methods omitted for brevity...

        [HttpPost]
        [AllowAnonymous]
        public IActionResult CreateOrder([FromBody] Order order) {
            if (ModelState.IsValid) {

                order.OrderId = 0;
                order.Shipped = false;
                order.Payment.Total = GetPrice(order.Products);

                ProcessPayment(order.Payment);
                if (order.Payment.AuthCode != null) {
                    context.Add(order);
                    context.SaveChanges();
                    return Ok(new {
                        orderId = order.OrderId,
                        authCode = order.Payment.AuthCode,
                        amount = order.Payment.Total
                    });
                } else {
                    return BadRequest("Payment rejected");
                }
            }
            return BadRequest(ModelState);
        }
    }
}
```

Applying the Authorize attribute restricts access to all the action methods, but this policy is overridden by the AllowAnonymous attribute, which ensures that the CreateOrder action can be targeted by any users.

Restricting Access to Products

The final controller to secure is the ProductValuesController class, which should allow all users to view the data but only allow administrators to make changes. Some additional work is required for this controller to ensure that access to related data is handled consistently with the policy provided by the other controllers to avoid providing back-door access to data that is restricted elsewhere. To implement the authorization policy, make the changes shown in Listing 11-6.

Listing 11-6. Restricting Access in the ProductValuesController.cs File in the Controllers Folder

```
using Microsoft.AspNetCore.Mvc;
using SportsStore.Models;
using Microsoft.EntityFrameworkCore;
using System.Linq;
using System.Collections.Generic;
using SportsStore.Models.BindingTargets;
using Microsoft.AspNetCore.JsonPatch;
using Microsoft.AspNetCore.Authorization;

namespace SportsStore.Controllers {

    [Route("api/products")]
    [Authorize(Roles = "Administrator")]
    public class ProductValuesController : Controller {
        private DataContext context;

        public ProductValuesController(DataContext ctx) {
            context = ctx;
        }

        [HttpGet("{id}")]
        [AllowAnonymous]
        public Product GetProduct(long id) {
            IQueryable<Product> query = context.Products
                .Include(p => p.Ratings);

            if (HttpContext.User.IsInRole("Administrator")) {
                query = query.Include(p => p.Supplier)
                    .ThenInclude(s => s.Products);
            }

            Product result = query.First(p => p.ProductId == id);

            if (result != null) {
                if (result.Supplier != null) {
                    result.Supplier.Products = result.Supplier.Products.Select(p =>
                        new Product {
                            ProductId = p.ProductId,
                            Name = p.Name,
                            Category = p.Category,
                            Description = p.Description,
                            Price = p.Price,
                    });
                }
```

```
            if (result.Ratings != null) {
                foreach (Rating r in result.Ratings) {
                    r.Product = null;
                }
            }
        }
        return result;
    }

    [HttpGet]
    [AllowAnonymous]
    public IActionResult GetProducts(string category, string search,
            bool related = false, bool metadata = false) {
        IQueryable<Product> query = context.Products;

        if (!string.IsNullOrWhiteSpace(category)) {
            string catLower = category.ToLower();
            query = query.Where(p => p.Category.ToLower().Contains(catLower));
        }
        if (!string.IsNullOrWhiteSpace(search)) {
            string searchLower = search.ToLower();
            query = query.Where(p => p.Name.ToLower().Contains(searchLower)
                || p.Description.ToLower().Contains(searchLower));
        }

        if (related && HttpContext.User.IsInRole("Administrator")) {
            query = query.Include(p => p.Supplier).Include(p => p.Ratings);
            List<Product> data = query.ToList();
            data.ForEach(p => {
                if (p.Supplier != null) {
                    p.Supplier.Products = null;
                }
                if (p.Ratings != null) {
                    p.Ratings.ForEach(r => r.Product = null);
                }
            });
            return metadata ? CreateMetadata(data) : Ok(data);
        } else {
            return metadata ? CreateMetadata(query) : Ok(query);
        }
    }

    // ...other methods omitted for brevity...
    }
}
```

The Authorize attribute has been applied to the entire class but has been overridden by the AllowAnonymous attribute so that anyone can send requests to the GetProduct or GetProducts method. Within these methods the role membership of the user is checked to make sure that only authorized users will receive the Supplier data that is related to a Product object.

Testing the Restrictions

To see the effect of the attributes applied to the controllers, start the ASP.NET Core MVC application and use a browser to navigate to http://localhost:5000. The store part of the Angular project will work normally because it depends on web service action methods that can be accessed anonymously.

However, if you navigate to http://localhost:5000/admin, you will see that the administration features are a different story. Click the Products button, for example, and you will see that the list of products is displayed but that all of them are shown with (None) in the Supplier column because access is restricted to related data, as shown in Figure 11-2.

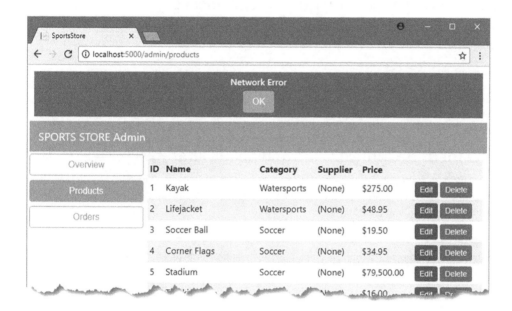

Figure 11-2. *The effect of authorization restrictions*

The Network Error message is displayed because some of the HTTP requests made by the administration features have failed completely. When the administration features are first displayed, requests are sent to the web service to get the product, supplier, and order data. The product request succeeds (although without related data), but the supplier and order requests fail, which produces the error shown in Figure 11-2.

If you look at the output from the ASP.NET Core MVC application, you will see that these requests have produced exceptions like this:

```
...
System.InvalidOperationException: No authentication handler is configured
to handle the scheme: Automatic
...
```

The Authorize attribute tells ASP.NET Core MVC to restrict access to action methods the application hasn't been configured with any way to establish the identity of users or provided with a database of users and roles. In the next section, I'll set up ASP.NET Core Identity and configure it to provide the missing functionality.

Installing and Configuring ASP.NET Core Identity

I am going to use ASP.NET Core Identity to provide ASP.NET Core MVC with the back-end support it needs for managing authentication and authorization. In the sections that follow, I add the ASP.NET Core Identity packages to the project and add the configuration that is required for a conventional MVC application. Once the pieces are in place, I explain how Identity can be used to support Angular applications through a RESTful web service.

Installing the ASP.NET Core Identity NuGet Package

To install the NuGet package for ASP.NET Core Identity, use a command prompt to run the commands shown in Listing 11-7 in the SportsStore folder.

Listing 11-7. Installing the NuGet Package

```
dotnet add package Microsoft.AspNetCore.Identity.EntityFrameworkCore --version 1.1.1
dotnet restore
```

Creating the Identity Context Class and Seed Data

The ASP.NET Core Identity system depends on Entity Framework Core for access to its data, which means that a database context class is required. Add a C# class file called IdentityDataContext.cs in the Models folder, with the code shown in Listing 11-8.

■ **Tip**   Close and reopen the project if your IDE cannot find the Identity namespaces required for the class shown in Listing 11-8.

Listing 11-8. The Contents of the IdentityDataContext.cs File in the Models Folder

```
using Microsoft.AspNetCore.Identity.EntityFrameworkCore;
using Microsoft.EntityFrameworkCore;

namespace SportsStore.Models {

    public class IdentityDataContext : IdentityDbContext<IdentityUser> {

        public IdentityDataContext(DbContextOptions<IdentityDataContext> options)
            : base(options) { }
    }
}
```

The IdentityDbContext base class provides the properties through which the data is accessed, and creating a subclass allows the Identity features to be customized and extended. I am using all the default options for this book, which are suitable for most projects; the main benefit of creating a context class is that it is easier to create and apply the migration that sets up the database schema, which I do later in this chapter.

When setting up Identity, it is helpful to seed the database with user account. Add a C# class file called IdentitySeedData.cs in the Models folder and add the code shown in Listing 11-9.

■ **Tip**   You must ensure that the seed data uses a password that meets the Identity password policy, which requires a mix of uppercase and lowercase characters, symbols, and digits. The database will not be seeded if you do not comply with the policy.

Listing 11-9. The Contents of the IdentitySeedData.cs File in the Models Folder

```
using System;
using System.Linq;
using Microsoft.AspNetCore.Builder;
using Microsoft.AspNetCore.Identity;
using Microsoft.AspNetCore.Identity.EntityFrameworkCore;
using Microsoft.EntityFrameworkCore;
using Microsoft.Extensions.DependencyInjection;

namespace SportsStore.Models {

    public static class IdentitySeedData {
        private const string adminUser = "admin";
        private const string adminPassword = "MySecret123$";
        private const string adminRole = "Administrator";

        public static async void SeedDatabase(IApplicationBuilder app) {
            (GetAppService<IdentityDataContext>(app)).Database.Migrate();

            UserManager<IdentityUser> userManager
                = GetAppService<UserManager<IdentityUser>>(app);
            RoleManager<IdentityRole> roleManager
                = GetAppService<RoleManager<IdentityRole>>(app);

            IdentityRole role = await roleManager.FindByNameAsync(adminRole);
            IdentityUser user = await userManager.FindByNameAsync(adminUser);

            if (role == null) {
                role = new IdentityRole(adminRole);
                IdentityResult result = await roleManager.CreateAsync(role);
                if (!result.Succeeded) {
                    throw new Exception("Cannot create role: "
                        + result.Errors.FirstOrDefault());
                }
            }

            if (user == null) {
                user = new IdentityUser(adminUser);
                IdentityResult result
                    = await userManager.CreateAsync(user, adminPassword);
                if (!result.Succeeded) {
                    throw new Exception("Cannot create user: "
                        + result.Errors.FirstOrDefault());
                }
            }
```

```
            if (!await userManager.IsInRoleAsync(user, adminRole)) {
                IdentityResult result
                    = await userManager.AddToRoleAsync(user, adminRole);
                if (!result.Succeeded) {
                    throw new Exception("Cannot add user to role: "
                        + result.Errors.FirstOrDefault());
                }
            }
        }

        private static T GetAppService<T>(IApplicationBuilder app) {
            return app.ApplicationServices.GetRequiredService<T>();
        }
    }
}
```

The static SeedDatabase method defined in the listing receives a parameter that defines the IApplicationBuilder interface, which will be provided by the Startup class and which can be used to access the services that have been defined during the application's configuration. This is used to get a database context object for the Identity database to ensure that the migrations have been applied and to ensure that there is an admin user in the database that has a password of MySecret123 and that is a member of the Administrator role.

■ **Note**   When you rely on a user account seeded in the database, it is good practice to change the password when the application has been deployed into production.

Adding Identity to the Application Configuration

To set up ASP.NET Core Identity so that it is integrated with the rest of the ASP.NET Core application, add the configuration statements shown in Listing 11-10 to the Startup class.

Listing 11-10. Configuring Identity in the Startup.cs File in the SportsStore Folder

```
using Microsoft.AspNetCore.Builder;
using Microsoft.AspNetCore.Hosting;
using Microsoft.Extensions.Configuration;
using Microsoft.Extensions.DependencyInjection;
using Microsoft.Extensions.Logging;
using Microsoft.AspNetCore.SpaServices.Webpack;
using SportsStore.Models;
using Microsoft.EntityFrameworkCore;
using Newtonsoft.Json;
using Microsoft.AspNetCore.Identity.EntityFrameworkCore;
```

```
namespace SportsStore {
    public class Startup {
        public Startup(IHostingEnvironment env) {
            var builder = new ConfigurationBuilder()
                .SetBasePath(env.ContentRootPath)
                .AddJsonFile("appsettings.json", optional: false, reloadOnChange: true)
                .AddJsonFile($"appsettings.{env.EnvironmentName}.json", optional: true)
                .AddEnvironmentVariables();
            Configuration = builder.Build();
        }

        public IConfigurationRoot Configuration { get; }

        public void ConfigureServices(IServiceCollection services) {

            services.AddDbContext<IdentityDataContext>(options =>
                options.UseSqlServer(Configuration
                    ["Data:Identity:ConnectionString"]));

            services.AddIdentity<IdentityUser, IdentityRole>()
                .AddEntityFrameworkStores<IdentityDataContext>();

            services.AddDbContext<DataContext>(options =>
                options.UseSqlServer(Configuration
                    ["Data:Products:ConnectionString"]));
            services.AddMvc().AddJsonOptions(opts => {
                opts.SerializerSettings.ReferenceLoopHandling
                    = ReferenceLoopHandling.Serialize;
                opts.SerializerSettings.NullValueHandling = NullValueHandling.Ignore;
            });

            services.AddDistributedSqlServerCache(options => {
                options.ConnectionString =
                    Configuration["Data:Products:ConnectionString"];
                options.SchemaName = "dbo";
                options.TableName = "SessionData";
            });

            services.AddSession(options => {
                options.CookieName = "SportsStore.Session";
                options.IdleTimeout = System.TimeSpan.FromHours(48);
                options.CookieHttpOnly = false;
            });
        }

        public void Configure(IApplicationBuilder app,
                IHostingEnvironment env, ILoggerFactory loggerFactory) {
            loggerFactory.AddConsole(Configuration.GetSection("Logging"));
            loggerFactory.AddDebug();
```

```
        app.UseDeveloperExceptionPage();
        app.UseWebpackDevMiddleware(new WebpackDevMiddlewareOptions {
            HotModuleReplacement = true
        });

        app.UseStaticFiles();
        app.UseSession();
        app.UseIdentity();
        app.UseMvc(routes => {
            routes.MapRoute(
                name: "default",
                template: "{controller=Home}/{action=Index}/{id?}");

            routes.MapSpaFallbackRoute("angular-fallback",
                new { controller = "Home", action = "Index" });
        });

        SeedData.SeedDatabase(app.ApplicationServices
            .GetRequiredService<DataContext>());
        IdentitySeedData.SeedDatabase(app);
    }
  }
}
```

The AddDbContext method called in ConfigureServices registers the database context class defined in Listing 11-8 with Entity Framework Core, while the AddIdentity method tells Identity to use the default classes to represent users and roles and to store the data through the context class. The UseIdentity method called in the Configure method adds Identity to the ASP.NET Core request pipeline to integrate it into the rest of the application.

To provide the connection string that tells Entity Framework Core where to store the Identity data, add the configuration entries shown in Listing 11-11 to the appsettings.json file (ensuring that the connection string is on a single line).

Listing 11-11. Adding a Connection String in the appsettings.json File in the SportsStore Folder

```
{
  "Logging": {
    "IncludeScopes": false,
    "LogLevel": {
      "Microsoft.EntityFrameworkCore": "Information",
      "Microsoft.AspNetCore.NodeServices": "Information",
      "Default": "Warning"
    }
  },
  "Data": {
    "Products": {
      "ConnectionString": "Server=localhost,5100;Database=SportsStore;User Id=sa;Password=my
      Secret123;MultipleActiveResultSets=true"
    },
```

```
    "Identity": {
      "ConnectionString": "Server=localhost,5100;Database=Identity;User Id=sa;
      Password=mySecret123;MultipleActiveResultSets=true"
    }
  }
}
```

The connection string uses the same SQL Server container that is storing the rest of the SportsStore data but uses a database called Identity.

Creating the Database Migration

To create the database migration, use a command prompt to run the command shown in Listing 11-12 in the SportsStore folder.

Listing 11-12. Creating a Database Migration

```
dotnet ef migrations add Identity --context IdentityDataContext
```

When the application is next started, the migration will be applied to the database before it is seeded with the admin user, which will be assigned the Administrator role.

Creating the Authentication Controller and View

Although ASP.NET Core Identity provides all the plumbing required to support authentication and authorization, it requires the addition of a controller to present the user with a login screen when trying to access a restricted action method. Create a C# class file called AccountController.cs in the Controllers folder and add the code shown in Listing 11-13.

Listing 11-13. The Contents of the AccountController.cs File in the Controllers Folder

```
using Microsoft.AspNetCore.Identity;
using Microsoft.AspNetCore.Identity.EntityFrameworkCore;
using Microsoft.AspNetCore.Mvc;
using System.ComponentModel.DataAnnotations;
using System.Threading.Tasks;

namespace SportsStore.Controllers {

    public class AccountController : Controller {
        private UserManager<IdentityUser> userManager;
        private SignInManager<IdentityUser> signInManager;

        public AccountController(UserManager<IdentityUser> userMgr,
                            SignInManager<IdentityUser> signInMgr) {
            userManager = userMgr;
            signInManager = signInMgr;
        }
```

```
    [HttpGet]
    public IActionResult Login(string returnUrl) {
        ViewBag.returnUrl = returnUrl;
        return View();
    }

    [HttpPost]
    public async Task<IActionResult> Login(LoginViewModel creds,
            string returnUrl) {

        if (ModelState.IsValid) {
            if (await DoLogin(creds)) {
                return Redirect(returnUrl ?? "/");
            } else {
                ModelState.AddModelError("", "Invalid username or password");
            }
        }
        return View(creds);
    }

    [HttpPost]
    public async Task<IActionResult> Logout(string redirectUrl) {
        await signInManager.SignOutAsync();
        return Redirect(redirectUrl ?? "/");
    }

    private async Task<bool> DoLogin(LoginViewModel creds) {
        IdentityUser user = await userManager.FindByNameAsync(creds.Name);
        if (user != null) {
            await signInManager.SignOutAsync();
            Microsoft.AspNetCore.Identity.SignInResult result =
                await signInManager.PasswordSignInAsync(user, creds.Password,
                    false, false);
            return result.Succeeded;
        }
        return false;
    }
}

public class LoginViewModel {
    [Required]
    public string Name {get; set;}
    [Required]
    public string Password { get; set;}
}
}
```

The Login action method that accepts GET requests renders a Razor view that will prompt the user for their credentials. The POST Login action method validates the credentials and signs the user in. The authentication is performed in the DoLogin method, which I have defined so I can use the same code for web service authentication later in the chapter.

To provide the view that will prompt the user for their credentials, create a `Views/Account` folder and add to it a Razor file called `Login.cshtml`, with the content shown in Listing 11-14.

Listing 11-14. The Contents of the Login.cshtml File in the Views/Account Folder

```
@model SportsStore.Controllers.LoginViewModel

<div class="m-2">
    <h3 class="bg-primary p-2">Log In</h3>
    <div class="text-danger" asp-validation-summary="All"></div>
    <form asp-action="Login" method="post">
        <input type="hidden" name="returnUrl" value="@ViewBag.returnUrl" />
        <div class="form-group">
            <label>Name</label>
            <input asp-for="Name" class="form-control" />
        </div>
        <div class="form-group">
            <label>Password</label>
            <input type="password" asp-for="Password" class="form-control" />
        </div>
        <div class="text-center">
            <button class="btn btn-primary" type="submit">Log In</button>
        </div>
    </form>
</div>
```

The view contains an HTML form that uses `input` elements to collect the username and password and send them to the `Account` controller.

Understanding the Conventional Authentication Flow

The controller and view in Listings 11-13 and 11-14 are the standard way to deal with authentication for traditional round-trip applications. To see how the flow of requests is handled, add the action method shown in Listing 11-15 to the `Home` controller so that there is a round-trip action method to target using the browser.

Listing 11-15. Adding an Action Method in the HomeController.cs File in the Controllers Folder

```
using Microsoft.AspNetCore.Mvc;
using SportsStore.Models;
using System.Linq;
using Microsoft.AspNetCore.Authorization;

namespace SportsStore.Controllers {
    public class HomeController : Controller {
        private DataContext context;

        public HomeController(DataContext ctx) {
            context = ctx;
        }
```

```
        public IActionResult Index() {
            ViewBag.Message = "Sports Store App";
            return View(context.Products.First());
        }

        [Authorize]
        public string Protected() {
            return "You have been authenticated";
        }
    }
}
```

The new action method is called Protected, and it has been decorated with the Authorize attribute, which means that any authenticated user will be able to access the action. Restart the ASP.NET Core MVC application and use a browser to request the URL http://localhost:5000/home/protected. When prompted for credentials, enter admin into the Name field and MySecret123$ into the Password field and click the Log In button to see the message produced by the protected action method, as shown in Figure 11-3.

Figure 11-3. *Round-trip authentication*

When ASP.NET Core MVC finds that the Authorize attribute has been applied to an action method, the browser is redirected to the /account/login URL so that the user can enter credentials. When the user submits their name and password, the sign-in process redirects the user back to the URL for the protected action method. This second redirection incudes a cookie that the browser will include in subsequent HTTP requests and that is used to identify the user without needing to prompt them for credentials again.

The use of the cookie means that the Angular application benefits for the login process, too. Navigate to http://localhost:5000/admin/products using the same browser tab with which you authenticated yourself, and you will see that the administration features work and that related data is displayed for each product. This happens because the browser automatically includes the authentication cookie in the HTTP requests sent by the Angular application, which means that authenticating using the round-trip part of the application also has the effect of authenticating for the web service part of the application, too.

CHAPTER 11 ■ SECURING THE APPLICATION

Authenticating Directly in Angular

As things stand, the user needs to know that they have to authenticate themselves before starting the Angular application to use the administration features, which is far from ideal. But, with a little work, it is possible to allow users to authenticate themselves within the Angular application so that the round-trip authentication system isn't required.

Creating a Web Service Authentication Method

The first step is to create an ASP.NET Core MVC action method that will allow clients to authenticate without trying to redirect them to a URL or return an HTML response, as well as creating a corresponding action that will end an authenticated session. Add the methods shown in Listing 11-16 to the Account controller.

Listing 11-16. Adding Action Methods in the AccountController.cs File in the Controllers Folder

```
using Microsoft.AspNetCore.Identity;
using Microsoft.AspNetCore.Identity.EntityFrameworkCore;
using Microsoft.AspNetCore.Mvc;
using System.ComponentModel.DataAnnotations;
using System.Threading.Tasks;

namespace SportsStore.Controllers {

    public class AccountController : Controller {
        private UserManager<IdentityUser> userManager;
        private SignInManager<IdentityUser> signInManager;

        public AccountController(UserManager<IdentityUser> userMgr,
                            SignInManager<IdentityUser> signInMgr) {
            userManager = userMgr;
            signInManager = signInMgr;
        }

        // ...other methods omitted for brevity...

        [HttpPost("/api/account/login")]
        public async Task<IActionResult> Login([FromBody] LoginViewModel creds) {
            if (ModelState.IsValid && await DoLogin(creds)) {
                return Ok();
            }
            return BadRequest();
        }

        [HttpPost("/api/account/logout")]
        public async Task<IActionResult> Logout() {
            await signInManager.SignOutAsync();
            return Ok();
        }
    }
}
```

```
    public class LoginViewModel {
        [Required]
        public string Name {get; set;}
        [Required]
        public string Password { get; set;}
    }
}
```

The new methods are simplified versions of the actions for round-trip clients, providing support for just authentication, without redirection or the need to provide HTML content to get the user's credentials.

Creating the Repository Method

The next step is to add methods to the Angular Repository class so that the client can perform authentication, as shown in Listing 11-17.

Listing 11-17. Performing Authentication in the repository.ts File in the ClientApp/app/models Folder

```
import { Product } from "./product.model";
import { Injectable } from "@angular/core";
import { Http, RequestMethod, Request, Response } from "@angular/http";
import { Observable } from "rxjs/Observable";
import "rxjs/add/operator/map";
import { Filter, Pagination } from "./configClasses.repository";
import { Supplier } from "./supplier.model";
import { Order } from "./order.model";
import { ErrorHandlerService, ValidationError } from "../errorHandler.service";
import "rxjs/add/operator/catch";

const productsUrl = "/api/products";
const suppliersUrl = "/api/suppliers";
const ordersUrl = "/api/orders";

@Injectable()
export class Repository {
    private filterObject = new Filter();
    private paginationObject = new Pagination();

    constructor(private http: Http) {
        this.filter.related = true;
        this.getProducts();
    }

    // ...other methods omitted for brevity...

    login(name: string, password: string) : Observable<Response> {
        return this.http.post("/api/account/login",
            { name: name, password: password});
    }
    logout() {
        this.http.post("/api/account/logout", null).subscribe(respone => {});
    }
```

```
    product: Product;
    products: Product[];
    suppliers: Supplier[] = [];
    categories: string[] = [];
    orders: Order[] = [];

    get filter(): Filter {
        return this.filterObject;
    }

    get pagination(): Pagination {
        return this.paginationObject;
    }
}
```

The login method sends an HTTP POST request to the web service, and unlike the other methods in the repository, it returns an Observable<Response>, which will allow the outcome of the authentication request to be monitored. Unlike the data-related operations that the SportsStore supports, authentication requires immediate feedback to the user. The logout method also sends an HTTP POST request to the web service but doesn't allow the response to be observed (but calls the subscribe method, without which the request will not be sent).

Creating the Authentication Service

The simplest way to manage authentication in an Angular application is with a simple service, which can provide access to the repository methods and provide a consistent view of whether the user is currently authenticated. Create the ClientApp/app/auth folder and add to it a TypeScript file called authentication. service.ts with the code shown in Listing 11-18.

Listing 11-18. The Contents of the authentication.service.ts File in the ClientApp/app/auth Folder

```
import { Injectable } from "@angular/core";
import { Repository } from "../models/repository";
import { Observable } from "rxjs/Observable";
import { Router } from "@angular/router";
import "rxjs/add/observable/of";

@Injectable()
export class AuthenticationService {

    constructor(private repo: Repository,
                private router: Router) { }

    authenticated: boolean = false;
    name: string;
    password: string;
    callbackUrl: string;
```

```
    login() : Observable<boolean> {
        this.authenticated = false;
        return this.repo.login(this.name, this.password)
            .map(response => {
                if (response.ok) {
                    this.authenticated = true;
                    this.password = null;
                    this.router.navigateByUrl(this.callbackUrl || "/admin/overview");
                }
                return this.authenticated;
            })
            .catch(e => {
                this.authenticated = false;
                return Observable.of(false);
            });
    }

    logout() {
        this.authenticated = false;
        this.repo.logout();
        this.router.navigateByUrl("/login");
    }
}
```

The service packages up access to the repository methods and provides an authenticated property that can be used to determine whether the user is currently authenticated. The login method uses the repository to send an HTTP request to the web service and observes the response to generate an observable true or false outcome.

Creating the Authentication Component

To create a component that will prompt the user for their credentials, add a TypeScript file called authentication.component.ts to the ClientApp/app/auth folder with the code shown in Listing 11-19.

Listing 11-19. The Contents of the authentication.component.ts File in the ClientApp/app/auth Folder

```
import {Component } from "@angular/core";
import { AuthenticationService } from "./authentication.service";

@Component({
    templateUrl: "authentication.component.html"
})
export class AuthenticationComponent {

    constructor(public authService: AuthenticationService) {}

    showError: boolean = false;
```

```
    login() {
        this.showError = false;
        this.authService.login().subscribe(result => {
            this.showError = !result;
        });
    }
}
```

The component uses its constructor to receive an AuthenticationService object through dependency injection so that it can be accessed from the template. It also defines a showError property that will signal to the template when an error message will be displayed, and there is a login method that starts the login process and uses the result to set the showError property.

To define the template, add an HTML file called authentication.component.html to the auth folder with the elements shown in Listing 11-20.

Listing 11-20. The Contents of the authentication.component.html File in the ClientApp/app/auth Folder

```
<div class="navbar bg-info mb-1">
    <a class="navbar-brand text-white">SPORTS STORE Admin</a>
</div>

<h4 *ngIf="showError" class="p-2 bg-danger text-white">
    Invalid username or password
</h4>

<form novalidate #authForm="ngForm">
    <div class="form-group">
        <label>Name:</label>
        <input #name="ngModel" name="name" class="form-control"
                [(ngModel)]="authService.name" required />
        <div *ngIf="name.invalid" class="text-danger">
            Please enter your user name
        </div>
    </div>
    <div class="form-group">
        <label>Password:</label>
        <input type="password" #password="ngModel" name="password"
                class="form-control" [(ngModel)]="authService.password" required />
        <div *ngIf="password.invalid" class="text-danger">
            Please enter your password
        </div>
    </div>
    <div class="text-center pt-2">
        <button class="btn btn-primary" [disabled]="authForm.invalid"
                (click)="login()">Login</button>
    </div>
</form>
```

The template presents form elements to the user to obtain their credentials, which Angular validation uses to ensure that the form cannot be submitted until values are provided. The component's showError property is used with the ngIf directive to show an error to the user when there is an authentication problem.

Creating the Authentication Route Guard

The Angular route guard feature is used to prevent navigation to a URL route until a specific condition is met, which will be authentication in this case. To create a route guard, add a TypeScript file called authentication.guard.ts in the auth folder and add the code shown in Listing 11-21.

Listing 11-21. The Contents of the authentication.guard.ts File in the ClientApp/app/auth Folder

```
import { Injectable } from "@angular/core";
import { Router, ActivatedRouteSnapshot, RouterStateSnapshot } from "@angular/router";
import { AuthenticationService } from "./authentication.service";

@Injectable()
export class AuthenticationGuard {

    constructor(private router: Router,
                private authService: AuthenticationService) {}

    canActivateChild(route: ActivatedRouteSnapshot,
            state: RouterStateSnapshot): boolean {
        if (this.authService.authenticated) {
            return true;
        } else {
            this.authService.callbackUrl = "/admin/" + route.url.toString();
            this.router.navigateByUrl("/login");
            return false;
        }
    }
}
```

The canActivateChild method is called when the user tries to navigate to a child URL protected by the guard. The canActivateChild method returns true if the user has been authenticated, which allows the navigation to proceed. If the user has not been authenticated, then the application is instructed to navigate to the /admin/login, which will allow them to authenticate. The guard uses the value of the target URL to set the callbackUrl property defined by the authentication service, which is automatically navigated to when authentication succeeds, reproducing the redirection scheme used for round-trip clients described earlier in the chapter.

Creating and Registering the Authentication Feature Module

Add a TypeScript file called auth.module.ts in the auth folder and use it to define the Angular feature module shown in Listing 11-22, which will allow the authentication service, component, and guard to be used in the result of the application.

Listing 11-22. The Contents of the auth.module.ts File in the ClientApp/app/auth Folder

```
import { NgModule } from "@angular/core";
import { FormsModule } from '@angular/forms';
import { BrowserModule } from '@angular/platform-browser';
import { RouterModule } from "@angular/router";
```

```
import { AuthenticationService } from "./authentication.service";
import { AuthenticationComponent } from "./authentication.component";
import { AuthenticationGuard } from "./authentication.guard";

@NgModule({
    imports: [RouterModule, FormsModule, BrowserModule],
    declarations: [AuthenticationComponent],
    providers: [AuthenticationService, AuthenticationGuard],
    exports: [AuthenticationComponent]
})
export class AuthModule { }
```

To register the new feature module with the rest of the application, add the statements shown in Listing 11-23 to the root module.

Listing 11-23. Registering a Feature Module in the app.module.ts File in the ClientApp/app Folder

```
import { BrowserModule } from '@angular/platform-browser';
import { NgModule } from '@angular/core';
import { FormsModule } from '@angular/forms';
import { HttpModule } from '@angular/http';
import { AppComponent } from './app.component';
import { ModelModule } from "./models/model.module";
import { RoutingConfig } from "./app.routing";
import { StoreModule } from "./store/store.module";
import { ProductSelectionComponent } from "./store/productSelection.component";
import { AdminModule } from "./admin/admin.module";
import { ErrorHandler } from "@angular/core";
import { ErrorHandlerService } from "./errorHandler.service";
import { AuthModule } from "./auth/auth.module";

const eHandler = new ErrorHandlerService();

export function handler() {
    return eHandler;
}

@NgModule({
    declarations: [AppComponent],
    imports: [BrowserModule, FormsModule, HttpModule, ModelModule,
        RoutingConfig, StoreModule, AdminModule, AuthModule],
    providers: [
        { provide: ErrorHandlerService, useFactory: handler},
        { provide: ErrorHandler, useFactory: handler}],
    bootstrap: [AppComponent]
})
export class AppModule { }
```

Configuring the URL Routes

To enable authentication, change the routing configuration to add support for the authentication components and to guard the administration components, as shown in Listing 11-24.

Listing 11-24. Configuring the URL Routes in the app.routing.ts File in the ClientApp/app Folder

```
import { Routes, RouterModule } from "@angular/router";
import { ProductSelectionComponent } from "./store/productSelection.component";
import { CartDetailComponent } from "./store/cartDetail.component";
import { CheckoutDetailsComponent }
    from "./store/checkout/checkoutDetails.component";
import { CheckoutPaymentComponent }
    from "./store/checkout/checkoutPayment.component";
import { CheckoutSummaryComponent }
    from "./store/checkout/checkoutSummary.component";
import { OrderConfirmationComponent }
    from "./store/checkout/orderConfirmation.component";
import { AdminComponent } from "./admin/admin.component";
import { OverviewComponent } from "./admin/overview.component";
import { ProductAdminComponent } from "./admin/productAdmin.component";
import { OrderAdminComponent } from "./admin/orderAdmin.component";

import { AuthenticationGuard } from "./auth/authentication.guard";
import { AuthenticationComponent } from "./auth/authentication.component";

const routes: Routes = [
    { path: "login", component: AuthenticationComponent },
    { path: "admin", redirectTo: "/admin/overview", pathMatch: "full"},
    {
        path: "admin", component: AdminComponent,
        canActivateChild: [AuthenticationGuard],
        children: [
            { path: "products", component: ProductAdminComponent, },
            { path: "orders", component: OrderAdminComponent },
            { path: "overview", component: OverviewComponent },
            { path: "", component: OverviewComponent }
        ]
    },
    { path: "checkout/step1", component: CheckoutDetailsComponent },
    { path: "checkout/step2", component: CheckoutPaymentComponent },
    { path: "checkout/step3", component: CheckoutSummaryComponent },
    { path: "checkout/confirmation", component: OrderConfirmationComponent },
    { path: "checkout", component: CheckoutDetailsComponent },
    { path: "cart", component: CartDetailComponent },
    { path: "store", component: ProductSelectionComponent },
    { path: "", component: ProductSelectionComponent }]

export const RoutingConfig = RouterModule.forRoot(routes);
```

The changes set up the /login URL for handling authentication and apply the route guard to prevent any of the administration routes from being activated until authentication has been performed. There is also an /admin route, which I have added so that the user can navigate to /admin without generating an error when the service navigates after a successful authentication.

Creating the Log Out Button

It is important to allow users to terminate a session, especially when they have access to administration functions. Add the code shown in Listing 11-25 to prepare to display a logout button to the user.

Listing 11-25. Preparing for Logout in the admin.component.ts File in the ClientApp/app/admin Folder

```
import { Component } from "@angular/core";
import { Repository } from "../models/repository";
import { AuthenticationService } from "../auth/authentication.service";

@Component({
    templateUrl: "admin.component.html"
})
export class AdminComponent {

    constructor(private repo: Repository,
                public authService: AuthenticationService) {
        repo.filter.reset();
        repo.filter.related = true;
        this.repo.getProducts();
        this.repo.getSuppliers();
        this.repo.getOrders();
    }
}
```

The changes receive the authentication service via dependency injection so that it can be accessed through the template. To create the logout button, add the elements shown in Listing 11-26 to the component's template.

Listing 11-26. Adding a Log Out Button in the admin.component.html File in the ClientApp/app/admin Folder

```
<div class="navbar bg-info mb-1">
    <div class="row">
        <div class="col">
            <a class="navbar-brand text-white">SPORTS STORE Admin</a>
        </div>
        <div class="col text-right">
            <button class="btn btn-sm btn-warning"
                (click)="authService.logout()">
                Log Out
            </button>
        </div>
    </div>
</div>
```

```
<div class="row no-gutters">
    <div class="col-3">
        <button class="btn btn-block btn-outline-info" routerLink="/admin"
                routerLinkActive="active" [routerLinkActiveOptions]="{exact: true}">
            Overview
        </button>
        <button class="btn btn-block btn-outline-info" routerLink="/admin/products"
                routerLinkActive="active">Products</button>
        <button class="btn btn-block btn-outline-info" routerLink="/admin/orders"
                routerLinkActive="active">Orders</button>
    </div>
    <div class="col p-2">
        <router-outlet></router-outlet>
    </div>
</div>
```

The new button calls the logout method provided by the authentication service, which will send an HTTP request to the web service to end the user's session and prevent the user from accessing any of the administration features until they have authenticated again.

Disable Automatic Authentication Redirection for Web Services

The final step is to change the configuration so that clients are not sent redirection responses when authentication is required for web service requests. This is an optional step, but it is important for applications where the Angular application isn't the only client of the web services.

Add the configuration statements shown in Listing 11-27 to the Startup class to change the behavior for requests that target URLs that start with /api.

Listing 11-27. Configuring Authentication Redirection in the Startup.cs File in the SportsStore Folder

```
using Microsoft.AspNetCore.Builder;
using Microsoft.AspNetCore.Hosting;
using Microsoft.Extensions.Configuration;
using Microsoft.Extensions.DependencyInjection;
using Microsoft.Extensions.Logging;
using Microsoft.AspNetCore.SpaServices.Webpack;
using SportsStore.Models;
using Microsoft.EntityFrameworkCore;
using Newtonsoft.Json;
using Microsoft.AspNetCore.Identity.EntityFrameworkCore;
using Microsoft.AspNetCore.Authentication.Cookies;
using System.Threading.Tasks;

namespace SportsStore {
    public class Startup {
        public Startup(IHostingEnvironment env) {

            // ...statements omitted for brevity...
        }

        public IConfigurationRoot Configuration { get; }
```

```
public void ConfigureServices(IServiceCollection services) {

    services.AddDbContext<IdentityDataContext>(options =>
        options.UseSqlServer(Configuration
            ["Data:Identity:ConnectionString"]));
    services.AddIdentity<IdentityUser, IdentityRole>()
        .AddEntityFrameworkStores<IdentityDataContext>();
    services.AddDbContext<DataContext>(options =>
        options.UseSqlServer(Configuration
            ["Data:Products:ConnectionString"]));

    services.AddMvc().AddJsonOptions(opts => {
        opts.SerializerSettings.ReferenceLoopHandling
            = ReferenceLoopHandling.Serialize;
        opts.SerializerSettings.NullValueHandling = NullValueHandling.Ignore;
    });

    services.AddDistributedSqlServerCache(options => {
        options.ConnectionString =
            Configuration["Data:Products:ConnectionString"];
        options.SchemaName = "dbo";
        options.TableName = "SessionData";
    });

    services.AddSession(options => {
        options.CookieName = "SportsStore.Session";
        options.IdleTimeout = System.TimeSpan.FromHours(48);
        options.CookieHttpOnly = false;
    });

    services.Configure<IdentityOptions>(config => {
        config.Cookies.ApplicationCookie.Events =
            new CookieAuthenticationEvents {
                OnRedirectToLogin = context => {
                    if (context.Request.Path.StartsWithSegments("/api")
                            && context.Response.StatusCode == 200) {
                        context.Response.StatusCode = 401;
                    } else {
                        context.Response.Redirect(context.RedirectUri);
                    }
                    return Task.FromResult<object>(null);
                }
            };
    });
}

public void Configure(IApplicationBuilder app,
        IHostingEnvironment env, ILoggerFactory loggerFactory) {

    // ...statements omitted for brevity...
}
    }
}
```

ASP.NET Core Identity provides a series of events triggered at key states in the authentication and authorization process. The new statements in the ConfigureServices method replace the default behavior so that the 401 Unauthorized status code is returned for unauthorized requests to URLs that start with /api. This allows the rest of the URLs supported by the application to use the conventional redirection approach while excluding the web services.

Testing the Client Authentication Process

Restart the ASP.NET Core MVC application and use the browser to navigate to http://localhost:5000/ admin. The Angular application will load and display the /login URL. Enter admin into the Name field and MySecret123$ into the Password field and click the Log In button. The Angular application will use the web service for authentication and then navigate to the /admin URL. Click the Log Out button and you will be returned to the login prompt, as shown in Figure 11-4.

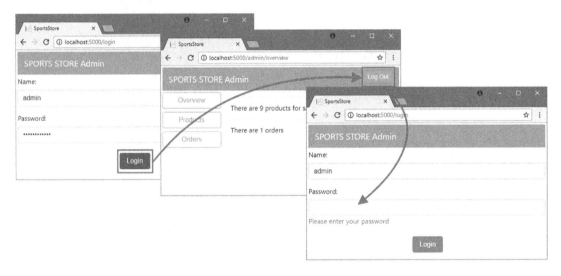

Figure 11-4. *Authenticating using the Angular application*

Authenticating the user within the Angular application provides a more integrated experience for the user but uses the same authentication system as for round-trip clients. When the Angular application provides valid credentials to the authentication web service, ASP.NET Core Identity adds a cookie to the response, which the browser automatically includes in future requests; this allows the identity of the user to be established and satisfies the restrictions applied using the Authorize attribute.

Summary

In this chapter, I explained how to use ASP.NET Core MVC and ASP.NET Core Identity to secure an application that has an Angular client. I showed you how to apply the Authorize attribute to restrict access to action methods and how to set up ASP.NET Core Identity to manage users and their roles. In the next chapter, I show you how to prepare the application for deployment.

CHAPTER 12

Preparing for Deployment

There are lots of ways to deploy an ASP.NET Core MVC application. I don't get into the options in this book, but there are some changes that are required regardless of how the application is hosted.

In this chapter, I show how to secure the web service against cross-site forgery attacks, using a feature that can be disruptive during development but that is essential for production applications. I also show you how to disable the developer-friendly features that have ensured that the database is kept up-to-date, that the TypeScript files are automatically compiled, and that changes in the Angular application are sent to the browser automatically. These are all useful features for the developer, but they should not be left enabled for production applications.

Preparing for This Chapter

This chapter uses the SportsStore project created in Chapter 3 and modified since. To reset the database and its contents, open a command prompt, navigate to the SportsStore folder, and run the commands shown in Listing 12-1.

■ **Tip** You can download the complete project for this chapter from https://github.com/apress/esntl-angular-for-asp.net-core-mvc. This is also where you will find updates and corrections for this book.

Listing 12-1. Resetting the Database

```
docker-compose down
docker-compose up
```

The first command removes the Docker database container from the previous chapter. The second command creates and starts a fresh container. Wait until SQL Server is up and running, open a second command prompt, and run the commands shown in Listing 12-2 in the SportsStore folder.

Listing 12-2. Preparing the Database

```
dotnet ef database update --context DataContext
dotnet ef database update --context IdentityDataContext
dotnet sql-cache create "Server=localhost,5100;Database=SportsStore;User Id=sa;
Password=mySecret123;MultipleActiveResultSets=true" "dbo" "SessionData"
```

© Adam Freeman 2017
A. Freeman, *Essential Angular for ASP.NET Core MVC*, DOI 10.1007/978-1-4842-2916-3_12

The first and second commands apply the migrations in the project to the database, which creates the SportsStore and Identity databases. The --context argument is required for these commands because there are two database context classes in the project and Entity Framework Core needs to know which one it should use to update the database.

The third command creates the additional table required to store session data. This command receives its connection string as an argument and doesn't use the context classes to set up its database, which is why no --context argument is required.

Start the application to add the seed data and begin handling HTTP requests. If you are using Visual Studio, you can do this by selecting Debug ➤ Start Without Debugging. If you are using Visual Studio Code or just prefer working with the command line, then run the command shown in Listing 12-3 in the SportsStore folder.

Listing 12-3. Starting the Application

```
dotnet run
```

Use a browser to navigate to http://localhost:5000 and you will see the content shown in Figure 12-1.

Figure 12-1. *Running the example application*

Preventing Cross-Site Request Forgery Attacks

Whenever you use cookies to identify a user, you must take care to protect your application from cross-site request forgery (CSRF) attacks. The idea of a CSRF attack is to trick the user into loading a malicious web page and sending an HTTP request to your application. The browser will automatically include any cookies it has received from your application in the request, which allows the attacker to perform operations while impersonating the user, typically to grant the attacker access to the application or to change or delete the application's data.

Protecting against CSRF attacks requires including a random cryptographic token in HTTP responses from the application and requiring that the client includes the same token in subsequent HTTP requests. For round-trip applications, the token is usually included as a hidden form field, but for Angular clients, the token is sent as a cookie. Angular detects the cookie and uses it to set the value of a header in HTTP requests, something that CSRF attacks cannot do, which identifies a request as coming from the Angular application and not from an attack. ASP.NET Core MVC includes built-in support for anti-CSRF tokens but requires some additional work to use them in a way that works with Angular, as described in the sections that follow.

Enabling Anti-CSRF Tokens

The first step to protecting against CSRF is to apply the attribute that tells ASP.NET Core MVC to accept requests only when they contain a valid cryptographic token. The simplest way to protect the application is to apply the ValidateAntiForgeryToken attribute to a controller that tells ASP.NET Core MVC to accept only those requests with valid tokens. Apply the attribute as shown in Listing 12-4 to protect the product API controller.

■ **Tip**   You can apply the IgnoreAntiforgeryToken attribute to an action method if you want to exclude to it from the anti-CSRF policy created by a class-wide ValidateAntiForgeryToken attribute.

Listing 12-4. Requiring Tokens in the ProductValuesController.cs File in the Controllers Folder

```
using Microsoft.AspNetCore.Mvc;
using SportsStore.Models;
using Microsoft.EntityFrameworkCore;
using System.Linq;
using System.Collections.Generic;
using SportsStore.Models.BindingTargets;
using Microsoft.AspNetCore.JsonPatch;
using Microsoft.AspNetCore.Authorization;

namespace SportsStore.Controllers {

    [Route("api/products")]
    [Authorize(Roles = "Administrator")]
    [ValidateAntiForgeryToken]
    public class ProductValuesController : Controller {
        private DataContext context;

        public ProductValuesController(DataContext ctx) {
            context = ctx;
        }

        // ...methods omitted for brevity...
    }
}
```

Apply the same attribute to the session API controller, as shown in Listing 12-5, so that session data can be stored using only the requests that contain a valid anti-CSRF token.

Listing 12-5. Requiring Tokens in the SessionValuesController.cs File in the Controllers Folder

```
using Microsoft.AspNetCore.Http;
using Microsoft.AspNetCore.Mvc;
using Newtonsoft.Json;
using SportsStore.Models;
using SportsStore.Models.BindingTargets;

namespace SportsStore.Controllers {

    [Route("/api/session")]
    [ValidateAntiForgeryToken]
    public class SessionValuesController : Controller {

        // ...methods omitted for brevity...
    }
}
```

Apply the attribute to the controller for supplier data, as shown in Listing 12-6.

Listing 12-6. Requiring Tokens in the SupplierValuesController.cs File in the Controllers Folder

```
using Microsoft.AspNetCore.Mvc;
using SportsStore.Models;
using SportsStore.Models.BindingTargets;
using System.Collections.Generic;
using Microsoft.AspNetCore.Authorization;

namespace SportsStore.Controllers {

    [Route("api/suppliers")]
    [Authorize(Roles = "Administrator")]
    [ValidateAntiForgeryToken]
    public class SupplierValuesController : Controller {
        private DataContext context;

        public SupplierValuesController(DataContext ctx) {
            context = ctx;
        }

        // ...methods omitted for brevity...
    }
}
```

Apply the attribute to the controller for order data, as shown in Listing 12-7.

Listing 12-7. Requiring Tokens in the OrderValuesController.cs File in the Controllers Folder

```
using Microsoft.AspNetCore.Mvc;
using Microsoft.EntityFrameworkCore;
using SportsStore.Models;
using System.Collections.Generic;
```

```
using System.Linq;
using Microsoft.AspNetCore.Authorization;

namespace SportsStore.Controllers {

    [Route("/api/orders")]
    [Authorize(Roles = "Administrator")]
    [ValidateAntiForgeryToken]
    public class OrderValuesController : Controller {
        private DataContext context;

        public OrderValuesController(DataContext ctx) {
            context = ctx;
        }

        // ...methods omitted for brevity...
    }
}
```

As a result of these changes, all the web service action methods can be accessed only if the request includes a token that has been provided by the application. Restart the ASP.NET Core MVC application and navigate to http://localhost:5000; you will see that the initial HTTP request succeeds and all of the subsequent requests fail, causing an application error, as shown in Figure 12-2.

Figure 12-2. *The effect of requiring anti-CSRF tokens*

Sending and Receiving Anti-CSRF Tokens

Angular looks for a cookie with the name XSRF-TOKEN in HTTP responses and will automatically use the cookie value to set a header called X-XSRF-TOKEN in subsequent requests.

To provide the Angular client with the cookie and tell ASP.NET Core MVC about the header that Angular uses, add the statements shown in Listing 12-8 to the Startup class.

Listing 12-8. Using Anti-forgery Tokens in the Startup.cs.cs File in the SportsStore Folder

```
using Microsoft.AspNetCore.Builder;
using Microsoft.AspNetCore.Hosting;
using Microsoft.Extensions.Configuration;
using Microsoft.Extensions.DependencyInjection;
using Microsoft.Extensions.Logging;
using Microsoft.AspNetCore.SpaServices.Webpack;
using SportsStore.Models;
using Microsoft.EntityFrameworkCore;
using Newtonsoft.Json;
using Microsoft.AspNetCore.Identity.EntityFrameworkCore;
using Microsoft.AspNetCore.Authentication.Cookies;
using System.Threading.Tasks;
using Microsoft.AspNetCore.Antiforgery;

namespace SportsStore {
    public class Startup {
        public Startup(IHostingEnvironment env) {
            var builder = new ConfigurationBuilder()
              .SetBasePath(env.ContentRootPath)
              .AddJsonFile("appsettings.json", optional: false, reloadOnChange: true)
              .AddJsonFile($"appsettings.{env.EnvironmentName}.json", optional: true)
              .AddEnvironmentVariables();
            Configuration = builder.Build();
        }

        public IConfigurationRoot Configuration { get; }

        public void ConfigureServices(IServiceCollection services) {

            // ...other statements omitted for brevity...

            services.AddAntiforgery(options => {
                options.HeaderName = "X-XSRF-TOKEN";
            });
        }

        public void Configure(IApplicationBuilder app,
                IHostingEnvironment env, ILoggerFactory loggerFactory,
                IAntiforgery antiforgery) {

            loggerFactory.AddConsole(Configuration.GetSection("Logging"));
            loggerFactory.AddDebug();

            app.UseDeveloperExceptionPage();
            app.UseWebpackDevMiddleware(new WebpackDevMiddlewareOptions {
                HotModuleReplacement = true
            });
```

```
app.UseStaticFiles();
app.UseSession();
app.UseIdentity();

app.Use(nextDelegate => context => {
    if (context.Request.Path.StartsWithSegments("/api")
            || context.Request.Path.StartsWithSegments("/")) {
        context.Response.Cookies.Append("XSRF-TOKEN",
            antiforgery.GetAndStoreTokens(context).RequestToken);
    }
    return nextDelegate(context);
});

app.UseMvc(routes => {
    routes.MapRoute(
        name: "default",
        template: "{controller=Home}/{action=Index}/{id?}");

    routes.MapSpaFallbackRoute("angular-fallback",
        new { controller = "Home", action = "Index" });
});

SeedData.SeedDatabase(app.ApplicationServices
    .GetRequiredService<DataContext>());
IdentitySeedData.SeedDatabase(app);
        }
    }
}
```

The new statements in the ConfigureServices method tell ASP.NET Core MVC to look for the anti-CSRF token in the HTTP header called X-XSRF-TOKEN. The new statements in the Configure method add a token to requests for the / URL and the URL that starts with /api.

Save the changes, restart the ASP.NET Core MVC application, and navigate to http://localhost:5000. Now that Angular is receiving and sending the tokens, ASP.NET Core MVC will process its requests, as illustrated by Figure 12-3.

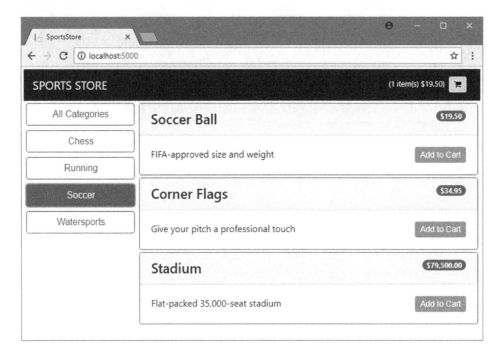

Figure 12-3. *Configuring anti-CSRF tokens*

Creating the Database Migration Command

Throughout this book, I relied on Entity Framework Core to apply database migrations when the ASP.NET Core MVC application starts, which ensured that the database schema was up-to-date.

You should not automatically apply migrations when your application is in production because schema changes can cause data loss when tables or columns are dropped and re-created. It still is useful to be able to initialize the database, but it is important to do so explicitly, rather than every time the ASP.NET Core MVC application starts. The way that I approach this is to add support for a configuration setting that can be supplied as an environment variable or as a comment-line argument. When the setting is true, the database will be initialized, and then the application will exit. When the setting is false or not supplied, then the ASP.NET Core MVC application will start up as normal.

To add the NuGet package that provides access to variables provided via the command line, run the commands shown in Listing 12-9 in the SportsStore folder.

Listing 12-9. Installing the Command-Line NuGet Package

```
dotnet add package Microsoft.Extensions.Configuration.CommandLine --version 1.1.1
dotnet restore
```

To add support for the configuration option, add the statements shown in Listing 12-10 to the Startup class.

```
┌─────────────────────────────────────────────────────────────────────────┐
│                    USING CONFIGURATION ENVIRONMENTS                       │
└─────────────────────────────────────────────────────────────────────────┘
```

ASP.NET Core provides support for configuration environments, where a configuration setting is used to specify the environment in which the application runs and which can be used to load different configuration files or to branch to different configuration code in the Startup class.

I have become wary of this feature recently. I am fortunate enough to talk to a lot of MVC developers about their projects, and a recurring theme has been production problems caused by errors in the configuration files for production environments. The configuration feature is fine, but few project teams have the capability or discipline to test the effect of the production settings before deploying the application, which leads to deployment failures and rollbacks.

The configuration environment feature won't present a problem if you have a well-organized test and deployment process. But for everyone else, I recommend going through an explicit preparation process before each deployment.

Listing 12-10. Adding Explicit Database Initialization in the Startup.cs File in the SportsStore Folder

```csharp
using Microsoft.AspNetCore.Builder;
using Microsoft.AspNetCore.Hosting;
using Microsoft.Extensions.Configuration;
using Microsoft.Extensions.DependencyInjection;
using Microsoft.Extensions.Logging;
using Microsoft.AspNetCore.SpaServices.Webpack;
using SportsStore.Models;
using Microsoft.EntityFrameworkCore;
using Newtonsoft.Json;
using Microsoft.AspNetCore.Identity.EntityFrameworkCore;
using Microsoft.AspNetCore.Authentication.Cookies;
using System.Threading.Tasks;
using Microsoft.AspNetCore.Antiforgery;
using System.Linq;

namespace SportsStore {
    public class Startup {
        public Startup(IHostingEnvironment env) {
            var builder = new ConfigurationBuilder()
                .SetBasePath(env.ContentRootPath)
                .AddJsonFile("appsettings.json", optional: false, reloadOnChange: true)
                .AddJsonFile($"appsettings.{env.EnvironmentName}.json", optional: true)
                .AddEnvironmentVariables()
                .AddCommandLine(System.Environment.GetCommandLineArgs()
                    .Skip(1).ToArray());
            Configuration = builder.Build();
        }
```

```
    public IConfigurationRoot Configuration { get; }

    public void ConfigureServices(IServiceCollection services) {

        // ...statements omitted for brevity...
    }

    public async void Configure(IApplicationBuilder app,
            IHostingEnvironment env, ILoggerFactory loggerFactory,
            IAntiforgery antiforgery) {

        loggerFactory.AddConsole(Configuration.GetSection("Logging"));
        loggerFactory.AddDebug();

        app.UseDeveloperExceptionPage();
        app.UseWebpackDevMiddleware(new WebpackDevMiddlewareOptions {
            HotModuleReplacement = true
        });

        app.UseStaticFiles();
        app.UseSession();
        app.UseIdentity();

        app.Use(nextDelegate => context => {
            if (context.Request.Path.StartsWithSegments("/api")
                    || context.Request.Path.StartsWithSegments("/")) {
                context.Response.Cookies.Append("XSRF-TOKEN",
                    antiforgery.GetAndStoreTokens(context).RequestToken);
            }
            return nextDelegate(context);
        });

        app.UseMvc(routes => {
            routes.MapRoute(
                name: "default",
                template: "{controller=Home}/{action=Index}/{id?}");

            routes.MapSpaFallbackRoute("angular-fallback",
                new { controller = "Home", action = "Index" });
        });

        if ((Configuration["INITDB"] ?? "false") == "true") {
            System.Console.WriteLine("Preparing Database...");
            SeedData.SeedDatabase(app.ApplicationServices
                .GetRequiredService<DataContext>());
            await IdentitySeedData.SeedDatabase(app);
            System.Console.WriteLine("Database Preparation Complete");
            System.Environment.Exit(0);
        }
    }
  }
}
```

If there is a configuration setting called INITDB and it is true, then the databases will be migrated and seeded. After the databases have been prepared, the application will exit. Notice that the listing applies the async keyword to the Configure method and prefixes the call to the IdentitySeedData.SeedDatabase method with await. The operations required to seed the Identity database are all asynchronous, and it is important to wait until they complete before terminating the application. Listing 12-11 shows a change to the result returned by the IdentitySeedData.SeedDatabase method that allows it to be used with the await keyword.

Listing 12-11. Changing the Method Result in the IdentitySeedData.cs File in the Models Folder

```
using System;
using System.Linq;
using Microsoft.AspNetCore.Builder;
using Microsoft.AspNetCore.Identity;
using Microsoft.AspNetCore.Identity.EntityFrameworkCore;
using Microsoft.EntityFrameworkCore;
using Microsoft.Extensions.DependencyInjection;
using System.Threading.Tasks;

namespace SportsStore.Models {

    public static class IdentitySeedData {
        private const string adminUser = "admin";
        private const string adminPassword = "MySecret123$";
        private const string adminRole = "Administrator";

        public static async Task SeedDatabase(IApplicationBuilder app) {
            (GetAppService<IdentityDataContext>(app)).Database.Migrate();

            // ...statements omitted for brevity...
        }

        private static T GetAppService<T>(IApplicationBuilder app) {
            return app.ApplicationServices.GetRequiredService<T>();
        }
    }
}
```

Disabling Logging Messages

To disable the debugging messages that show the SQL queries used by Entity Framework Core and the build messages from webpack, change the logging levels in the appsettings.json file with those shown in Listing 12-12.

Listing 12-12. Disabling Debugging Messages in the appsettings.json File in the SportsStore Folder

```
{
  "Logging": {
    "IncludeScopes": false,
    "LogLevel": {
      "Microsoft.EntityFrameworkCore": "Warning",
```

```
      "Microsoft.AspNetCore.NodeServices": "Warning",
      "Default": "Warning"
    }
  },
  "Data": {
    "Products": {
      "ConnectionString": "Server=localhost,5100;Database=SportsStore;User Id=sa;Password=my
      Secret123;MultipleActiveResultSets=true"
    },
    "Identity": {
      "ConnectionString": "Server=localhost,5100;Database=Identity;User Id=sa;
      Password=mySecret123;MultipleActiveResultSets=true"
    }
  }
}
```

Disabling Automatic Angular Builds and Hot Modules

It is useful to have the Angular code build and bundled automatically during development but not in production. To disable this feature, comment out the statements shown in Listing 12-13 in the Configure method in the Startup class. I have also removed the developer-friendly error pages, which are helpful during development but provide too much information for end users.

Listing 12-13. Disabling Angular Builds in the Startup.cs File in the SportsStore Folder

```
...
public void Configure(IApplicationBuilder app,
        IHostingEnvironment env, ILoggerFactory loggerFactory,
        IAntiforgery antiforgery) {

    loggerFactory.AddConsole(Configuration.GetSection("Logging"));
    loggerFactory.AddDebug();

    //app.UseDeveloperExceptionPage();
    //app.UseWebpackDevMiddleware(new WebpackDevMiddlewareOptions {
    //    HotModuleReplacement = true
    //});

    app.UseStaticFiles();
    app.UseSession();
    app.UseIdentity();

    app.Use(nextDelegate => context => {
        if (context.Request.Path.StartsWithSegments("/api")
                || context.Request.Path.StartsWithSegments("/")) {
            context.Response.Cookies.Append("XSRF-TOKEN",
                antiforgery.GetAndStoreTokens(context).RequestToken);
        }
        return nextDelegate(context);
    });
```

```
    app.UseMvc(routes => {
        routes.MapRoute(
            name: "default",
            template: "{controller=Home}/{action=Index}/{id?}");

        routes.MapSpaFallbackRoute("angular-fallback",
            new { controller = "Home", action = "Index" });
    });

    if ((Configuration["INITDB"] ?? "false") == "true") {
        System.Console.WriteLine("Preparing Database...");
        SeedData.SeedDatabase(app.ApplicationServices
            .GetRequiredService<DataContext>());
        IdentitySeedData.SeedDatabase(app);
        System.Console.WriteLine("Database Preparation Complete");
        System.Environment.Exit(0);
    }
}
...
```

Preparing the Angular Startup Sequence

A corresponding change is required for the Angular application to disable support for hot module replacements. No new modules will be created when the application is in production, so there is no need to maintain a connection to the HTTP server to receive update notifications. Comment out the statements shown in Listing 12-14 in the boot.ts file, which controls the Angular application startup sequence.

Listing 12-14. Disabling HMR in the boot.ts File in the ClientApp Folder

```
import { enableProdMode } from "@angular/core";
import { platformBrowserDynamic } from "@angular/platform-browser-dynamic";
import { AppModule } from "./app/app.module";

const bootApplication = () => {
    enableProdMode();
    platformBrowserDynamic().bootstrapModule(AppModule);
};

// if (module["hot"]) {
//     module["hot"].accept();
//     module["hot"].dispose(() => {
//         const oldRootElem = document.querySelector("app-root");
//         const newRootElem = document.createElement("app-root");
//         oldRootElem.parentNode.insertBefore(newRootElem, oldRootElem);
//         platformBrowserDynamic().destroy();
//     });
// }
```

```
if (document.readyState === "complete") {
    bootApplication();
} else {
    document.addEventListener("DOMContentLoaded", bootApplication);
}
```

This listing also adds a call to the enableProdMode function, which enables the Angular production mode. The production mode disables some developer-friendly checks that help to avoid common errors and that are not useful in production.

Performing the Production Dry Run

The final step is to do a dry run and ensure everything works as expected by following the instructions in the following sections.

Preparing the Database

When you come to deploy your projects, you will need to change the database connection strings to reflect your production environment, but I am going to continue with a Docker container running SQL Server on the local machine. Run the commands shown in Listing 12-15 to reset the Docker container and create a fresh SQL Server database.

Listing 12-15. Resetting the Database

```
docker-compose down
docker-compose up
```

Once SQL Server has finished its startup sequence, run the command shown in Listing 12-16 in the SportsStore folder to apply the database migrations and create the seed data. Pay close attention to the hyphens in this command.

Listing 12-16. Preparing the Database

```
dotnet run -- --INITDB=true
```

Next, run the command shown in Listing 12-17 in the SportsStore folder to create the schema for storing session data.

Listing 12-17. Preparing the Database for Session Data

```
dotnet sql-cache create "Server=localhost,5100;Database=SportsStore;User Id=sa;
Password=mySecret123;MultipleActiveResultSets=true" "dbo" "SessionData"
```

Building the Angular Application

Run the command shown in Listing 12-18 in the SportsStore folder to compile the TypeScript files and generate the JavaScript module files that will be sent to the application. This has been done automatically during development, but it is a good idea to perform one final build before deployment.

Listing 12-18. Building the Angular Application

```
npm run build
```

Starting the ASP.NET Core MVC Application

The final step is to start the application by running the command shown in Listing 12-19 in the SportsStore folder.

Listing 12-19. Running the ASP.NET Core MVC Application

```
dotnet run
```

Once the application has started, use a browser to navigate to http://localhost:5000 and you should see the list of products illustrated in Figure 12-4. Navigate to http://localhost:5000/admin and authenticate using admin as the username and MySecret123$ as the password to make sure that the integration with ASP.NET Core Identity is working, also shown in Figure 12-4.

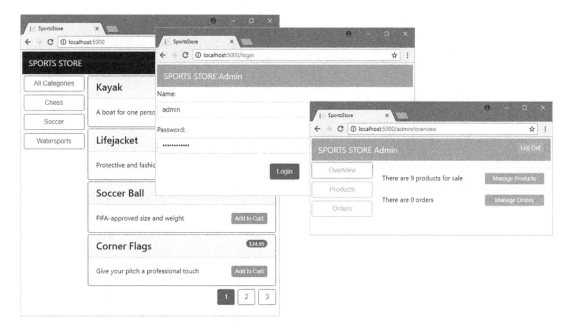

Figure 12-4. *Checking that the application works*

If everything works, you can make any final adjustments required, such as new database connection strings, and package the application for deployment.

Summary

In this chapter, I showed you how to prepare the application for deployment. I demonstrated how to add validation tokens to guard against cross-site request forgery, how to prepare the database using the command line, and how to disable the developer features so that the TypeScript files are not monitored for changes and hot module replacement is disabled.

That is all I have to teach you about using Angular and ASP.NET Core MVC together. I started by creating a project containing both Angular and ASP.NET Core MVC and showed you how to get them to work together, how to share data between them, and how to create and use web services. Along the way, I showed you how to use the core Angular building blocks to structure a client-side application.

I wish you every success in your Angular/ASP.NET Core MVC projects, and I can only hope that you have enjoyed reading this book as much as I enjoyed writing it.

Index

A

Add method, 109
AllowAnonymous attribute, 254
@angular/cli package, 21
@angular/core module, 138
@angular/http module, 75
@angular/router module, 148
appsettings.json file, connection string, 45, 262
ASP.NET Core Identity, 258
    authenticating users, 263
    authentication web service, 267
    configuring, 260
    seeding the database, 258
Attach method, 108
Authorize attribute, 253

B

Boostrap CSS, updating, 29
boot.ts file, 26
Bower, installing, 7, 13, 17, 30

C

Class binding, 176
@Component decorator, 64, 137, 139
Components, 137
    HTML template, 139
Connection string, 45
Cross-site requestforgery. *See* CSRF
CSRF, 280
    IgnoreAntiforgeryToken attribute, 281
    ValidateAntiForgeryToken attribute, 281
    XSRF-TOKEN cookie, 283
    X-XSRF-TOKEN header, 283
CSS classes, assigning, 176
Currency pipes, 170

D

Database context class, 48
Database migration, 50
Data binding classes, 106
[()] data bindings, 195
Data validation, 214
Decorators, 62
DeleteBehavior enumeration, 129
Deleting data, 128
Docker
    compose command, 53
    configuring, 8, 18
    installing, 8, 14, 17
    SQL Server container, 44
docker-compose.yml file, 44
dotnet add package, 24, 258
dotnet ef database, 279
dotnet ef migrations, 51, 129, 208, 263
dotnet new, 24
dotnet restore, 25, 258
dotnet run, 32, 43
dotnet sql-cache, 200, 279

E

Event bindings, 114, 171

F

Filtering data, 96
Font Awesome package, 181
Formatting data values, 170

G

Git, installing, 8, 13

© Adam Freeman 2017

A. Freeman, *Essential Angular for ASP.NET Core MVC*, DOI 10.1007/978-1-4842-2916-3

Get the eBook for only $5!

Why limit yourself?

With most of our titles available in both PDF and ePUB format, you can access your content wherever and however you wish—on your PC, phone, tablet, or reader.

Since you've purchased this print book, we are happy to offer you the eBook for just $5.

To learn more, go to http://www.apress.com/companion or contact support@apress.com.

Apress®